D0359202

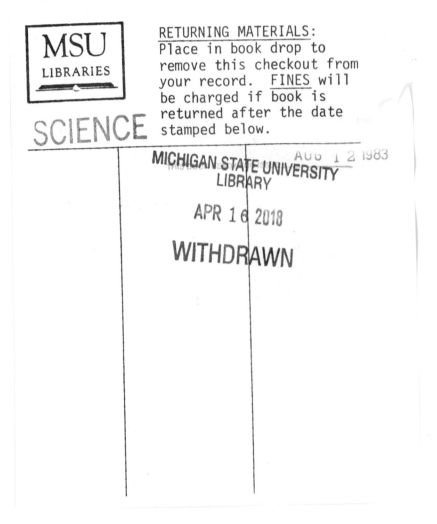

BRUSH MANAGEMENT

BRUSH MANAGEMENT

Principles and Practices for Texas and the Southwest

BY

CHARLES J. SCIFRES

TEXAS A&M UNIVERSITY PRESS

College Station and London

Library of Congress Cataloging in Publication Data

Scifres, Charles J   1941–
    Brush management.

        Bibliography: p.
        Includes index.
        1. Brush control—Texas. 2. Brush control—Southwest-
ern States. 3. Range management—Texas. 4. Range management—Southwestern States. I. Title.
        SB612.T4S25   633'.2   79-7407
ISBN 0-89096-080-1

Manufactured in the United States of America
FIRST EDITION

To Julia

Contents

Tables

Preface

WOODY plants dominate the vegetation of most of the rangeland plant communities of Texas and frequently pose the primary deterrent to effective range management throughout the Southwest. Effective methods of manipulating woody-plant communities have been developed by range scientists of the Texas Agricultural Experiment Station during the past twenty-five years, and research is being conducted on even more effective and economical systems of brushland management.

An increased public awareness of the need for improving the productivity of rangeland while maintaining the integrity of the environment has led to increased use of the terms *brush management* and *vegetation manipulation* instead of *brush control*, with its less palatable connotation. Terms such as *eradication* no longer have a realistic application to the problem. Some woody cover is desirable for livestock shade and browse. Woody plants provide quality wildlife habitat both for cover and for the food requirements of game animals. The need for brush has served as a point of philosophical difference between range scientists and wildlife scientists in the past. However, wildlife habitat can be improved while the production of domestic livestock is increased on rangeland by the judicious use of effective techniques of manipulating vegetation. The attitude among scientists and producers—that brush should not be controlled just for the sake of control—indicates that some woody plant cover is not only tolerable in livestock production but also desirable. This book was conceived on the premise that vegetation should be manipulated to optimize production from natural resources.

Theoretically, after the nature of the brush problem has been identified, the proper technology can be applied to alleviate the problem. However, research information on brush management is scattered throughout an array of publications, both technical and popular. Since organized research on the brush problem was initiated more than twenty-five years ago, the chance for duplication of work is increasing. My objectives are (1) to provide descriptive information for identifying selected woody plants of significance on Texas ranges and of importance in other range states, (2) to summarize available information on the ecology of these plants, and (3) to collate the applicable research findings with practical management methods. Information herein, developed as a guide, embraces only the more common, troublesome woody plants of Texas. Control methods are listed for some species, but the fact that these methods are given does not imply that control of these plants is warranted in all cases. The choice and implementation of control measures must be a management decision.

This book was developed with the desire that it be of use to land resource managers—landowners, ranchers, farmers—as well as technicians and students. It was undertaken with the knowledge that society is more educated than ever before and participates directly in making decisions concerning the management and fate of our natural resources. Therefore, I have included the principles which, in my opinion, are critical for effectively formulating decisions that affect the manipulation and use of rangeland vegetation. Because of my experience with range management in Texas, I discuss the application of the basic principles of brush management almost solely with reference to Texas problems. However, the principles of brush management are applicable throughout the Southwest if they are used properly and with due consideration for species susceptibility and for the influence of environment in dictating the rate and extent of vegetation response. Inasmuch as my capability allows, these principles are related in lay language. The reader with a deep interest in any given subject entertained herein will find, upon investigation of the literature, that any chapter could be developed into a book. I hope that this collation will facilitate the use of available research information and stimulate additional research in this important area of investigation.

I am indebted to S. L. Beasom, R. W. Bovey, J. D. Dodd, G. O. Hoffman, M. M. Kothmann, R. E. Meyer, R. E. Whitson, and D. N. Ueckert for their critical reading of selected parts of the manuscript at various stages of development and their constructive criticisms, encouragement, and additions of pertinent information. C. H. Meadors,

L. B. Merrill, J. L. Mutz, J. L. Schuster, R. E. Steger, G. Sultemeier, and H. T. Weidemann added important observations which were not available in printed form. All the coworkers who encouraged this undertaking are too numerous to mention here, but their direct contributions, especially those of my graduate students, can be noted in the research cited throughout the book, and the association with them made this effort not only possible but enjoyable as well. I am forever indebted to my wife, Julia, for her untiring support and encouragement, her persistence through the countless hours of typing, and her continual patience as I pursue my life's work.

C. J. SCIFRES

BRUSH MANAGEMENT

Brush Management
in Perspective

MOST rangeland in Texas supports an excessive cover of woody plants, a brush problem that must be managed for successful range animal production and for best use of the land for other purposes. During the past three decades significant technological advancements have been made toward coping with the brush problem. However, before we consider management approaches that include the new technology, the origin and cause of the problem should be discussed. Perhaps by understanding the nature of the factors that cause excessive woody plant cover, we may more effectively apply appropriate remedies and more readily formulate new approaches.

In this book the term *rangeland* will include all lands on which the potential (climax) native vegetation is predominantly grasses, grasslike plants, forbs, or shrubs suitable for grazing and browsing. Rangeland includes natural grasslands, savannahs, shrublands, most deserts, tundra, alpine communities, coastal marshes, and wet meadows in addition to land revegetated naturally or artificially to provide a forage cover that is managed like native vegetation. The term *brush* will refer to a growth of shrubs or small trees usually undesirable for livestock grazing or timber management but which may be of value for browse, wildlife habitat, and/or watershed protection. The term *brushland* will refer to areas covered primarily with brush.

The great diversity of vegetation in Texas reflects the state's extreme variability in environmental conditions, especially rainfall and soils (Fig. 1.1). This diversity allows effective application of brush management technology developed in Texas to problems common to most of the Southwest. Annual precipitation varies from about 8 inches in far western Texas to over 50 inches in portions of the

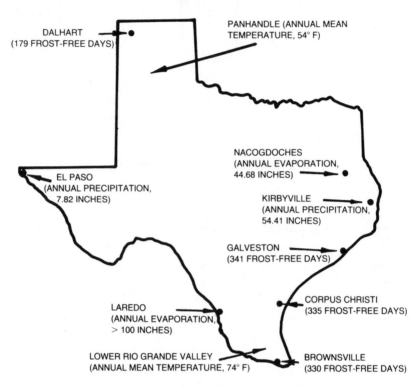

1.1. Environmental conditions vary greatly across Texas, contributing to the tremendous diversity in woody plant communities (109).

coastal zone. Total annual rainfall has been as little as 2 inches near El Paso and as much as 80 inches in East Texas. Evaporation exceeds 100 inches annually in the western part of the state but may be less than 45 inches in the eastern portion. Growing season increases from about 180 days near Dalhart to more than 330 days in the extreme south near Brownsville. Accordingly, woody-plant communities in the far west are typified by low-growing xerophytic (dry-country) species, with plants of notable stature occurring only along the drainageways and in the bottomlands. Conversely, densely storied woody-plant communities typified by a primary layer of trees, often covered with vines, and a secondary layer of bushes and shrubs forming dense thickets are characteristic of East Texas. Only the most shade-tolerant herbaceous species occur on the floors of these forests.

Soils of the state vary from deep alluvial sands along the lowlands to thin clays, often with rocky outcrops, on the uplands. Topography varies from the steep mountain slopes of the Trans-Pecos to the near level plains of the Coastal Prairie. Because of this diversity and the lack of descriptive information from some areas, detailed discussion of communities of woody plants on Texas rangeland is not included in this book. Instead, the generalized types of vegetation are discussed in chapter 2, where the major plant communities and dominant woody species are described.

Origin of the Brush Problem

Early writings tell of "waving seas of grass" extending across Texas. The mesas of West Texas and southern New Mexico were covered primarily by gramas a hundred or so years ago (338). Mesquite[1] was restricted to well-drained, gravelly hilltops, and juniper stands were primarily on mountain foothills. The prairies near San Antonio during the middle of the nineteenth century were largely covered by perennial grasses and supported only scattered bushes and small honey mesquite trees (161). Unfortunately, only a few are left who witnessed the original grasslands. Ernest Holdworth, Sr., described the early vegetation of Zavala County in the South Texas Plains:

In 1887 the first wire fences were built. Some of these were promptly cut, as some of the people didn't appreciate any of the country's being fenced. They were rebuilt and not very much trouble developed. Up to about this time, or the preceding year, the country was very much as Nature made it, but during the drought many cattle were moved in from farther east, and it was soon tramped out, has never since been like it was before and never will be again. It is rather hard to describe at this time, but I will do my best. At that time there was considerable prairie, especially around Loma Vista. This was all dotted with mesquite mottes. The grass was fairly solid on the hills; and in the hollows, which are mesquite thickets now, the grass was up to the stirrups in riding through. Some kinds of grass aren't seen here any more; the sedge and blackbeard were a solid mat and were sometimes cut for hay. As the country burned off periodically and the grass was so heavy, there was very little timber

[1] Scientific names for most plants are given in chapter 3. Scientific names of all plants not given in chapter 3 are listed alphabetically by common name in Appendix A.

in the hollows and flats. Farther west there was quite a lot of open country in what was known as the Bell Prairie. It was covered with smooth
mesquite grass, and though there was a bush here and there, you could
see a coyote a quarter of a mile away. The brush country was not as thick
as it is now, except for the blackbrush hills. The mesquite were what
we called "gotch"—you could see under them for some distance. There
weren't many "switches," as now. The creeks had good-sized water holes
and small lakes that generally had water. The Leona and Nueces were
running streams except in very severe droughts.

That is the country as God made it. There are few living who saw
it as it was then, and none will ever see it again.[2]

Because a high value was placed upon grazing lands in the early
days, and because there was a great desire to discover areas suitable
for settlement, there is good reason to accept such accounts without
question. The relative amount of open grassland has, without doubt,
seriously diminished since then. However, the proper perspective must
be maintained—*woody plants were present then but were restricted
to specific sites.* Under pristine conditions they only rarely migrated
from those specific sites into the grassland communities.

The relatively recent occupation of grasslands by brush has led
to the conclusion that the ecological ranges of many woody plants are
increasing. Although the ranges of a few species, such as huisache,
are suspected of increasing (250), the brush problem on rangeland
actually should be attributed to increases in the stature and density
of woody species rather than to changes in their distribution (161).
Formerly restricted primarily to the waterways and drainages or occurring as scattered individuals across the grassland, woody plants now
form an almost continuous cover over Texas rangeland. The brush
problem is of critical concern to the livestock producer, whose liveli-
hood depends largely on herbaceous forage, especially native grasses.

Encroachment of woody plants into previously brushless areas is
closely correlated with the intensification of the activities of modern
man (255). "People pressure" has complemented fluctuations in climate and local weather to allow increases in the severity of the brush

[2] Ernest Holdworth, Sr. Undated. "A history of Zavala County under
Spanish and Mexican flags." (Mimeographed. 29 pp. Copy on file in the Department of Range Science, Texas A&M University).

problem. Cyclic wet and dry periods and periodic wildfires shaped the ecological structure of the grasslands. However, before the white man's influence, the mobility of grazing animals naturally deferred the grassland from grazing during dry periods. Large numbers of herbivores grazed given areas for only short periods of time and then moved as the supply of forage decreased. Today, fences restrict the movement of grazing animals, making grazing deferment a part of man's management responsibility.

Man's high mobility and agricultural activities make him possibly the single most influential factor in the long-distance dispersal of plants that might otherwise remain near the parent plant. Also, man has always been a disturber of natural systems, and his ability to create disturbances quickly has increased as his technology has advanced. Thus, man is the primary biotic factor in the world ecosystem which determines the fate of the earth's natural resources. For example, man has largely suppressed naturally occurring fires, which once were an important factor in grassland development and maintenance. Repeated burning prevented the encroachment of woody plants into the climax vegetation of North American grasslands, and early man played a significant role in maintaining the influence of fire. Areas were burned to attract game animals, and fire was used to herd them. As man became increasingly sedentary, his domestic animals disturbed and overused many plant communities formerly closed to invaders, resulting in regression and undesirable shifts in the botanical composition of the vegetation. Thus, the speedy recent occupation of grasslands by woody species has been in response to reductions of grass cover, and the replacement of grass with brush coincides closely with intensive use of grasslands by the cattle industry.

Regression of vegetation through overuse and mismanagement may ultimately lead to extensive soil erosion and permanent damage to the ecosystem. In some cases, plant communities which replaced climax stands, referred to as "disclimaxes," have become fairly stable as the result of continued disturbance. A good example is the shortgrass plains, now so typical of northwestern Texas, which once were an extension of the mixed prairie. Remnants of the once dominant mid-grasses such as needlegrasses and western wheatgrass still exist only in protected areas. Overgrazing accentuated by periodic droughts resulted in a cover of sod grasses such as buffalograss, the shorter gramas, and species of *Hilaria*.

Influences of man in changing the vegetation cover of grasslands (Fig. 1.2) include

1. Restriction, even complete elimination over an extended period, of naturally occurring fires
2. Continual grazing pressure on the grassland by an increase in the number of grazing animals
3. Intentional and severe restriction of the movements of grazing animals by fencing
4. Cultivation and abandonment of grassland soils, which must begin the slow and tedious process of returning to their original state through secondary succession
5. The ever-increasing mobility of man and his animals which has augmented the dispersion of woody plant propagules
6. Introduction of woody plants such as Macartney rose as ornamentals which have escaped cultivation to become severe management problems.

Although the brush problem must be accepted as largely a man-made dilemma, it is one with which man may cope using improved technology and experience. This technology must be applied within the framework of the proper use of land resources to achieve effective "brush management"—the economical manipulation of stands of brush to meet specific management objectives.

Considerations for Society

The United States has a billion-acre resource in its range and pasture lands (303). More than 728 million acres in the West, 76 percent of the land area, can be classified as rangeland, with grazing by livestock and wildlife as the most important land use. More than 200 million acres are still used for range livestock production, with about 107 million acres used as rangeland in Texas alone.

The problem of woody plants has long posed the primary deterrent to maximizing use of much, if not most, of Texas rangeland. Losses to excessive cover of brush on rangeland affect virtually every citizen of the state. In 1948, Texas ranchmen lost an estimated $18.5 million to the brush problem (339). No recent estimates are available,

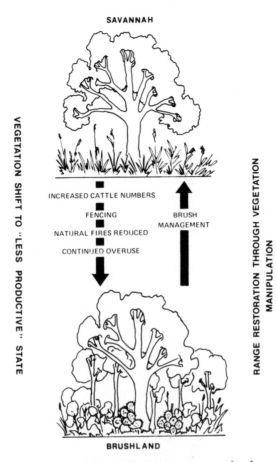

SAVANNAH

VEGETATION SHIFT TO "LESS PRODUCTIVE" STATE

RANGE RESTORATION THROUGH VEGETATION MANIPULATION

INCREASED CATTLE NUMBERS

FENCING

NATURAL FIRES REDUCED

CONTINUED OVERUSE

BRUSH MANAGEMENT

BRUSHLAND

1.2. Much, if not most, of the shift from open grasslands or savannahs dotted with trees toward the dominance of woody plants on Texas rangelands can be attributed to man's activities. Brush management is used to reverse the trend and to expedite secondary succession, the extent of which is dictated by weather, soils, management objectives, and economic constraints.

but today's losses can be expected to far surpass those of 1948. Presently, over 88 percent of rangeland in Texas is so heavily covered by brush that livestock production on it is reduced. No wonder it is not unrealistic to expect that effective brush management technology could double, even triple, the livestock production on western rangelands (303).

Solution of the brush problem in a reasonable time can be achieved only by integrating technology from a number of disciplines, including biology, ecology, chemistry, engineering, economics, and business management. Knowledge of the biology of the problem—the growth habits and requirements of both individual plants and the aggregations of individuals that occur on an area—is of great value in the development of brush management programs. Ideally brush management should be initiated only if the nature of the problem is thoroughly understood. The composition of natural vegetation is typically complex, with few cases of sharp boundaries between communities, and the composition of Texas ranges is no exception. Woody plant groupings may vary from almost pure stands of a single species to mixed stands with more than ten species, which further complicate the problem.

As research on brushland management has progressed, it has become evident that management problems of Texas rangelands must be approached systematically. Too often we have searched for the panacea when there is no single, simple answer to the problem. Management of rangelands is complex, and specific procedures vary as a result of the inherent heterogeneity of rangeland, variations in climate, available technology, economics, the production potential of the land, and individual management goals.

Brush management efforts must be approached with consideration of all potential uses for rangeland. Although this natural resource has traditionally been used primarily for livestock production, the value of trees and shrubs in furnishing wildlife habitat (food and cover) and the ever-growing recreation potential of Texas rangeland have added new dimensions to range management. Although many people view rangelands as land suitable *only* for grazing since they are not suitable for cultivation, a significant amount of rangeland in Texas has extremely high production potential and is suited to a multitude of agricultural uses. It is our primary reservoir of untapped cropland.

There is no reason to believe that brush management, properly applied, will detract from uses of rangeland for purposes other than livestock production. Descriptions of the grasslands before the turn of the century invariably included accounts of abundant wildlife, good argument against the concept that heavy cover is absolutely necessary for the survival of most game species. If heavy brush cover is now needed by game species, it is probably the result of the increased pressure of sharing habitats with man and his domestic animals.

Regardless of the impetus for brush management, ultimate success depends on the land manager's ability to develop a sound management plan and persistently pursue the objectives of that plan.

I cited man as the catalyst for converting much of Texas grasslands to brushlands, and I feel that he will continue to be the most significant ecological force in determining change in natural resources. Man decides the ultimate use of all resources based on his concept of human need, both material and aesthetic. Cognizant of his role in the ecosystem, and becoming increasingly aware of the ecological principles that regulate vegetation growth, development, and aggregation, man can now apply his knowledge to manipulate natural ecosystems for improved productivity while maintaining the integrity of the resources.

At one time, manipulation of range vegetation by brush management and the method to be used were essentially the business of the landowner. Traditionally, the general public has shown relatively little interest in the use and fate of rangelands. However, a general awareness of the value of natural resources, concern for their fate with present attitudes concerning land use, and the need for a perpetual source of red meat protein with a minimal expenditure of energy have stimulated public interest in rangeland during the last decade. Rangeland is no longer the almost exclusive province of ranchers, range researchers, and public land administrators (194). Society's interest in natural resources and their management will surely become even more intense in the future. It is imperative that land resource managers, public officials, educators, and researchers provide the public with the necessary information to understand needs for range resource management and to demonstrate wise stewardship of the land.

Brush management efforts must be viewed as an integral part of the overall system for wise, efficient use and conservation of grasslands. Available brush management and conservation methods are complex tools, the effectiveness of which depends primarily upon the resource manager's understanding of their proper application.

Energy from grassland plants must be converted to usable protein by grazing and browsing animals—an additional step in the food chain. Thus, those involved in brush management must have a working knowledge of plant ecology, an appreciation of practical range management needs and concepts, and an understanding of the economic implications of management/improvement procedures. As Shaw (283) has written, "weeds and their control are basically ecological and economical problems," and brush management, as an integral part of successful range management, is indeed *ecology applied.*

General Ecological Considerations

Compared to single-species cropping systems, native grasslands are ecologically complex. It is apparent from the varied botanical composition of the natural grasslands of Texas that climate varies greatly across the landmass of the United States (with species composition changing accordingly). Diversity of plants occupying rangeland is an attribute rather than a limitation, since complex ecosystems are more efficient than simple ones in using environmental resources (289). Diversity, as it influences average yield of products over a relatively long period, lends a long-term stability to natural vegetation. Whereas single-species stands must be constantly tended to prevent progressive reduction in yield, natural plant mixtures require only extensive treatment instead of intensive applications of fertilizer, water, and crop protection chemicals for sustained production, with variations in animal yield primarily reflecting fluctuations in weather.

However, the response of natural grasslands to improvement efforts is directly dependent upon soils and their capability, weather (especially rainfall immediately following treatment), and climate as it determines vegetation potential. Compared to the land manager who may control nutrient and water availability to cultivated systems, the range manager has little control over these factors. He truly must deal daily with the whims of nature, which lend an inevitable degree of risk and uncertainty to brush management.

Range improvement practices are directed towards promoting the growth and development of specific kinds of plants which exist in certain mixes of species. In the past, range livestock producers have fallen victim to the dogma that grasslands should be composed almost solely of grass. There is an unfortunate tendency to look upon any broad-leaved herbaceous plant (forb) as simply being a "weed." Although the grassland formation assumes its character primarily from the dominant grasses, most of which are bunch grasses, forbs are also characteristic of grasslands. Forbs usually fall into mixed societies according to season, site, and geographical location, but they give the distinctive tone to prairies. Many species of forbs furnish grazing for range animals, and some native legumes have significant nitrogen fixing capability. Removing the forbs and leaving only grasses changes the community structure from the true character of the prairie. The intent underlying range improvement should be not to change the character of the prairie but to reinstate the balance necessary to maintain its integrity.

"Desirability" of a plant species is a concept based on the comparative "usefulness" of a given plant at a specific time and in a particular mix of species. Traditionally, brush management practices have been applied to minimize "competition" (a common need for a limited resource) between the "desirable" and the "undesirable" species. However, the results of competition among plants are rarely straightforward, apparently because competitive ability must be related to environmental and other factors that are by no means static (289), especially in natural ecosystems. On natural grasslands relative competitive ability is expressed as the reactions of different plants to pressures such as those from grazing animals, pests, and diseases and variations in abiotic factors such as moisture, temperature, and light. A given plant species then, may be especially competitive in one situation and not adapted to another depending on site conditions, associated vegetation, and management programs. Of particular importance are the different reactions of plant species to management practices. For example, conventional herbicides are usually detrimental to trees, brush, and forbs, releasing grasses to increase in abundance. The land resource manager, then, can use herbicides to give the "competitive edge" to grasses. On the negative side of this principle, all grasses, regardless of value, are benefited by such spray applications. Therefore, the advent of efficient herbicides may cause grasses to become some of the most important weeds of grasslands (289) unless the chemicals are used wisely.

Since overuse and mismanagement have caused the deterioration of a large portion of our rangelands, some people propose complete protection of those lands from further use to restore them to their original condition. However, such a view is invalid from the standpoints that continual production of red meat protein is required for our society, grazing animals are an integral part of the grassland ecosystem, and the time required for "restoration" of our brush-infested rangeland would be intolerable. I have evaluated brush-covered areas in the Post Oak Savannah that have been excluded from all but wildlife for twenty to twenty-five years. The only notable changes have been apparent increases in shade-tolerant understory woody species. Complete protection from grazing animals and from fire over prolonged periods eliminate two natural ingredients in the evolution and reinstatement of grasslands. Taking the land out of use does not necessarily promote conservation, nor can this luxury be afforded from a practical standpoint.

Another example is the result of evaluations of a site in the Rolling Plains of North Texas after it was protected from grazing by domestic livestock and from fire for more than twenty-seven years. Although vegetation on the site had shifted toward the more productive mid-grass communities, total herbage production was only slightly improved over that of grazed pastures (266). As the botanical composition of the herbaceous species improved, establishment of undesirable species such as honey mesquite was definitely minimized. No new invasion of honey mesquite occurred after twenty-one years of exclusion of domestic livestock. However, a substantial portion of the honey mesquite plants present when grazing was terminated are still present today, nearly thirty-five years later. Once established, brush seedlings such as those of honey mesquite are extremely tenacious and competitive with herbaceous species, especially in the absence of fire. They may survive continual reductions of 70 to 90 percent of normal sunlight (256), extended dry periods, and repeated top removal (275). Honey mesquite seedlings may germinate under relatively dry conditions if soil temperatures are adequate (265), and their establishment is not necessarily related to high levels of rainfall (266). Thus, although the principles of secondary succession are definitely operating, the process usually requires such long periods, especially in the drier areas, that man is forced to speed up the natural processes with technology. In my experience, range improvement can be expedited by proper grazing and management in conjunction with judicious use of other range improvement methods.

Dependence on the "natural" rate of vegetation change may be contrasted with the results of a four-year study of a site in North Texas where spraying with the herbicide mixture 2,4,5-T ([2,4,5-trichlorophenoxy]acetic acid) plus picloram (4-amino-3,5,6-trichloropicolinic acid) was evaluated for the rate at which it promoted the restoration of rangeland. Spraying rapidly reduced the influence of honey mesquite and sand sagebrush, the principal woody species on the site (257). The reduction in density and foliar cover of live honey mesquite and sand sagebrush plants four years after the site was sprayed allowed range forage to increase and the range condition to show signs of improvement. Thus, desirable vegetation changes, promoted by use of an effective brush management technique, occurred in approximately one-fifth of the time required for "natural" changes to become apparent in the same general area and on the same soil type. This contrast must be viewed only as an example, since the rate of vegetation change may be accelerated or slowed somewhat depending on moisture conditions.

Both the timeliness and amount of rainfall must be considered to be the overriding factors that regulate the response of herbaceous species to reductions in woody plant cover, especially in semiarid and arid areas. The response of an increase in forage in the Rolling Plains of Texas occurs only in years of average or above-average rainfall following aerial spraying of rangeland infested by honey mesquite. However, considering overall moisture levels through the years, sprayed areas are more efficient in the conversion of moisture to forage. In one study, the sprayed, ungrazed area produced 19.5 pounds per acre more oven-dry grass per inch of rainfall received above the annual average than did the untreated, ungrazed area (257). Efficiency in the use of moisture following brush management by spraying in the wetter extreme southeastern portion of the state usually improves more dramatically (259).

The brush communities in southeastern Texas are mixed brush (*Prosopis-Acacia*), many species of which are not susceptible to 2,4,5-T alone but are controlled by 2,4,5-T plus picloram. In a year of "good" moisture conditions, application of 2,4,5-T alone improves the efficiency of moisture use solely by reducing the moisture demands on the ecosystem of susceptible species such as honey mesquite. In years of low rainfall, only the more effective herbicide treatment of 2,4,5-T plus picloram, which controls not only honey mesquite but also many of the associated brush species, increases grass production. Three years after spraying, treated areas may produce twice as much forage per inch of precipitation as do unsprayed pastures (259).

Importance of Grazing Management

Sound grazing management is a requisite for greatest range improvement. This interrelationship will be entertained more fully in the final chapter, but it is worth emphasizing here that brush management efforts cannot be expected to result in the recovery of desirable vegetation if that vegetation is grazed too heavily or at the wrong season. Moreover, grazing management must usually be combined with brush management for best results. Good grazing management techniques can control the establishment of undesirable woody plants but will not remove established plants unless those techniques, such as the inclusion of goats for brush control, are designed specifically for that purpose. For example, under grazing by cattle only, honey mesquite regrowth (in density, height, canopy cover, and weight) is always greater on the more mesic Deep Upland range sites with good grazing management than on the drier Rocky Hill and Rolling Hill range sites on the Rolling Plains of North Texas (272). Honey mesquite regrowth on the Deep Upland sites is apparently favored by deferred rotation grazing systems, presumably because of improved moisture relationships and other overall benefits of the proper grazing system on the range vegetation. This is not to say that good grazing management should be avoided to reduce brush, but that woody plants such as honey mesquite thrive under the same growth conditions as other plants. The better the growth conditions, the more vigorous the brush development *after the plants are established.*

The primary objective of brush management is to selectively manipulate rangeland vegetation to maximize the production of usable species (269). Brush management techniques are used to expedite secondary succession on grasslands. In essence, brush management may be used to reverse the trend in vegetation change resulting from mismanagement (Fig. 1.2).

Brush management may be used at any of the several stages of vegetation regression to direct change toward more desirable plant communities. The first sign of vegetation regression is the reduced vigor of perennial, perhaps climax, grasses. At this point grazing management may be the most effective range improvement method. While the community is closed to an influx of invading species, reduction in grazing use and rest from grazing during key growth periods will expedite the restoration of the vigor and stature of desirable species which normally decrease under heavy grazing pressure. Continuous heavy grazing opens the grass cover, allowing increases in species that livestock use less, a high proportion of which may be woody plants (Fig. 1.3). This late stage of rangeland degeneration is typical of many Texas ranges and is, unfortunately, when much of the emphasis is placed on improved management techniques.

Adaptations of Woody Plants

The adaptation of woody plants to Texas conditions can be attributed to their effective reproductive systems, their ability to withstand environmental extremes, and their ability to adapt to man's control efforts. Probably the single most important attribute of their undesirable nature is their ability to persist because of their reproductive mechanisms. Whereas annual and biennial species depend almost solely upon seed as the mechanism of survival and spread, woody plants are especially tenacious because of their ability to readily reproduce asexually.

The more pronounced ability of short-lived (annual and biennial) plants to produce large amounts of seed does not necessarily mean that the role of seed as a mechanism of propagation is any less important for perennial species. Honey mesquite, which may produce from one to four bean crops in a single growing season (89), is a good example of a long-lived perennial for which seed is important. Honey mesquite seeds are especially equipped for a long life in the harsh rangeland environment. Dormancy, the ability of seeds to remain inactive but maintain growth potential, is an attribute which allows woody plants such as mesquite to recur from growing season to growing season. Dormancy mechanisms allow seed and vegetative structures to survive low temperatures, dry growing conditions, and seasonal variations in environmental factors such as photoperiod and humidity. Seed-coat domancy allows viable velvet mesquite seeds to lie domant in the soil for as long as twenty-five years, thus assuring

1.3. Continuous overgrazing opens the grass cover of rangeland, eventually bares the soil, and allows species of low grazing value to increase in abundance. (*Photograph by O. E. Sperry*)

an infestation when environmental conditions are conducive to germination and the establishment of seedlings (307). Mesquite seeds do not have morphological adaptations such as wings that would carry them in the wind or barbs that would attach to the coats of animals. They are spread primarily by runoff water, but they are also transported intact by man or are ingested by wildlife and livestock and relocated to new areas.

Seeds of many woody species are innately dormant. Inherent factors which restrict their germination after they are dispersed include their need for after-ripening, natural inhibitors in them that are often localized in specific parts, and mechanically restrictive or impermeable seed coats. After-ripening, a period of further seed maturation following dispersal, may be required for rudimentary embryos or physiologically immature embryos. The seed coats may be impermeable to water, as are those of huisache (250) and honey mesquite (265), or impermeable to gaseous exchange. Seed coat dormancy is usually ended by mechanical abrasion of the seed coat, either by alternate freezing and thawing, which structurally reduces the seed coat, or by passage of the seeds through the digestive tracts of animals and birds.

Some woody species, such as winged elm, have no dormancy mechanism and, unless germination occurs, survive only a short time after they are disseminated (164). Such species may be equipped with appendages such as wings or a pappus (parachutelike attachment) to facilitate their spread by the wind.

Although seeds are essential for the spread of perennial species, asexual reproduction is their major survival mechanism. Woody plants depend for survival on vegetative reproduction from buds along stems, roots, and rhizomes and are capable of asexual reproduction at an early age. Honey mesquite is capable of resprouting within seven days after its seed germinates if the aerial portions of the seedling are damaged (275). Those aerial portions are replaced by new sprouts from branch axils or from buds beneath the bark (255). After it is established, honey mesquite may replace its aerial portions repeatedly following top removal (266).

Perennial plants may be classified as either simple or creeping based on their reproductive capability. Simple perennials such as honey mesquite spread only by seed. Creeping perennials such as sand shinnery oak reproduce from organs such as rhizomes or stolons which vegetatively increase the area occupied by the plant. Simple perennials are relatively susceptible to many control measures. Once the top growth is removed beneath the lowermost stem bud, the plant cannot regenerate. However, removing the top growth of creeping perennials results only in breaking apical dominance and releasing new sprouts from roots and rhizomes. As a result, disturbing the top growth actually increase the canopy cover of the woody species. For example, single-stemmed honey mesquite may be effectively removed by grubbing beneath the lowest stem bud, but removal of a Texas persimmon stem, regardless of the depth at which it is grubbed, releases buds on lateral roots to produce new shoots several feet from the original, central stem.

Before any brush management method is chosen, the sources of potential for vegetative regeneration of the target woody species should be considered. Most rangeland woody plant problems can be categorized as one of four growth types: (1) upright, single-stemmed trees, (2) bushes or trees with a running or creeping growth habit, (3) multistemmed bushes, and (4) those plants which grow as vines or canes (Fig. 1.4). Various species of oaks and original-growth honey mesquite are examples of the single-stemmed, upright growth form. The

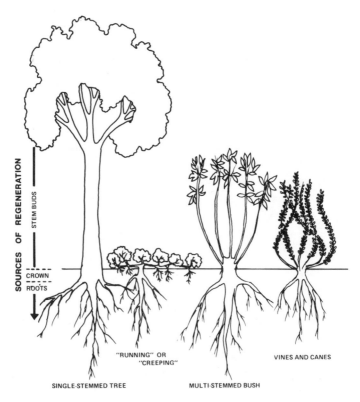

SOURCES OF REGENERATION

STEM BUDS

CROWN
ROOTS

"RUNNING" OR
"CREEPING"

VINES AND CANES

SINGLE-STEMMED TREE

MULTI-STEMMED BUSH

GROWTH TYPES

1.4. Woody plants occur in four basic growth forms which vary in regrowth potential, source of asexual regeneration, and response to conventional control methods.

running or creeping growth habit is typified by creeping mesquite, running live oak, and sand shinnery oak. The multistemmed bush is often the result of unsuccessful control efforts on single-stemmed trees. Small-statured, many-stemmed, bushy honey mesquite plants result from top removal of the single-stemmed tree, which releases buds along the remaining above-ground portions of the stem and from the crown. Macartney rose and saw greenbrier are examples of the vine type of growth. Upon top removal these species readily sprout from crown sections immediately beneath the ground line, from the roots, and, with Macartney rose, from displaced stem segments that may take root and sprout. Growth habits and the sources of vegetative regrowth of selected woody plants common to Texas rangeland are given in Table 1.1.

TABLE 1.1.
Growth Habit and Source of Vegetative Regrowth of Selected
Woody Species.

Woody Species	Usual Growth Habit*	Source of Sprout Development†
Agarito	UM	Cn
Allthorn	US	—
Blackbrush acacia	UM	St
Bluewood	US, UM	St
Buckeye	US	St
Burrobrush	US, UM	St
Catclaw acacia	UM	St
Cholla	US	P
Coralberry	UM	St
Coyotillo	US	—
Creosotebush	UM	St
Desert yaupon	UM	St
Devil's pincushion	LG	P
Eastern red cedar	US	St
Elbowbush	US, UM	St, R
Greenbrier	V	Cn, St, Ca
Guajillo	UM	St
Guayacan	LS-M	St
Hercules'-club	US	St
Huisache	US, UM	St, Cn
Javalina brush	US	St
Juniper, Ashe	US	St
Juniper, red-berry	UM	St, Cn
Kidneywood	US	St
Leatherstem	US	R
Lechuguilla	LG	Cn
Lime prickly ash	US	St
Lotebush	UM	St, R
Macartney rose	V	Ca, Cn, St, R
Mescal bean	US	St
Mesquite, honey	US, UM	St, Cn
Mesquite, creeping	Cr	St, Cn
Oak, blackjack	US	St
Oak, live	US, Cr	St, R
Oak, post	US	St
Oak, sand shinnery	Cr	St, R

TABLE 1.1 (Continued)

Woody Species	Usual Growth Habit*	Source of Sprout Development†
Oak, water	US	St
Paloverde	US	St
Persimmon, common	US	St, R
Persimmon, Texas	US, UM	St, R
Pricklypear	LG, UM	P
Retama	US	St
Salt cedar	US	St, R
Skunkbush	US, UM	St
Small soapweed	LG	Cn
Tarbush	US	St
Tasajillo	US	St
Texas colubrina	UM	St
Twisted acacia	US, UM	St
Wolfberry, Berlandier	US	St
Yaupon	US, UM	St, R

* UM, upright multistemmed; US, upright single-stemmed; LG, low-growing succulent; V, vine; LS, low-growing single-stemmed; LS-M, low-growing, single-stemmed to multistemmed; Cr, creeping (running).

† Cn, basal crown; St, stem sections; P, pads; R, roots; Ca, canes.

$$\boxed{2}$$

Woody Plant Problems by Resource Area

BECAUSE of the diversity in environment and vegetation throughout Texas, it is logical that the brush problem be considered on the basis of rather broad ecological units. Division by major land resource areas —general complexes of climate, vegetation, soils, and topography—is generally accepted as the most appropriate approach to delineating broad differences in land use and potential. One of the primary features which characterize the uniqueness of each of the ten major land resource areas in Texas (Fig. 2.1) is the composition of the woody cover, particularly brush. Since the effectiveness of each brush management technique depends largely on the nature of the target species and on environmental conditions, especially soils and rainfall, and since the objective of the landowner for undertaking brush management hinges on the potential use of his land, the following discussion was developed to relate brush problems in Texas to specific environmental conditions.

Pineywoods

The Pineywoods comprise about fifteen million acres primarily of forested land in eastern Texas. These pine-hardwood forests, which extend into Louisiana, Arkansas, and Oklahoma, are maintained by an average annual precipitation of 35–50 inches. Their soils are usually highly leached and vary from dark gray sands to sandy loams. Although the region is primarily forest, land use includes considerable amounts of cultivated cropland, tame pastureland, and some native grasslands (109).

Mechanical brush control is used more widely than herbicides in

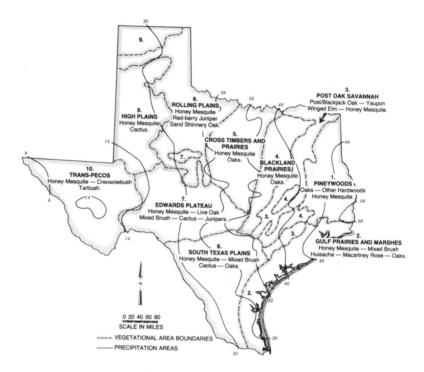

2.1. Primary woody plant problems based on vegetation areas and normal annual precipitation in Texas.

the Pineywoods because of the proximity of herbicide-sensitive cultivated crops and the anticipated uses for the land. Hardwoods, mostly low-value oaks such as post oak and blackjack oak, are the primary brush problems. Honey mesquite occurs here in lesser amounts than in most other physiographic provinces of Texas, but it can be a troublesome increaser. Understory brush species such as saw greenbrier and yaupon may form dense thickets that pose serious management problems for the forester and the range manager.

Brush control is practiced in much of the area as an initial step in the establishment of tame pastures. However, with rising production costs, particularly for energy and fertilizer, the trend may soon shift toward renewed emphasis on the use of native range species for grazing. Also, control of undesirable understory hardwoods in pine plantations can certainly augment development of grazeable forests.

Gulf Prairies and Marshes

The Gulf Prairies and Marshes vegetation area occupies approximately 9.5 million acres along the Texas coast. Gould (109) recognizes two major divisions of the coastal area, the Coastal Prairie and the Gulf Coast Marshlands. The Coastal Prairie, a nearly level, slowly drained plain, grades into the South Texas Plains on the west and the Post Oak Savannahs and the Pineywoods on the east. It is recognized as a needlegrass–bluestem (*Stipa-Andropogon*) association (70), with undisputed prominence of the bluestems. The Coastal Marsh is a narrow zone of low, wet marshland immediately adjacent to the coast (109).

Cultivated crops are becoming increasingly important at the expense of grassland on the better soils of the Coastal Prairie. Grain sorghum, rice, cotton, flax, and other crops flourish where prairie once prevailed. Average annual rainfall on the Gulf Prairies and Marshes varies from less than 30 inches to about 50 inches from west to east. The area is characterized by a growing season of more than three hundred days, warm temperatures, and high humidity.

Coastal Prairie soils are acid clays or clay loams interdispersed with relatively small areas of sandy loam. Most soils are slowly permeable and droughty. Topography is generally level and soils are poorly drained, but potential productivity of herbaceous vegetation is extremely high. Before the advent of white men, the area was probably fairly open grassland interspersed with honey mesquite and live oak mottes with scattered post and blackjack oaks. Primary range sites include blackland, sandy prairie, and lowland flats (109).

These Coastal Prairie sites may grade into the salt meadows and salt marshes of the Gulf Coast Marshlands. Potential vegetation of Coastal Prairie is tall- and mid-bunch grasses, with big bluestem, seacoast bluestem, switchgrass, and yellow Indiangrass common on well-managed sites. Introduced grasses such as common and coastal Bermudagrass and Bahiagrass are commonly used for tame pastures.

Distribution of woody vegetation follows the major soil types on the Coastal Prairie. Live oak savannahs are common in the southern and western portions. Live oak forms dense, almost pure stands on the deep sands or is associated on the heavier soils with various acacias such as huisache and with species such as spiny hackberry and lotebush. Post oak and blackjack oak occur with live oak or in isolated communities in the northwest part of the Coastal Prairie. The post oak–blackjack oak vegetation type is characterized by moderate to dense stands of underbrush including many species characteristic of the Post Oak Savannah.

Honey mesquite occurs throughout the Coastal Prairie but more sparsely than in other parts of the state except for the Pineywoods. In the extreme coastal zones of Kleberg, Kenedy, Willacy, and Cameron counties, large, single-stemmed honey mesquites occur singly or in small mottes often associated with pricklypear. This brush type is common as far inland as Starr, Jim Hogg, and Duval counties into the South Texas Plains. Honey mesquite inhabits deep loams and clays in the eastern portion of the area (Refugio, Bee, and Victoria counties). It intermingles with post oak, blackjack oak, and live oak on lighter soils and with low-growing, xerophytic mixed brush characterized by acacias on the uplands.

In addition to honey mesquite, the most characteristic troublesome species of the Coastal Prairie probably are huisache and Macartney rose. These species combine to form unique communities in some areas, especially on the heavy, slowly permeable soils. Such communities are typical in Victoria County on Victoria and Lake Charles clays where brush control is practiced regularly. Huisache is distributed throughout the Coastal Prairie (163). It may form dense, almost pure stands on lowland areas, and it thrives on the more mesic uplands in association with species typical of mixed-brush communities. Macartney rose may occur with an overstory of honey mesquite and huisache but may dominate the vegetation of heavier soils.

Post Oak Savannah

The Post Oak Savannah is a part of the true prairie (*Stipa-Sporobolus*) association of the grassland formation. It occupies over 8.5 million acres of gently rolling to hilly lands in East Central Texas. Annual rainfall varies from 35 inches to 45 inches, with most precipitation usually received in May or June. Soils are light-colored, acid sandy loams or sands on the uplands and acid, light brown to dark, sandy loams to clays on the bottomlands (109).

Savannah is open grassland within a grassland climate that supports isolated trees (77). The highly productive grasslands of the Post Oak Savannah are well suited to livestock production (Fig. 2.2). The optimum use for much of the area is as rangeland if proper range improvement and management procedures are applied. However, restriction of naturally occurring fires and continual overgrazing have converted much of the Post Oak Savannah from true savannah to complex, heavy thickets of woody plants which reduce forage production and present severe difficulties in the handling and care of livestock (Fig. 2.3). Post oak and blackjack oak form the overstory in

2.2. Post Oak Savannah, highly productive grassland well suited to livestock production, may be improved by aerial application of herbicides.

2.3. Restriction of naturally occurring fires and prolonged grazing abuse have resulted in the closing of the oaks and in the formation of thickets by invading understory species in the Post Oak Savannah (274).

the woody plant complex, and impenetrable thickets composed of species such as yaupon, winged elm, and common persimmon often form a secondary layer. Low-growing shrubs and vines common to these woodlands include saw greenbrier, skunkbush, southern dewberry, woollybucket bumelia, coralberry, and Mexican plum. On certain sites, downy hawthorne, sugar hackberry, spiny hackberry, common honey locust, and eastern red cedar may be present in limited quantities. Willow baccharis occurs frequently in the Post Oak Savannah, especially following disturbance (274). Honey mesquite may reinfest and form almost pure stands on abandoned cultivated lands of the area.

Small farms are common in the Post Oak Savannah, and increasing amounts of the area are being converted to tame pastures using Bermudagrass, Bahiagrass, and similar species which respond to intensive management, especially fertilization.

Aerial broadcast applications of herbicides can be used only to a limited extent in most of the Post Oak Savannah because of the proximity of susceptible crops (274). Herbicides may be applied to limited areas with ground equipment to reduce the drift hazard, but the primary brush control methods include bulldozing, chaining, and stacking and burning of debris.

Blackland Prairies

The Blackland Prairies occupy about 11.5 million acres of gently rolling to nearly level land in Central Texas. Average annual rainfall varies from 30 inches in the west to slightly more than 40 inches in the east. Soils are fairly uniform, dark, calcareous clays interspersed with gray, acid, sandy loams (109).

Much of the Blackland Prairies is under cultivation, especially with grain sorghum and cotton, but remnant native hay meadows typify the potential vegetation. Classification of the potential vegetation in the true prairie association is justified by the presence of species such as little bluestem (109). Honey mesquite is probably the most widespread brush problem in the area, especially on hardland sites of the southern portion of the Blackland Prairies. Post and blackjack oaks increase on the medium- to light-textured soils but generally without the complement of underbrush that occurs in the Post Oak Savannah. Mechanical brush control is practiced primarily to convert the brushland into native pastures or cultivated land rather than for the improvement of native range. Common Bermudagrass, coastal Bermudagrass, and Dallisgrass are used frequently to establish tame pastures.

Cross Timbers and Prairies

The Cross Timbers and Prairies occupy about 17 million acres, of which about 3 million acres compose the West Cross Timbers, about 1 million acres make up the East Cross Timbers, and about 6.5 million acres are included in the Grand Prairies. Average annual rainfall is 25–40 inches, with most precipitation received from April to June. Soils are slightly acid sandy or clay loams (109). Land use is predominantly for cultivated agriculture—grain sorghum, cotton, and wheat—but there are also many large cattle ranches. Brush problems, particularly in the lowlands, include post oak and blackjack oak forests similar to those described for the Post Oak Savannah. The Cross Timbers and Prairies grade into the Edwards Plateau on the south and

into the Rolling Plains on the west. Honey mesquite, red-berry juniper, Ashe juniper, and eastern red cedar form the brush complex on
the northern and eastern boundaries, especially on slopes and shallow
soils.

South Texas Plains

The South Texas Plains occupy more than twenty million acres of
level to rolling land dissected by streams flowing into the Gulf of
Mexico. Average annual precipitation is 16–35 inches, with monthly
rainfall usually lowest during January and February and highest in
May or June. Summer temperatures and evaporation rates are high,
and periodic droughts are common. Soils range from clays to sandy
loams, are calcareous to slightly acid, and vary in drainage and in
their capacities for moisture retention. Typical range sites include deep
sands, hardlands, shallow ridges, bottomlands, alkali flats, and mixed
sandyland. Most of the South Texas Plains is used as rangeland and
supports abundant white-tailed deer and other wildlife (109).

Potential vegetation of the South Texas Plains is highly productive grassland or savannah. It is a part of the mixed prairie (*Stipa-
Bouteloua*) association and grades into the desert plains grassland
(*Aristida-Bouteloua*) association on the west (70). Ranchers of the
region now face a severe problem with infestations of mixed-brush
communities or "chaparral," honey mesquite, post oak, live oak, cactus, and several acacias. The South Texas Plains support one of the
most diverse and difficult-to-manage brush problems in the state.

Compositions of plant communities and successional patterns
vary with range site in the South Texas Plains. Sandy loams are capable of supporting seacoast bluestem, bristlegrasses, false chloris, longspike silver bluestem, big sandbur, tanglehead, and species of *Setaria*,
Paspalum, and *Chloris*. Clay and clay loam may support longspike
silver bluestem, Arizona cottontop, buffalograss, common curlymesquite, bristlegrasses, gramas, and pappusgrasses. Gulf cordgrass, seashore saltgrass, and alkali sacaton are typical of low saline areas.

The complex brush communities of the South Texas Plains can
be most easily delineated by the soil preferences of the most common
woody plants. Davis and Spicer (67) suggest that before the white
man, the vegetation on fine, deep sands grading into loams and clays

was probably open savannah. Live oak savannahs represent one type of woody plant grouping on these soils. Live oak dominates the vegetation by forming dense mottes of mostly large trees with little underbrush. These live oak savannahs grade into open grasslands or open honey mesquite savannahs which support mottes of smaller live oak (sometimes "running" rather than upright live oak) surrounded by underbrush. Live oak savannahs are most common in the eastern portion of the South Texas Plains approaching or included in the Coastal Prairie. This vegetation is categorized as live oak–chaparral communities on the Welder Wildlife Refuge near Sinton, Texas (37).

Near the coastal zone in the southeastern tip of the state, extensions of honey mesquite and live oak savannahs are found in the isolated brush mottes. These unions are generally various mixtures of acacias, spiny hackberry, Texas persimmon, lotebush, and lime prickly ash forming the underbrush. Sites supporting these woody plants have potential for supporting tall bunch grasses. However, under moderate to heavy grazing they support *Chloris-Paspalum* associations which are rapidly reduced to annual grasses and weeds by overgrazing.

Davis and Spicer (67) list a "post oak subtype," typified by a post oak–blackjack oak union, for the South Texas Plains. The association between post oak and blackjack oak is so common that they should probably be considered as codominants in several vegetational areas. Post oak and blackjack oak apparently replace live oak, particularly northeastward, but for no apparent reason unless weather fluctuation and depth of soil have major influence (67). Post and blackjack oaks may be present in small amounts in the live oak savannahs. This aspect becomes rare west of a line from Starr County to Live Oak County. North of the line through southernmost Atascosa County it grades into the Post Oak Savannah of east central Texas. The post oak–blackjack oak union in South Texas is characterized by moderate to dense underbrush of species that are more xerophytic than those that occur in the Post Oak Savannah.

Honey mesquite dominates areas "varying from sandy loams to clay loams to heavy clays" with topsoils more than 20 inches deep (67). This most widespread woody vegetation grouping in South Texas is characterized by the presence of honey mesquite, especially along drainageways and valleys, with highly variable underbrush depending on geographical location and local topography. In Refugio,

Bee, and Victoria counties this vegetation is intermingled with post oak, blackjack oak, and live oak on the lighter soils and with low-growing, xerophytic, mixed brush characterized by acacias on the uplands. Before the advent of the white man these areas probably were savannahs interspersed with honey mesquite mottes in the west or honey mesquite–oak mottes in the east. Heavy honey mesquite stands probably followed the major drainageways, as is indicated by remnants of undisturbed vegetation supporting large, stately, single-stemmed trees. Areas supporting this vegetation have relatively high potential forage productivity increasing with rainfall and growing season from west to east.

Most of the western South Texas Plains is characterized by a variety of low-growing, xerophytic shrubs. Soils supporting this vegetation are shallow, heterogeneous, and generally of heavy texture. I agree with other writers (67, 161) that the vegetation, even before the coming of the white man, was low-growing brush of a variety of species. However, such low-growing woody plants have increased in density with the activities of civilization. Local conditions drastically affect composition, but two subtypes named by Davis and Spicer (67) can be typified. One characteristic grouping can be referred to as "guajillo ridges and mixed-brush uplands." This vegetation subtype is supported by rocky soils, outcrops, and gravel pavement ridges as fingers of the Balcones Escarpment (67). The ridges are dominated by guajillo in almost pure stands at the tops, grading downslope into communities with several acacias. Soil conditions, primarily fertility, apparently increase downslope and drainage is adequate. The lowlands often support moderate proportions of honey mesquite. However, the preponderance and uniformity of underbrush, commonly referred to as "chaparral," allow isolation of this vegetation (Fig. 2.4). This plant grouping provides excellent browse and cover for white-tailed deer, especially in the central to western portion of the South Texas Plains.

On the moist lowlands, especially along drainageways, retama becomes more common. Whitebrush may form dense, almost pure stands on the deep soil of lowlands (Fig. 2.5). A common component on upland slopes, whitebrush plays a relatively minor role there compared to its dominance of deep lowland soils. So typical is this association with deep, fertile soils that whitebrush is used as an indicator of soils most capable of cultivation.

2.4. As soil and moisture conditions improve downslope from the guajillo ridges, woody vegetation is dominated by honey mesquite, twisted acacia, blackbrush acacia, spiny hackberry, and lotebush, with lesser amounts of wolfberry, javelina brush, cenizo, agarito, cactus, and yuccas forming typical South Texas mixed brush.

2.5. On deep, productive lowlands of the South Texas Plains, whitebrush may form dense, almost pure stands.

Another grouping can be referred to as "hardlands vegetation." The hardlands have calcareous deposits just beneath the surface and support a variety of low-grading shrubs dominated by blackbrush, guajillo, and other acacias; notable amounts of spiny hackberry; cenizo; *Condalia* and *Ziziphus* species; and traces of species such as javelina brush, wolfberry, cactus, and yuccas. The soils usually contain considerable amounts of salts, especially of sodium. High salinity causes local vegetation to be dominated by creeping mesquite or, in extreme cases, to be absent. Salt-tolerant grasses and pricklypear usually inhabit the saline areas or are common around the periphery of the "slicks" (bare ground). In their discussion of communities on the Welder Wildlife Refuge near Sinton, Box and Chamrad (37) described the hardlands vegetation with the "chaparral–bristlegrass communities." Woody representatives in addition to those mentioned above are twisted acacia, agarito, Texas persimmon, and lime prickly ash. These communities are highly stable and increase in density upon disturbance.

Edwards Plateau

The Edwards Plateau, the "hill country" in west central Texas, occupies about twenty-four million acres of hilly, rocky land. The surface is rough, well drained, and dissected by several river systems. Average rainfall varies from less than 15 inches in the west to over 33 inches in the east. Soils are shallow, have a wide range of surface textures, and are underlain by limestone or caliche; rocky outcrops are common (301). Typical range sites include adobe hills, shallow uplands, rough, stony soils, and deep soils. The area is used predominantly as rangeland, with cultivation largely confined to the deeper soils in the valleys and near rivers (109).

The Edwards Plateau is bordered by the Trans-Pecos on the west, the Post Oak Savannah on the east, the Cross Timbers and Prairies and Rolling Plains on the north, and the South Texas Plains on the south (Fig. 2.1). Since the Edwards Plateau is the meeting point of most brush types of Texas, its woody plant problems are typified by honey mesquite, live oak, shin oak, and several junipers (44). Underbrush includes species such as cactus and Texas persimmon. On the thin, shallow soils and slopes, red-berry juniper, Ashe juniper, and eastern red cedar form almost pure stands.

Cattle or combinations of cattle with sheep and goats are stocked in the Edwards Plateau to make full use of the variety of plants. Goats are effective for the control of oaks, particularly of new sprouts following the removal of original top growth. Aerial spraying is used less than other brush control methods because of the rough terrain and species composition. Also, the brush communities are composed of several species of woody plants that are not highly susceptible to hormone herbicides. Mechanical brush control is practiced with caution because of the rocky, shallow soils. However, root plowing followed by reseeding with native grasses has been effective for range improvement at the Sonora Experiment Station (199).

Potential vegetation in the Edwards Plateau includes large amounts of little bluestem, yellow Indiangrass, and big bluestem (109). The cool-season species Texas wintergrass dominates many areas. Small-statured gramas, buffalograss, and species of *Aristida* occur on the shallow soils and under heavy grazing.

Rolling Plains

The Rolling Plains are an extension of the Great Plains of the central United States. They occupy almost twenty-four million acres of gently rolling to moderately rough topography in northwestern Texas. Average annual rainfall varies from about 22 inches in the west to nearly 30 inches in the east. Seasonal precipitation is highly variable but lowest during the summer when temperatures and evaporation rates are highest. Soils vary from coarse sands to redbed clays and shales. Typical range sites include hardland, mixed land, sandyland, sandy rough breaks, rocky hills, rolling hills, and bottomlands (109).

Cow-calf operations are the most common range livestock enterprises on the Rolling Plains. About two-thirds of the area is still in rangeland, with intermittent small cultivated areas dotting the landscape (109).

Potential vegetation of the Rolling Plains includes mid-grasses such as little bluestem and sideoats grama and, in lowland areas, western wheatgrass. On the more mesic sites, potential vegetation includes big bluestem, sand bluestem, yellow Indiangrass, and switchgrass. General aspect of the area is honey mesquite savannah with mostly shrubby, many-stemmed, widely spaced honey mesquite plants dotting the landscape (Fig. 2.6), which supports buffalograss, blue grama, common curlymesquite, tobosa, dropseeds, and species such as hooded windmillgrass.

On upland sites, lotebush, agarito, sand sagebrush, and small soapweed are associated with the honey mesquite on the lighter soils. Sandy valleys, particularly in the northern and northwestern portions of the area, are dominated by sand shinnery oak, which forms almost pure stands (Fig. 2.7). Sand sagebrush and small soapweed grow in association with sand shinnery oak on these sites. Forage production may almost be eliminated by the thick stands of sand shinnery oak. However, with brush control and sound grazing management, these areas may support little bluestem and other desirable and productive range forage species.

Rough rangelands, shallow soils, and slopes of the Rolling Plains are dominated by red-berry juniper (Fig. 2.8). This species was once

2.6. General aspect of the Rolling Plains is honey mesquite savannah with shrubby, multistemmed honey mesquite and mid- and short-grasses dominating the vegetation.

2.7. In the sandy valleys of the Rolling Plains, sand shinnery oak may form almost pure stands in association with scattered sand sagebrush and small soapweed.

2.8. Red-berry juniper dominates shallow soils, slopes, and rough rangeland of the Rolling Plains.

thought to be restricted almost solely to rough rangelands. However, the better soils, particularly bottomland areas intersecting the "cedar brakes," are also being invaded by red-berry juniper (252). Widely spaced agarito and lotebush plants are typically associated with red-berry juniper.

Waterways of the Rolling Plains may support tall, single-stemmed honey mesquite, salt cedar, cottonwoods, and willows. Salt cedar is extremely difficult to control and may rapidly invade the sandylands or bottomlands near waterways.

Aerial spraying, chaining, root plowing, and tree grubbing are widely practiced in the Rolling Plains. On the more favorable sites, mechanical brush control is often followed by artificial revegetation with native forage species. The relatively low average annual precipitation and the distribution of rainfall do not allow tame pastures to be as widely used as those in the eastern portion of Texas.

High Plains

The Texas High Plains occupy about twenty million acres of the Great Plains. The region is a relatively level high plateau separated from the Rolling Plains by the Caprock Escarpment. Its surface is spotted with playa lakes which sometimes cover considerable areas following heavy rains. Average annual rainfall is from 15 to 21 inches, with a dry midsummer period. The average frost-free period is from 180 to about 225 days. Much of the high plains region, particularly in the eastern portion, has been converted from native grasslands to the cultivation of grain sorghum, cotton, and wheat. The amount of cultivation has increased with the availability of underground irrigation water. The area from the Caprock Escarpment on the east to Amarillo on the northwest is almost totally cultivated (109).

The western extension of the High Plains is primarily rangeland and is classified as mixed prairie or short-grass prairie. Typical native grasses include buffalograss, blue grama, and sideoats grama. Little bluestem and western wheatgrass may occur on the more favorable sites. The High Plains typically support lower densities of woody plants than the Rolling Plains, but species composition is similar. The High Plains can be classified as honey mesquite shrubland or savannah. In some areas honey mesquite forms heavy stands with cholla

cactus, lotebush, plains pricklypear, agarito, and tasajillo. Small soapweed and sand sagebrush are common on the lighter soils. Sand shinnery oak may dominate sandylands, bottomlands, and valleys, though
to a lesser extent than in the Rolling Plains.

Trans-Pecos Mountains and Basins

The Trans-Pecos occupies some nineteen million acres of mountains and arid valleys in the extreme western portions of Texas. It is
bordered by the Edwards Plateau on the east, the Rio Grande on the
south, and New Mexico on the north. Environmental conditions are
extremely diverse, with vegetation heavily influenced by microenviron-
mental conditions. Average annual precipitation is less than 12 inches
over most of the area. However, there is extreme variability in annual
precipitation, and yearly rainfall of more than 30 inches has been
reported. Soils are generally calcareous and may accumulate alkali as
a result of poor drainage. Typical range sites include stony hills, clay
flats, sands, saline soils, gypsum flats, deep uplands, rough, stony
mountains, gravelly outwashes, and badlands (109). Most of the area
still remains in native rangeland and is in large landholdings. Farm-
lands are confined primarily to irrigated valleys. Ranges are usually
stocked with cattle and sheep or with combinations of cattle, sheep,
and goats (109).

Many vegetation types occur in the Trans-Pecos due to wide
variation in elevation. Potential grasses include sideoats grama, green
sprangletop, Arizona cottontop, bush muhly, plains bristlegrass, vine
mesquite, black grama, tobosa, and alkali sacaton. Although bordered
by shallow soils supporting little range forage, black grama sites in the
Trans-Pecos are some of the best grazing lands in the state. Although
it is of short stature, black grama is highly nutritious forage. Primary
brush problems are honey mesquite, creosotebush (Fig. 2.9), and
tarbush. These species, in association with catclaw acacia and catclaw
mimosa, form a desert-shrub community. The Trans-Pecos is indeed
an area of contrast, ranging from desert shrub to beautiful forests of
pine and oak within a few miles. On some of the more favorable sites,
especially at the higher elevations, junipers form almost open savannahs grading upward into pinyon pine and oak forests. Lowland areas,
particularly the more favorable sites, may support brush similar to that

2.9. Broad expanses of shallow soils in the Trans-Pecos are dominated by creosotebush with little production of usable livestock forage.

of the South Texas Plains, where honey mesquite grows in combination with several species of *Acacia*, *Yucca*, and *Quercus*. Due to the aridity and the resistance of most of the species to present control methods, brush control must be approached more carefully in the Trans-Pecos than in any other area of Texas. However, brush management in conjunction with other range improvement methods, such as water spreading, the contouring and shaping of the land to retain and effectively distribute precious rainwater, can result in dramatic increases in productivity.

3

Selected Brush Species: Ecology and Control

MANY references are available which facilitate identification of woody plant species. Therefore, the following taxonomic descriptions are provided only as an aid in diagnosing the brush problem. Only the more common brush species, listed alphabetically by common name, are included below. If more than one common name is listed for a species, the common name first mentioned, by which the species is alphabetized, is preferred. Technical terms used in the plant descriptions are defined in the Glossary.

Once the brush problem has been positively identified, the reader may consider control and management suggestions. However, before any control procedure is undertaken, the information in subsequent chapters relating to the proper implementation of the procedures should be consulted. In the case of herbicides, the reader should be sure that the chemical has current Environmental Protection Agency registration and that the target species is still included on the label. Otherwise the county Agricultural Extension Agent or the USDA Soil Conservation Service should be consulted for the most recent recommendations for managing the target species. All herbicide application rates are given as amount of active ingredient rather than as formulated product. Amount of commercial formulation required can be determined by consulting the herbicide label. Methods for calculating herbicide rates as active ingredient using a formulated product are given in chapter 5.

1. Agarito; algerito. *Berberis trifoliolata* Moric. (Berberidaceae). Hollylike evergreen shrub; usually less than 5 feet tall but rarely to 8 feet; trifoliate leaves stiff, spinescent, sessile, leaf margins 3- to

7-lobed, spiny-pointed; flowers bright yellow in axillary racemes; fruit a small, red berry (Fig. 3.1) (317).

Distribution and Ecology. Agarito is also referred to as *Mahonia trifoliolata* (Moric.) Fedde (Laredo mahonia) (317). The plant contains certain alkaloids once used for medicinal purposes. Agarito

3.1. Agarito is a widespread woody component of Texas range vegetation. Easily recognized by its hollylike leaves and bright yellow flowers, it is often found growing singly or in close proximity to larger-statured woody plants.

spreads readily by seed since the fruits are relished by birds and other forms of wildlife; its flowers may evidently be a source of food for bees. The growing tips are heavily browsed by deer and goats (199). Agarito is usually a minor component of brush stands and is more common in central and western portions of Texas than in the coastal zone (Fig. 2.1, areas 1–10). It is distributed into southern New Mexico and into the eastern portion of Arizona. In Texas it is often noted growing in close proximity to other plants such as honey mesquite and live oak, with apparent preference for clay loam (87) or shallow gravelly soils (199). The root tissue, from which extracts have been used as dye, is a deep yellow color. Agarito stems arise from a discrete crown which must be removed entirely for complete control. Excavation of the plants in early spring will reveal yellowish buds clustered on the crowns. Top growth is rapidly replaced after mechanical removal. Agarito is not usually a severe management problem on rangeland except in localized areas where previous brush control efforts have released it to a more important role.

Control. Grubbing to 4 to 6 inches deep (87, 196) or basal sprays with 2,4,5-T at 4 pounds per 100 gallons of diesel oil or kerosene when the soil is dry and not fused to the trunk will control agarito (141, 234).

Promising treatments. Picloram as a foliar spray or as a granular broadcast treatment at 1 pound per acre and individual-plant treatments with picloram pellets show promise for agarito control (87). Agarito is reported to decrease in abundance after burning and after roller chopping or after a combination of roller chopping followed by burning (71, 72).

2. Ashe juniper; blue-berry juniper. *Juniperus ashei* Buchholz (Pinaceae). Shrub or evergreen tree rarely to 25 feet; low-branched, trunks twisted; flowers minute, dioecious, about 0.17 inch long; fruit fleshy, very light-coned, about 0.25 inch long, bluish green, formed by compression of enlarged fleshy scales; leaves long, scalelike, opposite, oppressed; twigs gray to reddish; bark gray to reddish brown, often in shaggy strips (317) (Fig. 3.2).

Distribution and Ecology. Ashe juniper occurs primarily on limestone hills and valleys (199), reaching greatest proportions in the Edwards Plateau, where it intermingles with red-berry juniper and eastern red cedar (Fig. 2.1, areas 5, 7–10). It spreads by seed (199).

3.2. Ashe juniper reaches greatest proportions on the limestone hills and in the valleys of the Edwards Plateau. (*Courtesy D. N. Ueckert*)

The junipers are especially prominent on thin soils and slopes, forming cedar brakes on the Edwards Plateau. Huss (157) indicated significant invasion of Ashe juniper in Real County between 1850 and 1900. The increase is partially attributed to control of naturally occurring fires by prolonged overgrazing (331). Its forage is only occasionally browsed by goats and deer, but Ashe juniper furnishes food and cover for several important species of wildlife. It is most readily consumed by sheep, goats, and deer from December through March under heavy grazing (199).

    Control. Ashe juniper is usually controlled by mechanical methods such as bulldozing, chaining, or grubbing. It is not susceptible to broadcast application of phenoxy herbicides normally used for range improvement. During a dry spring when the amount of fine fuel is at least 1,000 pounds per acre, prescribed burning has killed 99 percent of Ashe juniper plants which did not exceed about 6 feet in height (331). Prescribed burning is recognized as an effective improvement technique for rangeland infested with Ashe juniper.

3. Berlandier wolfberry. *Lycium berlandieri* Dunal (Solanaceae). Spinescent shrub; leaves spatulate-linear; flowers small, tubular, light blue to purple or white, borne singly or in small clusters; fruit a small red berry with numerous seeds (317) (Fig. 3.3).

3.3. Berlandier wolfberry is a persistent component of South Texas mixed brush. It is typified by the spatulate-linear leaves, which commonly occur singly or in groups of two, three, or four.

Distribution and Ecology. Berlandier wolfberry is a persistent component of mixed-brush stands of South Texas (Fig. 2.1, areas 2, 6, 7, 10). Little is known about the ecology of this species, but it appears to favor heavier-textured soils of good drainage. It spreads by seed and regrows from the stem base upon top removal (87). Rarely found alone in dense enough stands to constitute a brush problem, Berlandier wolfberry grows in association with a group of plants such as twisted acacia, Texas colubrina, blackbrush acacia, and catclaw which, collectively, present a severe range management problem.

Control. Berlandier wolfberry resists broadcast sprays of 2,4,5-T at rates normally used for range improvement. Apparently it is only moderately susceptible to broadcast applications of picloram. Picloram plus 2,4,5-T (1:1) at 2 pounds per acre has not effectively controlled Berlandier wolfberry (31), but the species decreased in relative abundance following burning of South Texas ranges (40). It is susceptible to any mechanical method which uproots the entire plant (87), such as root plowing, but it is not controlled by methods of simple top removal such as shredding, chopping, dragging, or chaining.

4. Blackbrush acacia; blackbrush. *Acacia rigidula* Benth. (Leguminosae). Shrub or small tree with dark green leaves and dark, almost black, stems; flowers small, white or light yellow, in densely flowered, white to yellow spikes; fruit slender, mostly 2 to 3.1 inches long, constricted between the seeds, glabrous; leaves bipinnate, pinnae one to two pairs, leaflets two to five pairs with heavy yellow midrib; spines straight, short (usually less than 0.4 inch), usually paired at nodes; bark light to dark gray, smooth (Fig. 3.4).

Distribution and Ecology. Restricted primarily to South Texas, blackbrush acacia now infests almost nine million acres of rangeland (286) (Fig. 2.1, areas 2, 6, 7, 10). It grows in association with most other species in the South Texas mixed-brush complex on a variety of soils. In pure stands it forms almost impenetrable thickets. Blackbrush acacia usually does not exceed 15 feet in height and is highly branched from the base. It becomes a serious management problem on rangeland, especially where associated species have been removed.

Control. Blackbrush acacia tolerates moderate rates of phenoxy herbicides as aerial sprays. It has been known to increase in abundance following burning of South Texas ranges (40). Root plowing or root plowing followed by raking has had little influence on the presence of blackbrush acacia in the South Texas Plains (71). However, the treatment sequence of roller chopping, shredding, and prescribed burning has decreased the density of this species by almost 40 percent (72). Two full years were required for completion of the treatments, with shredding in the spring followed by a late summer burn the same year.

3.4. Blackbrush acacia, a component of South Texas mixed brush, may also form almost pure stands on shallow, gravelly, well-drained soils.

Promising treatments. Aerial sprays, in the spring or fall, containing picloram are especially effective for blackbrush acacia control. A mixture of 0.25 pound of picloram plus 0.25 pound of 2,4,5-T per acre has resulted in good control, but response varies with location and season (91). However, blackbrush acacia may be most effectively controlled by picloram alone (31). Picloram pellets applied at 1 to 2 pounds per acre in the spring or in the fall appear promising (196).

5. Blackjack oak. *Quercus marilandica* Muenchh. (Fagaceae). Deciduous tree to 15 feet, growing occasionally to 50 feet; flowers as catkins; fruit light brown acorns; leaves obovate usually with 3 lobes at apex; bark usually black, rough (Fig. 3.5).

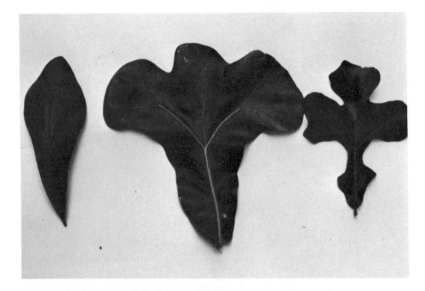

3.5. Blackjack oak (center), post oak (right), and water oak (left) are most easily differentiated based on leaf characteristics, although leaf shape is highly variable among individuals within each species.

Distribution and Ecology. Blackjack oak is distributed throughout the southern half of Texas, becoming rare only in the extreme western portions (Fig. 2.1, areas 1–3, 6–8). In the drier portion of its range, blackjack oak is restricted primarily to bottomland sites and drainageways. Although the species is a serious management problem in the central and eastern portion of Texas, scattered individuals are prized for animal shade and cover, especially in the outer limits of its range. It sprouts readily from any trunk segment remaining after top removal (274). Blackjack oak is usually found in close association with post oak, especially in the Post Oak Savannah.

Control. Individual blackjack oak trees may be treated with ammate (AMS) (140) by applying about 2 ounces of crystals per gallon of water poured into frills or 0.5 ounce of crystals per inch of tree diameter applied to cut stumps. Frill or remove the tops of trees up to 5 inches in diameter and apply 2,4,5-T solution to the cut stump. Applications of picloram or 2,4,5-T plus picloram (1:1) at 1 pound per acre in the spring have effectively controlled blackjack oak near College Station, Texas (26, 274). Granular picloram has not been as effective as sprays at the same rates and dates (29). Air temperatures above 86° F, relative humidity below 60 percent, poor spray coverage, and excessive spray swath widths have significantly reduced defoliation of blackjack oak with 2,4,5-T in Oklahoma (80). Application rates of less than 2 pounds per acre were not as effective as higher rates of 2,4,5-T for blackjack oak control.

6. Bluewood; Brasil. *Condalia obovata* Hook. (Rhamnaceae). Thorny shrub or small tree; flowers small, greenish, in small axillary cluster; leaves obovate to spatulate; fruit a small, shiny black drupe (317).

Distribution and Ecology. Bluewood generally occurs as a shrub rarely dense enough to form heavy thickets. Rarely attaining heights of over 12 feet, usually less than 6 feet, bluewood is a minor but common component of the mixed-brush complex of South Texas (Fig. 2.1, areas 2, 6, 7, 10). It is common on various soils except those with extremely poor drainage. Bluewood sprouts readily from stem and root tissues. Old bark of bluewood is typically smooth and grayish, whereas new growth is usually bluish green with large thorns.

Control. Most mechanical methods are effective, and good control of bluewood is possible with individual-plant treatments using 8 pounds of 2,4,5-T in 100 gallons of diesel oil or kerosene (141). Bulldozing or grubbing of light stands or root plowing of dense stands followed by seeding has also been successful. Foliar broadcast sprays of phenoxy herbicides are usually not effective. Aerial application of 1 pound of 2,4,5-T plus picloram per acre has given fair to good control (87).

7. Border paloverde. *Cercidium macrum* I. M. Johnst. (Leguminosae). Small deciduous tree or shrub, rarely growing to 15 feet; small yellowish flowers; fruit dark brown, elongate, flattened, apex pointed; leaves doubly pinnate, olive to dark green, less than 0.25 inch long; branches smooth, light green when young, turning dark green to brown with age; spines alternate at each node, green to black, slightly curved, less than 0.25 inch long, slightly curved or straight, sharp (317) (Fig. 3.6).

Distribution and Ecology. Restricted to the western portion of the Coastal Prairie and the South Texas Plains, border paloverde is usually most evident on shallow, well-drained rocky soils as an underbrush species. It spreads by seed and regrows from a persistent crown upon disturbance of top growth (87).

Control. Root plowing and grubbing have successfully controlled

3.6. Border paloverde is usually found on shallow, well-drained rocky soils.

border paloverde (87). Aerial application of 1 pound of 2,4,5-T plus picloram (1:1) per acre appears promising for control (87).

8. Burrobrush. *Hymenoclea monogyra* T. & G. (Compositae). Thicket-forming shrub, 2 to 8 feet tall, highly branched with numerous simple, alternate leaves 1 to 3 inches long (Fig. 3.7). Leaves are linear-fili-form and entire; numerous small, unisexual heads; staminate heads with flattish 4- to 6-lobed involucre; pistillate flower solitary. Fruiting involucre about 0.16 inch long, wings 7 to 12 in a single series, whorled thin, silvery white, 0.04 to 0.1 inch long (317).

Distribution and Ecology. Burrobrush occurs in the western portion of the Edwards Plateau and throughout the Trans-Pecos along streams and on alluvial soils. It also occurs in New Mexico, Arizona, California, and northern Mexico. Burrobrush presents severe management problems on certain sites, especially drainageways and foothills in the Trans-Pecos (244). Based on growth form and vegetative structures, burrobrush is often confused with *Baccharis* species.

Control. Based on limited unpublished research by the author, burrobrush was not highly susceptible to broadcast applications of 2,4-D, 2,4,5-T or dicamba at 1–2 pounds per acre. Stands of burro-

3.7. Burrobrush may create severe management problems in bottomlands and along streams in the western Edwards Plateau and in the Trans-Pecos.

brush are generally too thick for effective application of individual-plant treatments. Shredding may be used to suppress burrobrush.

9. Catclaw; catclaw acacia; cat's-claw. *Acacia greggii* Gray (Leguminosae). Spiny shrub or subshrub; flowers small, cream-colored, in dense spikes, mostly 0.8 to 2 inches long; thorns short, stout, and curved at the end like a cat's claw; fruit a flat, usually curved pod, constricted between the seeds (317).

Distribution and Ecology. Catclaw grows in association with other *Acacia*s in the mixed-brush complex of South Texas and West Texas. Catclaw is distributed throughout South Texas but is most common in central and western portions of the area on drier sites (Fig. 2.1, areas 2, 6–8, 10). Although it has been described as "sometimes becoming small trees" (317), it usually forms part of the understory as a small shrub. Catclaw appears to be highly adapted to gravelly loam and sandy loam sites (87). Although it is of relatively small stature, catclaw can make up relatively high amounts of ground cover in some brush stands. In some areas catclaw forms heavy, solid stands seriously limiting range forage production and restricting efficiency of working and handling livestock. It provides excellent cover in drier areas for upland game birds. It spreads by seed and persists after top removal by vegetative reproduction from the stem base (crown) (87).

Control. Aerial sprays of 2,4,5-T are not effective for control of catclaw. Individual plants can be successfully controlled with basal sprays of 8 pounds of 2,4,5-T per 100 gallons of diesel oil or kerosene when the soil is dry (141). Grubbing and root plowing give effective control of catclaw (87).

Promising treatments. Sprays containing picloram usually result in fair to moderate control of catclaw, but results have been variable. Good control has resulted from 2 pounds per acre of a 1:1 mixture of 2,4,5-T plus picloram aerially applied (31).

10. Catclaw mimosa. *Mimosa biuncifera* Benth. (Leguminosae). Spiny shrub, rarely to 8 feet; thorns curved similarly to those of catclaw acacia and lime prickly ash, spines single or paired; flowers pale pink to whitish; legume 0.75 to 1.5 inches long, slightly curved or straight, constricted between the seeds; 4 to 10 pairs pinnae per leaf, petioles 0.5 to 1.5 inches long, leaflets glabrous or slightly pubescent (317).

Distribution and Ecology. Catclaw mimosa occurs primarily in the Trans-Pecos as a xeric shrub (Fig. 2.1, areas 5, 7–10). It occurs on clay loam soils in solid stands or in association with honey mesquite (87). Catclaw mimosa spreads by seed and reproduces vegetatively from a basal crown (87).

Control. Catclaw mimosa is not susceptible to broadcast applications of phenoxy herbicides at rates normally used for range improvement. Aerial application of 0.5 to 1 pound of 2,4,5-T plus picloram per acre has resulted in good control, and root plowing and grubbing are effective (87).

11. Cenizo; Texas silverleaf; purple sage. *Leucophyllum frutescens* (Berl.) I. M. Johnston (Scrophulariaceae). Evergreen, low shrub with stout stems, usually less than 4 to 6 feet tall, occasionally to 10 feet; flowers whitish to pink, showy; obovate leaves whitish gray to grayish green, giving strong contrast to flowers (317) (Fig. 3.8).

Distribution and Ecology. Cenizo reaches greatest proportions on the South Texas Plains (Fig. 2.1, areas 2, 6, 7, 10). It grows primarily on upland, rocky, shallow sites and only occasionally dominates the aspect. Cenizo plants are usually widely spaced, growing in

3.8. Cenizo, a showy, low-growing shrub common to droughty, shallow sites of the western half of Texas, is also commonly used as an ornamental.

association with acacias such as blackbrush acacia, twisted acacia, and guajillo. It spreads by seed and regrows from the base upon top removal (87). Used as an ornamental, cenizo is not considered to be a severe brush control problem relative to the area it covers as an individual species. However, since it resists most conventional control methods, it becomes a difficult problem in local areas in association with other species.

Control. Apparently cenizo is not susceptible to broadcast applications of hormone herbicides at rates normally used for range improvement. In scattered stands grubbing may be the best approach to its control (87). Root plowing followed by raking, dragging, or dragging followed by root plowing effectively reduces stands of cenizo in the South Texas Plains (71).

12. Cholla. *Opuntia imbricata* Haw. var. *imbricata* (Cactaceae). Large, upright cactus reaching 10 to 13 feet tall, occasionally in dense thickets but usually widely spaced (Fig. 3.9); flowers terminal 1.5 to 2.75 inches long, purple; fruit yellow, dry; seeds 0.08 to 0.16 inches in diameter; points cylindric, branchlike, very spiny; leaves 1 to 3.2 inches long, deciduous; spines 0.7 to 1.25 inches long, barbed, white to green (317).

Distribution and Ecology. Cholla is referred to as "walking-stick cholla" by the Weed Science Society of America (321). It is described by Vines (317) as occurring in Texas, northward to Oklahoma and Kansas, and westward to New Mexico. Cholla reaches its greatest proportions in the High Plains and Trans-Pecos of Texas (Fig. 2.1, areas 9, 10). It grows in association with honey mesquite in savannah vegetation. Cholla occurs on clay and clay loam soils or foothills in West Texas, especially the High Plains and Trans-Pecos (196). It spreads by seed and vegetatively by removal of the joints.

Control. Individual-plant treatment with herbicides such as 2,4,5-T successfully controls sparse stands of cholla. Broadcast, aerial applications of herbicides containing picloram are more effective than phenoxy herbicides alone. Individual-plant treatments such as grubbing or removal with a fork lift (196), allowing the plant parts to desiccate, and stacking are also effective. If disrupted, as by dragging or chaining when the soil is moist, the cholla pads quickly take root and establish new plants, forming dense thickets. Chaining should be accomplished before winter (196).

3.9. Cholla is a severe range management problem in the High Plains and parts of Trans-Pecos Texas. Upon separation from the parent plant, cholla joints readily take root in moist soil. (*Courtesy Soil Conservation Service*)

13. Common honey locust. *Gleditsia triacanthos* L. (Leguminosae). Usually thorny tree attaining heights of more than 45 feet; branches erect; bark smooth and pale; flowers 3 to 4 inches long; fruit orange yellow, straight or falcate legume; leaves compound, 12- to 22-foliate, leaflets oblong ovate, upper surface dark green and lustrous (317).

Distribution and Ecology. Common ·honey locust is especially prevalent in central and eastern Texas, reaching its greatest numbers in the Brazos River area of the Post Oak Savannah (Fig. 2.1, areas 1–7). Used to some extent as an ornamental, it becomes a range management problem only as it occurs in association with other species.

Control. Common honey locust is not highly susceptible to broadcast foliar applications of phenoxy herbicides. Poor to fair control with 1 to 2 pounds of 2,4-D or 2,4,5-T per acre has been reported (167).

14. Common persimmon. *Diospyros virginiana* L. (Ebenaceae). Tree usually less than 40 feet tall; flowers greenish yellow and thick, pollen light and powdery, staminate and pistillate flowers on separate trees; fruit a persistent berry which is astringent when green, somewhat sweeter when ripe; leaves simple, alternate, entire, ovate, oblong to elliptic, deciduous; bark brown to black with deep fissures; wood a dark brown to black (317).

Distribution and Ecology. Common persimmon is distributed across the state but is most common in the eastern two-thirds of Texas (Fig. 2.1, areas 1–5, 8). A vigorous root sprouter (95), it occurs on an array of soil types occasionally in densities adequate to be considered a severe brush problem.

Control. Common persimmon is apparently highly sensitive to foliar, soil, or basal-bark applications of dicamba. In Missouri, foliar sprays of 4 pounds of dicamba per acre or 1 to 2 pounds of picloram per acre applied in the spring have killed over 90 percent of the common persimmons (225). Basal sprays of 2,4-D or 2,4,5-T were also effective. Fair control can be expected from 1 pound of silvex per acre as a broadcast foliar spray (167). There is no apparent differential response between male and female trees to individual-plant herbicide treatments (95). Application of AMS (8 pounds per 100 gallons of water) to cut stumps is also an effective treatment for control of common persimmon.

15. Coralberry; buckbrush. *Symphoricarpos orbiculatus* Moench. (Caprifoliaceae). Thicket-forming shrub, spreading by stolons; usually 2 to 6.5 feet tall; flowers greenish white to pinkish; fruit a berrylike drupe, pink to light coral red; leaves numerous, opposite, oval to ovate, upper surface dull green; twigs slender, brown, with shreddy bark (Fig. 3.10) (317).

Distribution and Ecology. Coralberry occurs in central to north

3.10. Coralberry is typified by numerous oval to ovate, dull green leaves and light coral red fruits.

central Texas, into Oklahoma, and eastward into Arkansas and Louisiana (317). It reaches greatest proportions in the northeastern quarter of Texas (Fig. 2.1, areas 1–5, 7). Coralberry serves as excellent
wildlife food and cover, but in heavy stands it reduces the production
of desirable range forage. Seeds are spread primarily by birds and
animals (87).

Control. Broadcast applications of 1 to 2 pounds of 2,4-D or
2,4,5-T per acre will give fair control of coralberry (167); grubbing
or root plowing results in effective control.

16. Coyotillo. *Karwinskia humboldtiana* (R. & S.) Zucc. (Rhamnaceae). Evergreen shrub, rarely a small tree; spineless with mostly
opposite, pinnately veined, lanceolate to oval leaves; generally 1 to 5
feet tall, occasionally to 10 feet, rarely to 18 feet; flowers small, greenish, in small axillary clusters; calyx five-lobed; five petals, five stamens
and a compound pistil; fruit small, brown or black, ovoid drupe; fruits
containing from one to four seeds (317) (Fig. 3.11).

Distribution and Ecology. Coyotillo is a poisonous species (291)
which infests rangelands of South Texas and extends into Mexico and
to California (292) (Fig. 2.1, areas 2, 6, 7, 10). Its fruits mature in
late summer and fall, but their rate of development may not be uniform. Coyotillo reaches greatest development on moist, deep soils,
although it grows on hills and ridges and in arroyos and river canyons.
It evidently prefers calcareous soils and is usually confined to shallow
sites. It may grow in association with guajillo and has similar site requirements.

Control. Broadcast, foliar treatments with 2,4,5-T usually do not
give satisfactory results, and results from basal applications evidently
are erratic (291). Excellent control from broadcast applications of
silvex has been reported (167). Best results are obtained from basal
treatments of 2,4,5-T in diesel oil. Injection of 2,4,5-T, 2,4-D, or a
combination of the herbicides into the soil at the base of the plants is
evidently effective on deep soils. Grubbing or bulldozing of scattered
plants or root plowing when associated with thick chaparral is recommended (234). Root plowing or root plowing followed by raking in
the South Texas Plains will provide effective control (71).

17. Creeping mesquite. *Prosopis reptans* Benth. var. *cinerascens*
(Gray) Burk. (Leguminosae). Low-spreading shrub, usually not over

3.11. Coyotillo is a poisonous woody plant which occurs on rangeland from South Texas into Mexico and California.

4 to 5 feet tall; flowers yellow, borne in headlike clusters; fruit a thick, tightly coiled, woody-walled legume, mostly 0.6 to 2 inches long; leaves and twigs very similar to those of honey mesquite (317).

Distribution and Ecology. Vegetative characters of creeping mesquite, commonly called "running mesquite," are morphologically similar to those of honey mesquite, but the species differ in that creeping mesquite assumes an almost prostrate growth habit. It grows on alkaline or gypsum soils of the South Texas Plains, with the largest infestations along the Nueces and Frio watersheds (Fig. 2.1, areas 2, 6). In areas of greatest adaptation creeping mesquite is a formidable brush problem, growing in solid stands to the exclusion of forage species.

Control. Two or three successive annual applications of 0.67 pound of 2,4,5-T per acre are usually necessary for acceptable control of creeping mesquite (142). Aerial application is accomplished by dispensing the herbicide in 1 gallon of diesel oil and enough water to make 5 gallons of spray solution per acre. As with honey mesquite, the best results are obtained from aerial application of herbicides forty to ninety days after leaf growth appears or when the foliage turns from light to dark green. Creeping mesquite, because of its growth form, is not susceptible to most mechanical methods, root plowing being the exception.

18. Creosotebush. *Larrea divaricata* Cav. (Zygophyllaceae). Evergreen aromatic shrub, occasionally growing to 10 feet; flowers yellow, one-seeded and dehiscent; fruit a small, globose capsule; leaves bifoliate; leaflets two, small, opposite, thick, dark green to yellowish green, resinous and strong scented; twigs brown, with conspicuous nodes, bark dark gray to black (317). The Weed Science Society of America (321) accepts *L. tridenta* (DC.) Coville (Fig. 3.12).

Distribution and Ecology. Creosotebush reaches its greatest proportion in western Texas and presents a serious range management problem in the Trans-Pecos (Fig. 2.9). Scattered through western portions of the Edwards Plateau and Rio Grande Plain, it occupies only the more xerophytic sites, especially shallow, gravelly sites (87) in this eastern portion of its range (Fig. 2.1, areas 6, 7, 10). Creosotebush usually occurs on soils underlain by a hardpan. It is usually not eaten by cattle and is poisonous to sheep. It grows in thick, dense stands in areas of its greatest adaptation, usually to the exclusion of forage species. Creosotebush may be found growing in association

3.12. Creosotebush is an evergreen shrub most common in the western portion of the South Texas Plains and Edwards Plateau and in the Trans-Pecos. It occupies broad expanses of shallow gravelly sites almost to the exclusion of herbaceous forage species. (*Courtesy Soil Conservation Service*)

with tarbush, forming tarbush-creosotebush flats, especially in the Trans-Pecos.

Control. Creosotebush is not susceptible to broadcast application of most herbicides at commonly used rates (2 pounds or less per acre) for range improvement. Creosotebush has been controlled with high rates (8 pounds per acre) of the propylene glycol butyl ether ester of 2,4,5-T in Arizona (240). Greatest herbicidal activity occurs within thirty days following effective summer rains, when the creosotebush plants are in full flower to fruiting. Nevertheless, creosotebush requires 2 to 4 pounds of 2,4-D or 2,4,5-T per acre for effective control (241). Effective control of creosotebush was accomplished by root plowing followed by reseeding with adapted grasses (87, 131). However, creosotebush usually inhabits lands where high investment for mechanical control is not feasible and revegetation programs are risky.

Promising treatments. Picloram sprays at 0.25 to 1 pound per acre have effectively controlled creosotebush (241).

19. Desert yaupon. *Schaefferia cuneifolia* Gray (Celastraceae). Evergreen shrub growing to 7 feet tall; densely branched with alternate or fasciculate leaves, petioles greatly reduced; leaves cuneate, obovate or rarely oval, rounded apex, glabrous (Fig. 3.13); bark gray and smooth (317).

3.13. Desert yaupon is a common component of mixed-brush communities, especially in the western portion of the South Texas Plains. Easily recognized by its ovate to obovate leaves, it is highly branched and rarely over 3 feet tall.

Distribution and Ecology. Desert yaupon occurs primarily in western and southwestern Texas (317), although I have collected specimens near Refugio, Texas, in a heavy mixed-brush community (Fig. 2.1, areas 2, 6, 7, 10). Desert yaupon rarely occurs in such abundance as to be considered alone as a range management problem, but it is a persistent component of South Texas mixed-brush complexes.

Promising treatments. Root plowing or root plowing followed by raking appear promising for control of desert yaupon (71).

20. Devil's pincushion; devil's head. *Echinocactus texensis* Höpffer (Cactaceae). Low, stiff-spined perennial; pink to light purple showy flowers; stem hemispheric, 0.8 to 3 inches tall, usually simple; spines in clusters of 8 or 9, heavy; fruits red (Fig. 3.14) (317).

Distribution and Ecology. Devil's pincushion is an inconspicuous component of the prairies and plains from the Rolling Plains of North Texas to the South Texas Plains into Mexico (Fig. 2.1, areas 2, 5, 6–10). It rarely reaches such proportions that it is considered a range

3.14. Devil's pincushion, a low-growing cactus with stiff spines and showy flowers, is highly adapted to shallow, gravelly clay soils.

management problem except in association with other species or in localized areas. It is used to some extent as an ornamental (196). The thick, sharp spines readily penetrate shoe soles and implement tires. It is apparently most highly adapted to shallow, gravelly clay soils (87), although it occurs on sandy clay loams to clay loams (196).

Control. Grubbing below the base, generally less than 4 to 6 inches deep, assures removal of the entire plant. Treatment of individual plants with 2,4,5-T at 16 pounds per 100 gallons of diesel oil or kerosene will also control devil's pincushion (196).

21. Eastern red cedar. *Juniperus virginiana* L. (Pinaceae). Evergreen tree varying in shape occasionally to 45 feet; flowers dioecious; catkins golden brown; female cones fleshy purplish; fruit a berrylike cone, pale blue; leaves scalelike and dark green or awl-shaped, sharp-pointed, and glandless; some leaves intermediate between the two forms; twigs reddish brown, bark light reddish brown, occasionally separating into long, fibrous strips (317).

Distribution and Ecology. Eastern red cedar distribution is apparently not as closely dictated by soil characteristics as distribution of red-berry and Ashe junipers. It ranges from central and west central Texas northward through Oklahoma, Kansas, and Nebraska and into the Dakotas (Fig. 2.1, areas 1, 3, 4, 7). It occurs in many varieties and forms and reaches greatest proportions in the Cross Timbers and Prairies, Post Oak Savannah, and Edwards Plateau of Texas. Usually a minor component of oak forest vegetation, eastern red cedar combines with red-berry juniper and Ashe juniper to form a heavy evergreen complex on slopes and thin soils of the Edwards Plateau. Invasion of open prairies by eastern red cedar is apparently correlated with the restriction of naturally occurring fires.

Control. Individual plants may be grubbed. Larger individuals may be chained. Some plants may be used for posts, but the remaining plants should be stacked and burned. Following initial control efforts, new sprouts may be cut by hand to prevent reinvasion. Eastern red cedar is highly susceptible to fire, particularly before the plants reach a height of 1.5 to 3 feet (22, 220). Picloram injected into the trees will kill 70 to 100 percent of the population, but injections of 2,4,5-T are ineffective (22). Wetting sprays of picloram alone or picloram combined with 2,4,5-T or 2,4-D applied to the foliage or the stems effectively control eastern red cedar. Broadcast foliar applications of most herbicides are less effective than individual-plant treatments. Mowing of small trees is fairly effective, but 25 percent or more of the population may be expected to regrow following top removal.

22. Elbowbush; downy forestiera. *Forestiera pubescens* Nutt. var. *pubescens* (Oleaceae). Shrub, sometimes small tree to 15 feet tall; flowers preceding leaves in the spring, greenish; fruit a drupe, in clusters, bluish black, 0.25 to 0.3 inch long, fleshy, one-seeded; leaves simple, opposite, deciduous, dull green and glabrous or slightly pubescent, lower surface yellowish green; twigs green to yellowish when young, light to dark gray and glabrous at maturity (317).

Distribution and Ecology. Elbowbush occurs primarily along waterways in Texas, New Mexico, and Oklahoma (Fig. 2.1, areas 1, 3–5, 7, 8). Elbowbush is very palatable to deer and goats, and the berries are consumed by wild turkeys and quail (199). It is apparently adapted to a wide range of growing conditions but reaches greatest proportions in the Edwards Plateau of Texas. It is most common on shallow and rocky sites of low stony hills (199). Elbowbush is an understory species that presents a range management problem usually only in association with other mixed-brush species. Elbowbush spreads by seeds, sprouts at the joints where limbs come in contact with the soil surface, and sprouts readily from the roots (199).

Control. Browsing by goats is an effective means of elbowbush control (199). Information is limited, but elbowbush is not considered susceptible to commonly used herbicides at normal rates of broadcast application of range improvement.

Promising treatments. Aerial application of 0.5 pound per acre of 2,4,5-T plus picloram appears promising (87).

23. Flame-leaf sumac. *Rhus copallina* L. (Anacardiaceae). Slender-branched shrub occasionally a small tree, 20 to 25 feet tall; leaves alternate, pinnate, 5 to 12 inches long; leaflets 7 to 17, elliptic or ovate to lanceolate, entire to lightly toothed, glabrous to pubescent above, hairy and glandular beneath, 1 to 3.5 inches long; rachis winged (Fig. 3.15); flowers 0.125 inch across; petals greenish white, 0.08 to 0.1 inch long; fruit in compact panicles, a red drupe, seeds solitary and smooth.

Distribution and Ecology. Flame-leaf sumac occurs mostly in the eastern two-thirds of Texas, being found in the western portion only

3.15. Flame-leaf sumac is characterized by pinnate leaves with winged rachises and large greenish white flowers. It usually occurs as a shrub or a small tree.

on the more mesic sites (Fig. 2.1, areas 1–6). It also occurs in Oklahoma, Arkansas, and Louisiana. It occurs in several varieties, including *R. copalina* L. var. *lanceata* Gray.

Control. Individual-plant treatment as basal spray or foliar or stump treatment with 2,4,5-T at 8 pounds per 100 gallons of diesel oil or kerosene (141).

Promising treatments. Ground broadcast sprays in 18 to 20 gallons of water per acre when the leaves are fully developed (April–May), using 2,4-D at 2 pounds per acre or at 1 pound per acre combined with 0.5 pound 2,4,5-T per acre (167).

24. Guajillo. *Acacia berlandieri* Benth. (Leguminosae). Shrub with many stems from base or small tree rarely over 10 feet tall; essentially thornless or thorns small and inconspicuous; flowers as white heads; fruit linear to oblong, flat, thin, velvety and bearing five to ten dark brown seeds; leaves doubly pinnate, linear to oblong, leaflets 0.125 to 0.25 inch long, dark green (317) (Fig. 3.16).

Distribution and Ecology. Restricted primarily to the South Texas Plains, guajillo now infests nearly 6 million acres of rangeland (286) (Fig. 2.1, areas 2, 6, 7). It is common along caliche ridges and occasionally on sandy loam or clay sites (162). Guajillo is a desirable browse species for livestock and white-tailed deer and commonly occurs in South Texas mixed-brush or "chaparral" communities. It spreads by seed and persists after top removal by sprout development from basal stem segments left intact (87, 196).

Control. For the management of guajillo the USDA Soil Conservation Service recommends chaining, chopping, or shredding so that livestock can reach browse (286). Dense stands should be root-plowed when it occurs with other mixed-brush species (87). The presence of guajillo increased following root plowing followed by raking in the South Texas Plains (71). Dragging, such as with a heavy rail iron, did not change the presence of guajillo. It often reaches greatest development on rocky hills where mechanical methods are not feasible.

Promising treatments. Aerial application of 1 pound per acre of 2,4,5-T plus picloram (1:1) in the spring or in the fall has effectively controlled guajillo (87), and 1 pound of picloram pellets per acre appears promising for control.

3.16. Guajillo occurs primarily in the South Texas Plains and is desirable browse for deer. The thornless bushes develop rather large, flat, velvety fruits. (*Photograph by O. E. Sperry*)

25. Guayacan. *Porlieria angustifolia* Engelm. (Zygophyllaceae). Evergreen shrub; leaves pinnate with oblong leaflets; flowers rather large and showy, purple, borne singly or in small clusters on short pedicels or peduncles; fruit a two-celled capsule, 0.5 to 1 inch broad, orbicular in general shape, but with protruding winged margins and persistent style base at apex; seed usually two per fruit, yellow or orange to red (317) (Fig. 3.17).

Distribution and Ecology. Guayacan is distributed throughout the southern half of Texas except for eastern and northern portions of the Coastal Prairie (Fig. 2.1, areas 2, 5–7, 10). Typically a low-growing species; it may reach 10 to 15 feet tall under good growing conditions. It is characteristic of the South Texas mixed-brush complex. It sprouts from stem segments, although regrowth is not as prolific as with most species when the tops are removed. Although it is usually present, guayacan is considered a secondary brush species because of its usual small stature.

Control. Guayacan is not controlled by broadcast applications of phenoxy herbicides at rates commonly used for range improvement. Guayacan has been effectively controlled by root plowing (87) or root plowing followed by raking in the South Texas Plains (71).

Promising treatments. Picloram sprays or tebuthiuron pellets at 1 pound or more per acre may give effective control of guayacan.

26. Honey mesquite. *Prosopis glandulosa* Torr. var. *glandulosa* (Torr.) Cockll. (Leguminosae). Deciduous shrub or tree; leaves bipinnate, leaflets 0.75 to 1.2 inches long; flowers small, yellowish green, numerous in catkinlike racemes; fruit a linear, indehiscent, greenish yellow pod, usually 5 to 10 inches long (Fig. 3.18).

Distribution and Ecology. Honey mesquite is probably the most troublesome woody plant on Texas rangeland (Fig. 2.6). Almost synonymous with the brush problem, it is widespread, infesting over 56 million acres of rangeland (Fig. 2.1, areas 1–10). Growth form of honey mesquite varies from a many-stemmed shrub to an upright, single-stemmed tree (204). It ranges from elevations to 4,200 feet and where the growing season is at least two hundred days (92). It is a prolific seed producer, and the pods and seeds are relished by wildlife and are used by cattle. Passage through the digestive tracts of animals affords scarification of honey mesquite seeds and aids their dispersion. The seeds are long-lived in the soil (307) but germinate readily after

3.17. Guayacan, a common component of southwestern Texas, is usually considered a secondary brush species because of its small stature.

scarification (264) and when the temperatures in the surface soil reach 70° to 75° F (263, 265). Newly established honey mesquite seedlings survive under relatively heavy shade (255, 256) and withstand repeated top removal (275). Disturbance of the tops of mature plants results in rapid sprouting from buds along a compressed, buried section of stem called the "crown" (204).

Control. Since a monograph was recently published with details

3.18. Whether present as an attractive, single-stemmed tree or a multi-stemmed bush, honey mesquite is a persistent species well adapted to a wide range of growing conditions. (*Courtesy R. E. Meyer*)

of honey mesquite control (279), only a cursory discussion will be presented here. Mechanical methods which have proven successful for honey mesquite control are hand grubbing, power grubbing, chaining of the tree-sized growth under adequate soil moisture, bulldozing, and root plowing (89, 143, 153, 267). Shredding (337) or any mechanical method which does not remove the entire stem from the soil does not give lasting control. Basal sprays of 8 pounds of 2,4,5-T per 100 gallons of oil are also effective for honey mesquite control (141). Individual trees may be treated with 2,4,5-T in water applied to wet all the foliage. Aerial applications of 0.5 pound of 2,4,5-T per acre, picloram plus 2,4,5-T at 0.25 plus 0.25 pound per acre, or 2,4,5-T plus dicamba at 0.25 plus 0.25 pound per acre in 3 to 5 gallons of a 1:3 or 1:4 diesel oil:water emulsion per acre are used to control large acreages of honey mesquite (258).

The 2,4,5-T plus picloram herbicide combination is now one of the most widely used for honey mesquite control. The combination is synergistic (64). Morphological reactions of honey mesquite to picloram are similar to those shown with 2,4,5-T (209); curling of the stem tips and death of the growing points are the most obvious effects.

Regardless of the herbicide used, the best time for foliar applications is usually from May 10 to June 15, when the honey mesquite foliage is fully developed but not cutinized. Susceptibility of honey mesquite to foliar sprays is strongly influenced by environmental variables such as soil temperature (59). Best control of honey mesquite may be obtained when the soil temperature at 18 inches depth reaches 70° to 75° F (59, 288). Of five methods used to reduce sprayed honey mesquite in the Rolling Plains of Texas, chaining was the most economical when most of the sprayed trees exceeded 5 inches in diameter (318). For smaller trees, basal sprays with diesel oil were most economical.

The mesquite twig girdler (*Oncideres rhodosticta* Bates) may have promise as a biological control agent for mesquite (313). In some years over 90 percent of the trees are attacked, but the regrowth potential of mesquite withstands such top removal.

Fire holds promise for manipulation of honey mesquite, especially as a secondary practice (144). Mortality of honey mesquite from prescribed burning varied from 0 percent to 24 percent in north central Texas (42). Wind speed, relative humidity, and the size of the mesquite plants influenced ignition and burning rate (42, 315). Larger trees (5 inches or more in diameter) burned for a longer time, increasing mortality.

27. Huisache; sweet acacia. *Acacia farnesiana* (L.) Willd. (Leguminosae). Shrub or small tree; bark reddish brown on small stems, becoming grayish; thorns long and slender in parts at base of leaves and fruits; flowers in small yellowish heads; fruit a thick, hard-walled pad mostly 1 to 2.25 inches long, highly constricted between the seeds; leaves pinnately compound, pinnae two to eight pairs; leaflets ten to twenty-five pairs, 0.08 to 0.25 inch long (317) (Fig. 3.19).

Distribution and Ecology. Huisache is a formidable management problem and is estimated to occupy more than 2.5 million acres of Texas grassland (286) (Fig. 2.1, areas 2–4, 6, 7). Tree forms may

3.19. Huisache fruits are hard-walled pods which are highly constricted between the seeds. (*Courtesy Soil Conservation Service*)

grow to 25 or 30 feet tall in almost pure dense stands on the better range sites. Huisache is tolerant of low, poorly drained sites of light- to medium-textured soils. Huisache exhibits fragrant flowers and produces small, hard, olive to tan spherical seeds. Germination and seedling growth requirements are very similar to those for honey mesquite. Seed scarification results in rapid germination, and huisache seedlings readily establish and can withstand severe top disturbance when only a few weeks old (250). Following top removal, all new branches are formed from stem tissues. Primary seedling branches arise from cotyledonary axils following disturbance of the central stem. Distributed throughout South Texas, huisache forms thick stands of trees on bottomland soils and shrubby growth on the drier, upland sites. It forms dense stands as far north as Brazos County.

Control. High rates (at least 2 pounds per acre) of 2,4,5-T as broadcast spray are required for a moderate level of huisache control. Sprays of picloram or picloram plus 2,4,5-T or picloram pellets are more effective than 2,4,5-T (31). Foliar applications of 2,4,5-T plus picloram have occasionally improved control as compared to picloram alone (26). However, adding 2,4,5-T is usually less important than applying the minimum required rate of picloram for hiusache control. Individual-plant treatment with foliage or basal-bark sprays containing 8 pounds of 2,4,5-T per 100 gallons of diesel oil or kerosene will control huisache. Generally, foliar treatments of picloram at 2 pounds per 100 gallons of an oil:water (1:3) emulsion are more effective than basal treatments of 8 pounds of picloram per 100 gallons of oil. Broadcast applications of 2,4,5-T plus picloram at 0.5 or 1 pound per acre have been more effective for control of huisache when applied in June or September than in July or August (33). Soil applications of picloram have been more effective than foliar treatments for control of greenhouse-grown huisache (27). Oiling, pouring 1–2 quarts of diesel oil or kerosene around the tree bases, is effective for huisache control but is limited to thin stands and should be done when soil is dry and not fused to the trunk.

Huisache has increased in abundance following burning of South Texas ranges (39). It also has not been controlled by root plowing or root plowing followed by raking in the South Texas Plains (72). Huisache rapidly resprouts from stem buds upon disturbance of the tops, so shredding offers only temporary control. Root plowing, chaining of larger trees, and power grubbing are effective if accomplished under proper environmental conditions. Grubbing is effective only when the trunks are removed to the first lateral root.

28. Javelina brush. *Microrhamnus ericoides* Gray (Rhamnaceae). Highly branched, spiny, low-growing shrub; flowers yellow; fruit a brown or black drupe; leaves small (less than 0.25 inch long), oblong to linear, dark green, entire margins; shape irregular, twigs often ending in spines, gray and somewhat rough on old stems (317) (Fig. 3.20).

3.20. Javelina brush is a small xerophytic shrub with leaves less than 0.25 inch long. Growth habit of javelina brush is similar to that of knife-leaf condalia, but comparison of leaf shapes and sizes allows quick differentiation of the two species. (*Courtesy Soil Conservation Service*)

Distribution and Ecology. Javelina brush is a common component of the underbrush of the xerophytic South Texas mixed-brush communities. Associated with species of *Lycium* and *Condalia*, and with cenizo, it evidently prefers well-drained, drier sites. Although rarely found in densities that warrant control, javelina brush is difficult to control and is an important species in the mixed-brush stands.

Control. Javelina brush is not susceptible to broadcast aerial applications of hormone-type herbicides at rates normally used for range improvement.

29. Knife-leaf condalia. *Condalia spathulata* Gray (Rhamnaceae). Small evergreen, thorny shrub, rarely to 8 or 10 feet; very spiny green branches; greenish flowers; fruit a black drupe, juicy, solitary seed; leaves in clumps, small (less than 0.5 inch long); obovate to spatulate, apex usually rounded, light green; dark gray, smooth bark (317) (Fig. 3.21).

Distribution and Ecology. Knife-leaf condalia occurs in widely scattered stands as a minor component of the mixed-brush complex of South Texas (Fig. 2.1, areas 2, 6, 7, 10). This low-growing shrub reaches its greatest proportions on xeric, rocky, shallow sites in the western portion of its range. It is usually found in low brush on gravelly caliche slopes or on thin soils, often in association with bluewood and lotebush.

Control. Virtually no formal information is available, but knife-leaf condalia can apparently be controlled with individual-plant treatments such as basal sprays of 2,4,5-T (8 pounds per 100 gallons of oil) or by grubbing.

3.21. Knife-leaf condalia is typified by small obovate to spatulate leaves, less than 0.5 inch long, which occur in tight clumps. (*Courtesy Soil Conservation Service*)

30. Leatherstem; sangre de drago; rubber-plant. *Jatropha dioica* Sesse *ex* Cerv. var. *dioica* (Euphorbiaceae). Deciduous, single-stemmed, usually less than 1.5 feet tall (Fig. 3.22); spineless; dioecious; flowers extremely small, white to pinkish; thick stem, dark brown, of rubbery appearance and feel; leaves clustered in groups of three or four, shiny green, obovate.

Distribution and Ecology. Leatherstem is most common in the western and deep southern portions of Texas (Fig. 2.1, areas 2, 6, 7). It occurs in clumps or circular colonies varying in size from small groups to areas 100 feet or more in diameter. Leatherstem evidently spreads by seeds and rhizomes (87). The localized colonies usually occur in open spaces instead of being associated with species of greater stature. In extreme cases leatherstem becomes so thick that it severely restricts forage production. It is a typical component of mixed-brush stands but is rarely considered alone as a severe brush problem.

Control. Although control measures are rarely directed toward leatherstem, the species is only moderately susceptible to aerial appli-

3.22. Leatherstem occurs in circular colonies or as scattered individual plants. It is typified by dark brown stems that are rubbery in appearance and by small globular fruits.

cations of 2,4,5-T. It is apparently susceptible to 0.5 pound or more of picloram per acre or herbicide combinations containing picloram as aerial sprays. Applications of 2,4,5-T plus picloram (1:1) at 1 pound per acre have controlled 75 percent of the leatherstem (31). Root plowing alone or followed by raking has not controlled leatherstem in the South Texas Plains (71).

Promising treatments. Picloram pellets at 1 to 2 pounds per acre have appeared promising in a limited number of experiments (87).

31. Lechuguilla. *Agave lecheguilla* Torr. (Liliaceae). Resembles species of *Yucca*; flower stalk is 6 to 12 feet tall (Fig. 3.23), rising in a cluster of numerous, thick basal leaves, 16 to 30 in number and usual-

3.23. Lechuguilla, a poisonous plant, is highly adapted to the rocky, arid hillsides of southwestern Texas. Leaves of lechuguilla resemble those of yucca but with marginal prickles hooked downward. (*Photograph by O. E. Sperry*)

ly 8 to 16 inches long and 1 to 1.5 inches wide; flowers greenish or yellowish white; fruit a brown to black capsule, 0.5 to 0.6 inches in diameter and 0.6 to 1 inch long; seeds numerous, flat, black and shiny; leaves grayish green to yellowish green, apex terminating in a stout spine, prickles on leaf margins hooked downward (317).

Distribution and Ecology. Lechuguilla occurs primarily in southwestern Texas, southeastern New Mexico, and northern Mexico (20). However, it may be used as an ornamental for a considerable distance outside of its native range if it is planted on well-drained areas. In Texas it reaches greatest proportions in the Trans-Pecos, occasionally in stands dense enough to seriously limit forage production (Fig. 2.1, areas 6, 7, 10). Lechuguilla is highly adapted to rocky, arid hillsides up to considerable elevations. It is poisonous to livestock, especially sheep and goats.

Control. Little information is available, but lechuguilla apparently can be controlled by treating individual plants with 2,4,5-T at 8 pounds per 100 gallons of diesel oil.

32. Lime prickly ash; colima. *Zanthoxylum fagara* (L.) Sarg. (Rutaceae). Prickly, aromatic, evergreen shrub or small tree, usually at least 15 feet tall, rarely to 30 feet; flowers small, greenish yellow, in clusters on the previous year's branches; fruit a small, pointed, reddish brown capsule, ripening in late summer or early fall, splitting at maturity; leaves alternate, pinnately compound on a broad, winged rachis, leaflets obovate to oblong; bark gray, smooth to slightly furrowed; thorn curved similar to catclaw (acacia) and catclaw mimosa (317) (Fig. 3.24).

Distribution and Ecology. Lime prickly ash is distributed from the coast in deep South Texas westward to south central Texas (Fig. 2.1, areas 2, 6, 7). It is palatable to deer and goats (199). Goats use the foliage throughout the year and will strip off the bark in winter. Lime prickly ash is usually subdominant, but in some locations it is found in high incidence, occasionally appearing to form almost pure stands. It is most common on rocky sites in the Edwards Plateau (199), but it occurs on a variety of soils from clays to sands in the coastal zones. Due to the thorn shape, lime prickly ash is often referred to locally as "catclaw," but it is not to be confused with catclaw (acacia) or catclaw mimosa. It spreads by seed and resprouts from the base upon top removal (87).

3.24. Lime prickly ash, also called colima and catclaw, can be distinguished from catclaw (acacia) and catlaw mimosa by the broad-winged rachis and the larger leaflets.

Control. Lime prickly ash apparently is not controlled by most hormone herbicides at rates normally used for range improvement, and it increases in density following simple top removal by roller chopping or shredding (72). Browsing by goats, root plowing, and grubbing will give effective control (87, 199).

33. Lindheimer pricklypear. *Opuntia lindheimeri* Engelm. (Cactaceae). Heavy, thick cactus with large pads growing in clumps to 5 or even 10 feet tall; definite trunk often prostrate; flowers bright and showy, yellow to orange or red; fruit large (to 3 inches long), red to purple; joints green to bluish green, obovate; spines variable, absent on some joints, white or yellow (Fig. 3.25).

Distribution and Ecology. There are numerous *Opuntia* species with the general growth form of Lindheimer pricklypear across Texas. However, *O. lindheimeri* is probably the most common and troublesome on rangelands. Also called nopal pricklypear, Lindheimer pricklypear varies from low and wide-spreading to treelike in growth form (146). It spreads by seed and by transportation of the cladophylls.

3.25. Lindheimer pricklypear is spread throughout the southern half of Texas but is most common in the western portion of the state. (*Photograph by O.E. Sperry*)

It is distributed throughout the southern half of Texas but is most common in the western portions (Fig. 2.1, areas 1–4, 6, 7, 10). It occurs on most soils but may be most abundant on shallow, gravelly or rocky sites (199). Ranchmen may burn the spines off pricklypear during the winter to allow its use as a supplemental cattle roughage. Lindheimer pricklypear provides protection for quail and other birds (87) and is important to most wildlife, especially javelina (19). The fruits, called "pear apples," are eaten by most animals, and the cladophylls are heavily used by deer, cattle, and goats. However, pricklypear alone is not usually adequate for maintaining animals without weight loss.

Control. Grubbing, piling, and other individual-plant treatments (2,4,5-T or silvex at 8 pounds per 100 gallons of diesel oil) successfully control light stands of Lindheimer pricklypear. Mechanical bruising (railing) followed by broadcast sprays of silvex or 2,4,5-T at 1 to 2 pounds per acre or spraying followed by stacking are also effective. Mechanical methods should be completed when the soil is dry to assure desiccation of all plant parts. Root plowing breaks up and spreads the cladophylls of pricklypear, often drastically increasing the stand density (71, 145, 146).

Promising treatments. Picloram sprays at 0.5 to 1 pound per acre are effective for controlling small Lindheimer pricklypear. Plants over 10 pads tall require 2 pounds per acre of picloram. Granular picloram at 1 to 2 pounds per acre (ultimate control dependent on timeliness of rainfall) or hexaflurate at 1 to 4 pounds per acre broadcast with ground equipment has resulted in excellent control (43, 137, 145, 202, 243).

34. Live oak. *Quercus virginiana* Mill. var. *virginiana* (Fagaceae). Evergreen tree or small shrub; flowers and fruits as in post oak; leaves typically smaller than those of post oak, ovate, shiny green, entire to toothed or lightly lobed. Trees have been noted on the Welder Wildlife Refuge near Sinton, Texas, that appear to be hybrids between live oak and post oak.

Distribution and Ecology. Live oak is distributed throughout South Texas but reaches greatest proportions in the central and eastern portions of the area (Fig. 2.1, areas 2, 3, 6, 7). It occurs in mottes (Fig. 3.26) which provide excellent shade for livestock and browse and cover for wildlife. It also assumes a low, running growth form referred to as "running" live oak. Leaves, young shoots, and acorns are eaten to varying degrees by goats, deer, sheep, cattle, and horses (199). The running form spreads by sprouts developing from rhizomes and forms stands similar to those of Vasey oak and other scrub oaks; it is most common in the eastern portion of its range. It usually occupies highly productive areas, but thick stands severely restrict forage production. In the Edwards Plateau, *Q. virginiana* var. *fusiformis* (Small) Sarg. (plateau oak) is a common variety. Plateau oak is quite similar to live oak, differing primarily by having oblong to obovate leaves with an acute apex, dentate margins, and a smaller acorn. Distinctions are often difficult, since intermediate forms between the variety and the species are common.

Control. Treat individual plants, using the frill, stump, or notch method, with 4 pounds of 2,4,5-T per 100 gallons of diesel oil or kerosene anytime during the year. Live oak is usually not controlled with rates of phenoxy herbicides commonly broadcast for range improvement. It has not been controlled by single or repeated aerial applications of 2,4,5-T at 2 or 4 pounds per acre (34).

3.26. Live oaks may occur as large trees of high value for livestock shade, in mottes, or in a low running form that greatly restricts range forage production.

Grubbing and root plowing will effectively control live oak (87). Methods such as chaining and dozing are used depending on stand density and growth form of the live oak. Browsing by goats is often used as a maintenance treatment following chaining (34).

Promising treatments. Live oak is effectively controlled by fall or spring applications of picloram as a broadcast aerial spray or with picloram pellets (34). A mixture of 2,4,5-T plus picloram (1:1) at 2 pounds per acre in November (26, 28) has been effective. Applications of the combination in the summer were not as effective. Absorption of picloram by live oak leaves is promoted by 2,4,5-T (16), accounting for the effectiveness of the combination.

35. Lotebush; lote. *Zizyphus obtusifolia* (T. & G.) Gray (Rhamnaceae). Thorny shrub, stiff, highly branched, rarely over 6 feet tall; deciduous. Whereas the leaves of bluewood are typically obovate, the leaves of lotebush are ovate, almost oblong, with margins entire to coarsely serrate; branches grayish green with alternate, formidable thorns; bark smooth, light gray to bluish colored except at the base, where it may be cracked and dark brown; flowers and fruits similar to those of bluewood (317).

Distribution and Ecology. Lotebush generally occurs as a small shrub. It is a minor but common component of the mixed-brush complex in association with bluewood in South Texas and of honey mesquite savannahs in the Rolling Plains. Lotebush is more common to the plains than to the coastal zones and is somewhat less prevalent in southern than in northern and northwestern Texas (Fig. 2.1, areas 2, 5–8, 10). It sprouts readily from the base and from short rhizomes (87, 271) upon top removal and dominates brush stands only in localized cases. Lotebush spreads by seed and provides excellent cover for quail (87).

Control. Broadcast sprays of phenoxy herbicides have been reported to be only slightly effective for lotebush control (207). However, effective control has resulted from aerial applications of picloram at 2 pounds per acre or 2,4,5-T plus picloram at 1 pound per acre of each herbicide in the spring. Lotebush may be controlled with individual-plant treatments of picloram pellets or basal sprays of 2,4,5-T plus picloram (271). Lotebush has increased in abundance following burning of South Texas ranges (40), but root plowing and root plowing followed by raking have effectively controlled lotebush in the South Texas Plains (71). Lotebush was also controlled by roller chopping followed in one year by shredding in the spring, after which the areas were burned in late summer (72). Grubbing to 12 or 14 inches deep will also control lotebush (325).

36. Macartney rose; rose hedge; hedge; wild rose; Cherokee rose; Chickasaw rose. *Rosa bracteata* Wendl. (Rosaceae). Evergreen shrub climbing and trailing from large clumps which may merge, forming impenetrable thickets; flowers large, white; fruit as large hips, orange red; leaves compound, shiny green with obovate or oval leaflets; stems as spreading canes, hairy; thorns paired at the nodes; bark reddish brown on young canes, grayish on old stems and canes (317) (Fig. 3.27).

Distribution and Ecology. Macartney rose was evidently introduced from China into the Gulf Coast about 1870 as a potential hedge species (234). It spread rapidly and now occupies about 275,000 acres of productive land (Fig. 2.1, areas 1–4). It sprouts from roots and spreads by seed and rooting of canes at the nodes (147). It has some value as wildlife browse and cover, so strips of Macartney rose are maintained in certain areas for game habitat. The seeds germinate readily following scarification, particularly after passing through the digestive tracts of animals (190).

3.27. Macartney rose is easily identified by its long, trailing, thorny canes and showy white flowers.

Control. Shredding was once a widespread method of attempting to control Macartney rose. Although top growth is reduced, few plants are killed by mowing or shredding, which may transplant cane segments and ultimately aggravate the problem. Following disturbance of top growth, low-growing Macartney rose that has regrowth at least six months old but no older than three years can be treated broadcast with 2 pounds of 2,4-D per acre from March 1 to June 15 (117). Early applications from March 1 to May 1 with the amine formulation may be effective, but later treatments should be made with the low-volatility ester (147), assuming that there are no adjacent susceptible crops. The low-volatility esters may also be applied in the early fall. Ground applications should be made with 10 to 15 gallons of spray solution. Swath widths must be narrow enough to ensure that the foliage is completely covered with the spray. At least two consecutive annual spray applications of 4 pounds per acre of 2,4-D in the spring or 3 pounds per acre in the fall are required to control undisturbed dense stands of Macartney rose. Individual plants can be treated with 8 pounds of 2,4-D in 100 gallons of water plus 0.5 to 1 percent (by volume) of wetting agent. High pressure is needed with hand applications to ensure that the canopy is penetrated by the spray. All plant parts must be thoroughly wet by the spray.

Picloram, applied broadcast in the spring or fall, is more effective than 2,4-D (247, 248). Picloram is more effective when applied in the spring than in the fall (117), but the reverse is apparently true with 2,4,5-T plus picloram (33). A single application of picloram at 2 pounds per acre controlled over 90 percent of the Macartney rose eighteen months after application (173).

37. Mescal bean; mountain laurel. *Sophora secundiflora* (Ort.) Lag. *ex* DC. (Leguminosae). Evergreen shrub or small tree; flowers large in showy terminal racemes, petals light purple; fruit a hard, thick-walled, indehiscent, densely brown-pubescent pod, constricted between the seeds (317) (Fig. 3.28).

3.28. Mescal bean produces showy purple flowers and hard, thick-walled pods constricted between the seeds. *(Courtesy Soil Conservation Service)*

Distribution and Ecology. Mescal bean occurs from the Trans-Pecos and Edwards Plateau throughout the South Texas Plains, mostly on shallow to shallow gravelly and rocky sites (199) (Fig. 2.1, areas 2, 4, 6, 7, 10). Mescal bean is a secondary invader following brush control and fire in the southwest (291). The seeds are poisonous but so hard that they are usually expelled and not digested by livestock.The leaves are also toxic but usually are not consumed in lethal quantities. The toxic agent in mescal bean is the narcotic cytisine or sophorine (294), which affects the central nervous system (290). The seeds are abundant in the soil near mature plants and maintain viability for several years. Scarified seeds germinate in three to five days, and seedlings emerge after about two weeks (290).

Control. Basal treatment with 8 pounds of 2,4,5-T in 100 gallons of diesel oil applied under optimum growth and moisture conditions during the summer and early fall will control mescal bean (291). Individual-plant treatments with 2,4,5-T sprays are most effective on plants less than 2 feet tall (291). Aerial application of 2,4,5-T at 1 pound per acre has given fair top kill, but picloram at 0.5 pound per acre has not controlled mescal bean (290).

38. Mexican plum. *Prunis mexicana* Wats. (Rosaceae). Shrub or small tree to 25 feet; flowers white, 0.75 to 1 inch in diameter; fruit a drupe, dark purplish red; flesh juicy; stone ovoid to oval; leaves alternate, simple, deciduous; upper surface yellowish green, glabrous and shiny; twigs stiff, grayish brown; bark gray to black (317).

Distribution and Ecology. Mexican plum occurs throughout eastern Texas, northward into Oklahoma, and eastward into Louisiana and Arkansas (317) (Fig. 2.1, areas 1–5, 7). It is a common component of the Cross Timbers and Prairies but reaches its greatest proportions in the southeastern portion of the Post Oak Savannah and into the Pineywoods. Mexican plum becomes a range management problem in association with other underbrush species of oak forest vegetation. However, it does not form heavy thickets, and the fruit may be used by wildlife.

39. Plains pricklypear. *Opuntia polyacantha* Haw. (Cactaceae). Small, low-growing, spreading cactus, usually less than 1.5 feet tall; flowers bright and showy, usually yellow to orange; fruit red; pads light green.

Distribution and Ecology. Plains pricklypear is most common in the northwestern quarter of the state and southward into the Trans-

Pecos. It occurs in scattered patches in the honey mesquite savannahs of the Rolling and High Plains (Fig. 2.1, areas 7–10). It is apparently most highly adapted to clay loam to sandy clay loam soils (87, 196). Under severe overgrazing, plains pricklypear slowly thickens to form large, circular, solid patches but serves some purpose by protecting highly palatable forage plants from overgrazing under heavy stocking (87). Plains pricklypear spreads by seed and by the scattering of plant parts. It also evidently serves as a source of cover for small rodents. The fruits are consumed by raccoons, birds, and coyotes and make excellent jelly (146).

Control. Individual-plant treatment with 2,4,5-T, 2,4,5-T plus dicamba, silvex alone, or 2,4,5-T plus picloram (1:1) aerially applied in the spring (87) will control plains pricklypear. Apply 6 to 8 pounds of herbicide per 100 gallons of diesel oil and thoroughly wet all pads.

Promising treatments. Night applications of 0.5 or 1 pound of 2,4,5-T or silvex in diesel oil per acre; 1 to 2 pounds of picloram per acre; and bruising the pads followed by 1 pound of picloram, dicamba, silvex, or 2,4,5-T per acre appear to be promising for the control of plains pricklypear (243, 324).

40. Poison ivy. *Rhus toxicodendron* L. var. *vulgaris* (Michx.) DC. (Anacardiaceae). Woody vine; flowers small, greenish white, in axillary panicles; fruit a small whitish drupe; leaves glossy green, ovate, smooth-margined, in groups of three (317).

Distribution and Ecology. Poison ivy is widespread and a common component of many Texas brush communities. A winding vine best known for its allergenic properties, poison ivy reaches its greatest proportions in lowland, moist areas (Fig. 2.1, areas 1, 3–5, 7, 8, 10).

Control. AMS, amino triazole, 2,4,5-T, silvex, or 2,4-D sprays applied in the spring, summer, or early fall directly to the rapidly growing foliage will control poison ivy (139). AMS and amino triazole are more effective when mixed at 1 pound of formulated herbicide per gallon of water with 1 or 2 ounces of household detergent. Thoroughly wet the foliage; two or more treatments are usually needed for complete control. Fair control may be attained with 1 pound of MCPA per acre as a broadcast spray (139, 167).

41. Post oak. *Quercus stellata* Wang. (Fagaceae). Deciduous tree to 25 feet or taller; leaves with two to four lobes on each side (Fig. 3.5), flowers small, unisexual, borne in separate catkins on the same tree; fruit an acorn.

Distribution and Ecology. Same as blackjack oak. These two species form a union in most areas of adaptation.

Control. Individual trees may be treated with ammate (AMS) or 2,4,5-T as described for blackjack oak. Effective control from aerial spraying usually requires two successive applications of 2,4,5-T (141). Sprays should be applied in the spring after leaves become full-sized but before summer dormancy. First treatment should be with 2 pounds of 2,4,5-T per acre in a 1:4 diesel oil:water emulsion, and the second application should be 1 to 1.75 pounds of 2,4,5-T per acre.

42. Red-berry juniper. *Juniperus pinchotii* Sudw. (Pinaceae). Small shrub or evergreen tree rarely reaching 25 feet; lower branches often close to the ground; cones small, dioecious; fruit a very light cone, 0.25 to 0.35 inch long, red, thin-skinned; seeds solitary, 0.125 to 0.25 inch long, ovoid; leaves scalelike, yellowish green to dark green, expressed in ranks of twos or threes; twigs rigid and greenish to red with age; bark gray to reddish brown, often in long, shaggy strips (317) (Fig. 3.29).

Distribution and Ecology. Red-berry juniper is most common on rough rangeland, particularly on the dry hillsides and canyons in the Rolling Plains, Edwards Plateau, and Cross Timbers and Prairies (Fig. 2.1, areas 5, 7–10). At one time junipers were evidently restricted primarily to shallow rocky sites on well-drained slopes called cedar brakes. Age and distribution of junipers on an isolated butte in Garza County, Texas, indicate that north-facing mid-slopes form the centers of distribution of red-berry juniper (81). Initial establishment probably occurred on the slopes about 1800, with about 10 percent of the trees that infest the lower portion of the slope established in the last fifteen years. Recently red-berry juniper has invaded fertile lowland ranges, particularly those below, or associated with, rough, shallow-soiled rangeland where it is the primary problem (Fig. 2.8) (252). Red-berry juniper spreads only by seed evidently transported by birds and animals (242). Upon top removal, new sprouts develop from the crowns. This plant is becoming recognized as one of the primary brush problems of north central Texas.

Control. Bulldozing is effective for red-berry juniper control (234). Broadcast sprays of phenoxy herbicides are not usually effective. Aer-

3.29. Red-berry juniper may occur as a low-growing shrub or as a bush, 10 to 12 feet tall, and is most common on thin, shallow soils. (*Courtesy Soil Conservation Service*)

ial sprays of picloram are less effective for control than broadcast applications of 2 or 4 pounds (actual ingredient) of pellets per acre (236). Soil-applied picloram has been more effective than dicamba in northwest Texas (252). From 0.02 to 0.04 ounce (active ingredient) of picloram pellets per foot of canopy diameter has killed over 95 percent of the plants within one year after herbicide application. Dicamba granules and monuron pellets were less effective than picloram pellets for controlling red-berry juniper. This species may be susceptible to fire if it is less than twelve years old because the bud zone may still be exposed above the soil line (242). Red-berry juniper regrowth following chaining can be suppressed with goats (199).

On some sites red-berry juniper serves as a soil stabilizer, furnishes cover for wildlife, and probably should not be controlled. It is low-value browse (242), and on higher potential sites it may be one of the primary limitations to forage production. Red-berry juniper occurs as many-stemmed bushes which, in dense stands, almost completely eliminate forage production. The larger trees are occasionally used for fence posts, but the plants are usually too small for any widespread usefulness.

43. Retama; Mexican paloverde. *Parkinsonia aculeata* L. (Leguminosae). Spiny, deciduous tree or shrub; bark greenish, at least on younger stems; leaves bipinnate, leaf rachis long and flat, persistent after the leaflets fall; leaflets 0.2 inch or less long; flowers large, yellow, in showy racemes; fruit a slender pod mostly 1.5 to 4 inches long, with one to eight seeds; pod constricted and flattened between the seeds (317).

Distribution and Ecology. Retama occurs in most of the southern half of Texas (Fig. 2.1, areas 2–7, 10). It is commonly associated with drainageways, lowland areas, and better upland sites. Retama is used to certain extent as an ornamental because of its shape, growth form, and showy flowers.

Control. Individual plants may be treated with basal sprays containing 8 pounds of 2,4,5-T per 100 gallons of diesel oil or kerosene (141). Trees with trunks exceeding 5 inches in diameter should be frilled for treatment. The Soil Conservation Service (234) also recommends dozing or grubbing of scattered plants but indicates that basal treatment with 2,4,5-T is the most practical treatment.

44. Salt cedar; French tamarisk. *Tamarix gallica* L. (Tamaricaceae). Shrub or tree to 30 feet with twisted trunk; flowers white or pink; fruit a very small capsule, 0.1 to 0.14 inch long; seeds numerous, minute, tufted with hairs; leaves delicate, grayish green, scalelike, alternate; branches drooping, often sweeping to the ground; grayish to reddish gray (317) (Fig. 3.30).

Distribution and Ecology. Salt cedar was introduced from Europe but now grows under cultivation and in native situations from eastern New Mexico through Texas into Florida (Fig. 2.1, areas 2, 5–10). It is most common on low, moist areas along waterways, and it may grow in association with species such as willows and cottonwoods (46). It spreads by seeds and resprouts vigorously from roots following top removal (87). However, on the more mesic bottomland soils salt cedar grows to the exclusion of most woody species. It is found in essentially all of Texas and is a range management problem on much of the lowland areas.

Control. Salt cedar is not susceptible to broadcast applications of 2,4-D or 2,4,5-T at rates normally used for range improvement. However, fairly high rates of silvex are used as repeat treatments for salt cedar control (167).

Salt cedar sprouts from root sections upon disturbance of top

3.30. Salt cedar, an introduced species, is restricted to low, moist areas where it restricts forage production and free movement of water through drainages.

growth (152), so methods of simple top removal are not effective. Shoot growth is erratic and is difficult to correlate with environmental variables. Control with broadcast applications of foliar-active herbicides is also erratic and not correlated with physiological factors such as carbohydrate reserves of salt cedar (57). Salt cedar with trunks 2 inches or less in diameter can be controlled with stump or basal applications of silvex in diesel oil (155). The stump treatment is more effective than basal sprays on trees with trunks greater than 2 inches. Mowing followed by broadcast spraying one year later with 2 to 4 pounds of silvex, silvex plus picloram (1:1), or picloram per acre has not controlled salt cedar (154). Spray treatments of 4 pounds of silvex per acre controlled 60 percent of the salt cedar population. Two successive annual applications of silvex at 2 pounds per acre each or a single application of a 1:1 mixture of silvex plus picloram at 2 pounds per acre controlled about 40 percent of undisturbed salt cedar. Where possible, root plowing and grubbing have been used for effective control.

Promising treatments. Picloram pellets at 2 pounds active ingredient per acre appear promising for control of salt cedar (87).

45. Sand sagebrush; sand wormwood. *Artemisia filifolia* Torr. (Compositae). Small, aromatic shrub usually less than 3 feet tall; freely branched (Fig. 3.31); flowers in dense, leafy panicles; fruit an achene, glabrous, without pappus; alternate leaves sessile, often fascicled, usually entire, lower leaves often dividing into threadlike divisions; twigs slender, pubescent, dark gray to black.

Distribution and Ecology. Distribution of sand sagebrush follows very closely that of sand shinnery oak. It is abundant to altitudes of 6,000 feet growing in association with sand shinnery oak and small soapweed and in pure stands (196). An indicator of sandy soils, it is particularly abundant in northwestern Texas from the Rolling Plains into the panhandle of Oklahoma on the north and into New Mexico on the west (Fig. 2.1, areas 8–10). It occurs also in Arizona, Nevada, Colorado, and Utah. Sand sagebrush is a range management problem in localized areas, particularly sandy valleys and hillsides. It spreads by movement of seed and persists by virtue of a shallow bud zone (196). Although it is browsed by cattle when other forage is unavailable, sand sagebrush is of little other known value (196).

Control. Foliar sprays from May 1 to June 15 under good grow-

3.31. Sand sagebrush, a freely branched shrub usually less than 3 feet tall, is a range management problem in the sandy valleys and hillsides in the northern and western parts of Texas. It is characterized by leaves which separate into threadlike divisions.

ing conditions when the leaves are fully developed will control sand sagebrush (141). Recommended are low-volatility esters of 2,4-D at 1 pound per acre in 1 gallon of diesel oil per acre and adequate water to make 5 gallons of total solution per acre using aerial broadcast sprays with swath widths adequate to ensure complete coverage. Good control can be obtained with 1 to 2 pounds of MCPA, 2,4,5-T, or silvex per acre as broadcast foliar sprays (167).

Promising treatments. Effective control of sand sagebrush has been noted where 2,4,5-T plus picloram (1:1) were applied at 0.5 to 1 pound per acre. Repeated mowing may also be effective (87), especially for control of small infestations.

46. Sand shinnery oak; Havard oak. *Quercus havardii* Rydb. (Fagaceae). Shrub usually less than 3 feet tall, in occasional mottes to 15 feet; flowers borne in separate male and female catkins; male catkins pubescent; fruit a large acorn, chestnut brown, lustrous and glabrous glaucescent; leaves alternate, deciduous, leathery, variable in size and

3.32. Sand shinnery oak forms dense stands on sandy soils and spreads by means of rhizomes and acorns.

somewhat variable in shape or obovate, margin entire, slightly undulate, coarsely toothed or lobed (Fig. 3.32).

Distribution and Ecology. Sand shinnery oak occurs on deep sands occasionally as a small tree in circular mottes and forms thick stands by means of a heavy system of rhizomes (Fig. 2.7). Sand shinnery oak occurs across northwestern Texas into the panhandle, eastern New Mexico, and Oklahoma. It reaches greatest proportions in the Rolling and High Plains, becoming of lesser importance in the Edwards Plateau, and is relatively rare in the Trans-Pecos (Fig. 2.1, areas 7–10). The acorns are eaten by some wildlife, particularly prairie chickens, bobwhite quail, and feral hogs. A serious management problem, sand shinnery oak limits range forage production and occasionally causes livestock poisoning (7, 294). Sand shinnery oak often grows in association with sand sagebrush, small soapweed, and little bluestem.

Control. Broadcast methods are the most effective for control of sand shinnery oak because of stand density and growth form. It can be controlled with broadcast ground or aerial applications of 0.5 to

1 pound of silvex or 2,4,5-T per acre. At least two applications of
2,4,5-T within a 3-year period are usually required for effective control. Combinations of silvex or 2,4,5-T with picloram have shown to
be synergistic for control of sand shinnery oak and have substantially
increased grass production in the Rolling Plains of Texas (251). Although less effective than 2,4,5-T or silvex, 2,4-D is sometimes used
on sand shinnery oak. Combinations of picloram plus 2,4-D, dicamba
plus 2,4,5-T, or dicamba plus silvex are usually not as effective as
combinations of 2,4,5-T plus picloram or silvex plus picloram for sand
shinnery oak control (251). A combination of water and surfactant
was as effective as the diesel oil:water emulsion (1:4) as a herbicide
carrier for control of sand shinnery oak (254). Granular dicamba or
picloram pellets at 2 pounds active ingredient or less per acre has
not effectively controlled sand shinnery oak in the Rolling Plains
(253). Reduced effectiveness of dry herbicides, compared to equivalent application rates of sprays, may be attributed to the inherent
resistance of the species to soil applications of herbicides and to the
need for rainfall for movement of adequate amounts of the herbicide
into the root zone. Satisfactory control results from use of 2,4,5-T or
silvex at 0.5 to 1 pound per acre as aerial sprays in swath widths
which will insure complete foliage cover. Sprays should be applied in
about 1 gallon of diesel oil and adequate water to make up 4 gallons
of spray solution. Recommended season of application is from May 1
to June 15 when the leaves are fully formed and under good growing
conditions. Sprays should not be applied following late freezes in the
spring.

47. Saw greenbrier. *Smilax bona-nox* L. (Liliaceae). Twining vine
with tough, green, spiny stems; flowers small, greenish, unisexual, the
staminate and pistillate ones in separate axillary umbels on the same
plant; fruit a small black berry (317) (Fig. 3.33).

Distribution and Ecology. Saw greenbrier occurs in all but the
western quarter of the state but is most common in the eastern half of
the state (Fig. 2.1, areas 2–8). Saw greenbrier reproduces from a
heavy crown and develops rapidly by anchoring to trees and shrubs.
The heavy, spiny vines may form almost impenetrable barriers.

Control. Saw greenbrier is not susceptible to broadcast applications of phenoxy herbicides at rates normally used for range improvement. Spot treatment with 2,4,5-T at 8 to 16 pounds in 100 gallons

3.33. Saw greenbrier is an aggressive vine that is not effectively controlled by available brush management methods. It occurs in fences, as an understory species, and occasionally grows into the tops of trees 30 feet or taller, especially in the Post Oak Savannah.

of diesel oil:water (1:4) emulsion will effectively control saw greenbrier. The species has not been controlled by broadcast applications of picloram or 2,4,5-T plus picloram (203). Cutting gives only temporary control, especially in years of good rainfall.

48. Skunkbush; fragrant sumac. *Rhus aromatica* Ait. var. *flabelliformis* Shinners (Anacardiaceae). Thicket-forming, irregularly branched shrub occasionally to 10 feet; flowers borne in clusters, yellowish green; fruit a persistent drupe, red and hairy; leaves alternate, deciduous, aromatic, three-foliate, ovate or obovate, margins usually crenate to dentate; twigs slender, brown, pubescent (317).

Distribution and Ecology. Skunkbush occurs from West Texas northward into Oklahoma and eastward into Arkansas and Louisiana in many varietal forms and with many synonyms. It spreads by seeds and reproduces vegetatively from the roots (196) or crown upon top removal (87). It reaches greatest proportions in the northern Post Oak Savannah and into the Cross Timbers and Prairies of Texas, where it may present a range management problem (Fig. 2.1, areas 4, 5, 7, 8). Skunkbush is highly adapted to sandy and shallow gravelly clay soils. It is desirable cover for quail (87). In the Edwards Plateau it is most common on rocky sites and generally occurs in conjunction with other shrubs such as live oak, shin oak, and junipers (199). Skunkbush spreads by seed and by root sprouts following top removal (196). It is very palatable to deer and goats (199, 299).

Control. Broadcast applications of 0.5 to 1 pound of 2,4,5-T per acre or individual-plant treatments (8 pounds per 100 gallons) control skunkbush (87). Heavy browsing by goats apparently eliminates skunkbush from pastures in the Edwards Plateau (199). Apparently skunkbush increases following burning (199), probably due to its ability to resprout from the root system.

49. Small soapweed. *Yucca glauca* Nutt. (Liliaceae). Occurs singly or in small clumps; flowers 1.4 to 2.4 inches long, showy, white; fruit oblong, brown to black capsule, six-seeded, about 2.75 inches long; seeds shiny black; leaves usually less than 1.65 feet long, hard and rigid; stems decumbent (317) (Fig. 3.34).

Distribution and Ecology. Small soapweed reaches its greatest proportions in the western half of the state, particularly in the Rolling and High Plains (Fig. 2.1, areas 7, 8, 10). It is common on many range sites but is usually of highest densities on sandy soils. Small soapweed blooms are browsed by cattle (87).

Control. Broadcast applications of 0.67 pound of silvex or 2,4,5-T per acre aerially applied in 4 gallons of a 1:4 oil:water emulsion per acre are recommended for control of small soapweed (142). The herbicides applied at 0.5 pound per acre during early bloom stage effectively control small soapweed (87). Individual-plant treatment with 2,4,5-T or silvex will also control the species.

3.34. Small soapweed is common in the Rolling Plains and High Plains vegetation regions. Common on most sites, it reaches greatest proportions on sandy sites similar to those common to sand shinnery oak and sand sagebrush.

50. Soaptree yucca. *Yucca elata* Engelm. (Liliaceae). Tree usually to 6 feet or less tall, rarely to 20 or 25 feet; flowers white, fragile, numerous; fruit a dry, persistent, brown capsule; leaves green in radiating clusters, 10 to 30 inches long, straight, smooth, ending in brownish spine (317) (Fig. 3.35).

Distribution and Ecology. Soaptree yucca spreads by seed and prefers semiarid to desert environments, especially shallow, droughty

3.35. Soaptree yucca is usually found on shallow, droughty sites but may occur on better sites if drainage is adequate. It rarely exceeds 6 to 8 feet in height.

sites (87). It reaches its greatest proportions in the Trans-Pecos of Texas and extends south to Mexico.

Control. The only known method of effective control of soaptree yucca is grubbing (87).

51. Spiny allthorn; allthorn. *Koeberlinia spinosa* Zucc. (Koeberliniaceae). Highly branched, shrubby or treelike to 15 feet; irregular shape determined by growth of stiff green spines; apparently leafless; flowers greenish to yellow; fruits clusters of four to eight small black berries; leaves minute, persistent for only short time so plant is usually leaf-

3.36. Spiny allthorn is well adapted to the dry conditions of western and southern Texas. The stiff spines cause irregular growth, the plant is essentially leafless, and the fruit is a small black berry.

less; branches ending in green, thick, smooth, sharp thorn (317) (Fig. 3.36).

Distribution and Ecology. Referred to simply as allthorn by the Weed Science Society of America (321), spiny allthorn is more common in the southern and western portions of South Texas than in the coastal zone. It also occurs on the edge of the Rolling Plains as the vegetation grades into that of the Edwards Plateau (Fig. 2.1, areas 2, 6–8, 10). It is usually a minor component of the mixed-brush understory but is a formidable plant to encounter.

Control. Allthorn is not susceptible to broadcast aerial applications of 2,4,5-T at rates normally used for range improvement (0.25 to 1 pound per acre). Individual-plant treatments with herbicides or mechanical removal are suggested where the species poses a problem. Effective control has been accomplished by root plowing alone or root plowing followed by raking in the South Texas Plains (71).

52. Spiny hackberry; granjeno. *Celtis pallida* Torr. (Ulmaceae). Densely branched, spiny, evergreen shrub; bark smooth, gray, with long, stout spines; spines alternate on old stems and opposite on new growth; leaf margins entire to serrated around top half, with three prominent, palmate veins and alternate, simple, ovate, rounded and acute at top; flowers and fruits as in sugar hackberry, but fleshy fruit yellow or orange (317).

Distribution and Ecology. Spiny hackberry is an important component of mixed-brush stands in South Texas. It occurs throughout South Texas on a variety of soils from the coastal zone to New Mexico and northward to the Post Oak Savannah (Fig. 2.1, areas 2, 6, 7, 10). Spiny hackberry usually occurs as a shrub 8 feet tall or less but occasionally reaching 12 to 15 feet on the more fertile range sites. It spreads by seed and resprouts from the base upon disturbance of the top (87). Although it is a definite management problem on rangelands, spiny hackberry flowers are used by bees, the fruits are relished by birds, and the foliage is browsed.

Control. Spiny hackberry is not susceptible to conventional sprays of 2,4,5-T. Occasionally it has been effectively controlled by sprays of picloram or 2,4,5-T plus picloram (31), but rates suggested for control of other species (1 pound per acre or less) are usually not satisfactory for spiny hackberry (91). Spiny hackberry decreased significantly following root plowing or combining root plowing and raking of rangeland in the South Texas Plains (71).

Promising treatments. Dry herbicide formulations appear promising for control of spiny hackberry. Both tebuthiuron and picloram pellets at 1 pound per acre have controlled over 80 percent of the population.

53. Sugar hackberry. *Celtis laevigata* Willd. (Ulmaceae). Tree with warty gray (or dark) bark; flowers small, greenish, solitary on short pedicels in the leaf axils; leaves alternate, simple, entire with few weak teeth near apex, ovate to lanceolate, light green, prominent three veins originating from base; branches gray to light brown; fruit a small brown or orange red drupe (317).

Distribution and Ecology. Sugar hackberry is widespread, occurring in most areas of Texas along stream banks and in lowlands. Sugar hackberry is more common to the plains than to the coastal zones of South Texas. It is distributed northward into the Edwards Plateau, where it inhabits gravelly or rocky sites (199), and eastward to the Post Oak Savannah (Fig. 2.1, areas 1–3, 5–10). It spreads by seed and is palatable browse for deer and goats (199). The trees are often 45 feet or more tall, and their desirable characteristics, as livestock shade, for example, usually outweigh their undesirable traits (199).

Control. Sugar hackberry is susceptible to many mechanical and chemical control methods. Aerial application of 0.5 pound of 2,4,5-T plus picloram (1:1) per acre will control sugar hackberry (87). AMS (ammate) as a cut, frill, or stump treatment will control individual plants (140). One tablespoon of AMS crystals per cup of water is poured into the frills, or 0.2 ounce of crystals per inch of tree diameter is applied to cut stumps. Individual plants may also be controlled with basal sprays of 8 pounds of 2,4,5-T in 100 gallons of diesel oil or kerosene (141). Trees over 5 inches in diameter should be frilled for treatment. Chaining followed with browsing by goats has been used to control sugar hackberry in the Edwards Plateau (199). Root plowing or tree grubbing also provides effective control of the species (87).

54. Tarbush. *Flourensia cernua* DC. (Compositae). Shrub, 1.5 to 6 feet tall, highly branched and leafy (Fig. 3.37); flowers small, in groups of 12 to 20, yellow; fruit an achene, 0.25 inch or less long; leaves simple, alternate, persistent, elliptic to oblong or ovate to oval, margin entire; upper surface green, somewhat resinous, lower surface paler and glabrous; aromatic and hoplike odor associated with leaves; twigs light brown to gray (317).

Distribution and Ecology. Tarbush is restricted in Texas primarily to the western Edwards Plateau, eastern South Texas Plains, and Trans-Pecos, occurring on dry soils of valleys, mesas, and flats (Fig. 2.1, areas 6, 7, 10). It also occurs abundantly in New Mexico, Arizona, and Mexico. Tarbush develops thick, persistent stands, especially where rangeland has been abused by mismanagement such as over-

3.37. Tarbush is most common on dry soils of southwestern Texas, especially the Trans-Pecos. It produces a bright yellow but small flower, and the leaves have an aromatic hoplike odor.

grazing. It spreads by seeds and resists top removal by resprouting from a persistent crown (87). Tarbush is often found in association with creosotebush, the two forming a complex which excludes range forage species. Tarbush is used during stress periods by white-tailed deer and sheep (87); the branch tops, flowers, and fruits are the most toxic portions (238).

Control. Tarbush is not highly susceptible to aerial broadcast applications of phenoxy herbicides at rates commonly used on rangelands. Although individual-plant treatments are usually not feasible because typical tarbush infestations are very thick and cover broad expanses, basal sprays of 2,4,5-T at 16 pounds per 100 gallons are effective for control (87).

Promising treatments. Control of tarbush with 2 to 4 pounds of 2,4-D or 2,4,5-T per acre; 0.25 to 1 pound of picloram per acre; or

2 pounds of fenuron or monuron per acre has been reported (240, 241). Broadcast applications of picloram may hold most promise. Herbel and his colleagues (131) reported effective control of tarbush by root plowing. However, root plowing should be restricted to sites with good moisture relations and with potential for revegetation.

55. Tasajillo; pencil cactus. *Opuntia leptocaulis* DC. (Cactaceae). Bushy appearance; usually less than 5 feet tall (Fig. 3.38); stems cylindric; small, inconspicuous greenish flowers; fruit globular, small (less than 1 inch long), red, fleshy; pads small (0.5 inch or shorter); branches slender, jointed and easily detached; spines slender white, variable, 0.75 to 2 inches long (317).

Distribution and Ecology. Tasajillo is distributed northward through the Rolling and High Plains and westward to the Trans-Pecos and south into Mexico (Fig. 2.1, areas 2–10). It is limited only in the extreme eastern portion of South Texas. Rarely a formidable management problem alone, it is usually not a dominant in brush stands. However, tasajillo is a common component of woody-plant communities except in the eastern quarter of the state. It is usually most abundant on sandy loam and clay loam soils and is often found in association with honey mesquite (87). It spreads by seed, especially as fruits are moved by birds, coyotes, and other animals, and by transportation of the joints. The berries are readily eaten by wild turkeys and other game birds (199).

Control. Tasajillo is not susceptible to aerial application of 2,4,5-T; individual-plant treatments with 2,4,5-T at 8 pounds per 100 gallons of diesel oil or kerosene result in effective control. (141).

Promising treatments. Broadcast sprays of 0.5 to 1.0 pound of picloram per acre applied in September and October, aerial applications of picloram or 2,4,5-T plus picloram (1:1) at 0.5 to 1 pound per acre in spring (87), prescribed burning, and root plowing followed by raking have controlled tasajillo (71, 72).

56. Texas buckeye. *Aesculus glabra* Willd. var. *arguta* (Buckl.) B. L. Robinson (Hippocastanaceae). Shrub to tree occasionally reaching 30 feet; flowers dense, yellow; fruit a brown capsule with two or three valves; leaves deciduous, opposite, palmately compound, elliptic to lanceolate, margins serrate, dark green, pubescent on lower side; bark gray to black (317) (Fig. 3.39).

Distribution and Ecology. Texas buckeye reaches greatest pro-

3.38. Tasajillo is a common component of range vegetation except in the eastern quarter of the state. (*Courtesy M. M. Kothmann*)

portions in the Edwards Plateau (231) but is distributed westward and into Oklahoma (Fig. 2.1, areas 1, 3–5, 7). Texas buckeye is a poisonous species. It is most often found along streams and adjacent low hills (317). It may occur in pure stands or in association with hardwoods and rapidly resprouts from an extensive root system upon top removal.

    Control. Texas buckeye is not susceptible to simple top removal

3.39. Texas buckeye, a poisonous plant, reaches its greatest proportions in the Edwards Plateau. (*Photograph by O. E. Sperry*)

or to burning but is susceptible to wetting basal sprays of 2,4,5-T, 2,4-D plus 2,4,5-T, or MCPA as 2 percent solutions in water (231). The same herbicides are more effective when applied in notches than when applied to the trunk bases.

57. Texas colubrina; hog plum. *Colubrina texensis* (T. & G.) Gray (Rhamnaceae). Deciduous, low, much-branched shrub with short but not spinescent branchlets; leaves oval to elliptic or oblong; flowers small, yellow, in axillary clusters; fruits of two to three dark brown nutlets (317) (Fig. 3.40).

Distribution and Ecology. Texas colubrina is more common in the South Texas Plains than in the coastal zone, but it occurs throughout South Texas and northward into the Post Oak Savannah (Fig. 2.1, areas 2, 5–7). Most common on deep sandy sites (87), it reproduces from seed and basal resprouts. Texas colubrina grows closely, forming heavy thickets of underbrush rarely over 8 to 10 feet tall.

Control. Relatively little information is available on control, since Texas colubrina usually occurs as a secondary species in the mixed-brush complex. Aerial application of phenoxy herbicides has

3.40. Texas colubrina, also called hog plum, is a common species in the South Texas Plains and Post Oak Savannah. It is characterized by short, stiff, almost spinelike branchlets and leaves with prominent venation.

not been effective (87). However, effective control of Texas colubrina from aerial applications in the spring of 2 pounds of picloram per acre or a combination containing 1 pound each of 2,4,5-T plus picloram per acre has been reported (31). Picloram plus 2,4,5-T at 0.5 pound of each herbicide per acre has not controlled Texas colubrina, but roller chopping followed by shredding and burning has effectively controlled this species (109). The grassland was shredded in the spring one year after roller chopping. Prescribed burnings were applied in late summer following shredding.

Promising treatments. Individual-plant treatment with picloram pellets is promising (87).

58. Texas kidneywood. *Eysenhardtia texana* Scheele (Leguminosae). Deciduous shrub, rarely attaining heights of 6.5 to 8 feet; flowers papilionaceous, white, small, in terminal racemes; fruit a small, glan-

3.41. Texas kidneywood is a small, deciduous shrub the leaves of which emit an unpleasant odor when wounded. *(Courtesy Soil Conservation Service)*

dular-dotted pod, usually with two to four seeds; several pods maturing on the raceme (317) (Fig. 3.41).

Distribution and Ecology. Plant parts of Texas kidneywood emit an unpleasant odor when wounded. It is a prolific seed producer if undisturbed by goats and deer (199). It occurs throughout southern Texas but more so in the northern portion of the South Texas Plains and southern Edwards Plateau than in the coastal zone or in far West Texas (Fig. 2.1, areas 2, 4–7, 10). Texas kidneywood also occurs as far south as Coahuila, Mexico (317). It is an irregularly shaped shrub, usually with a number of stems arising from the base. It is most prevalent on rocky sites such as low, stony hills in the Edwards

Plateau (199). Texas kidneywood is palatable to goats and deer and probably cattle and sheep.

Control. Little information is available, but Texas kidneywood has been controlled with 2 pounds of picloram and 2,4,5-T (1:1) per acre (31). Merrill (199) suggests that Texas kidneywood not be controlled but instead that a rotation program be developed, based on light grazing by goats for several years, to promote the species on Edwards Plateau rangeland.

59. Texas persimmon; Mexican persimmon; black persimmon. *Diospyros texana* Scheele (Ebenaceae). Small tree or large shrub; thick, leathery, dark green, oblong or obovate leaves; bark usually dark, characteristically splitting and flaking off, especially at the base of the main trunk, revealing light gray wood; dioecious, flowers small, with greenish white, urn-shaped corollas; fruit a large, globose berry, mostly 0.8 to 1.2 inches in diameter, dark purple or black at maturity; seeds hard, shiny, about 0.3 inch long (Fig. 3.42) (317).

Distribution and Ecology. Texas persimmon is a persistent species occupying about six million acres in central Texas, the Edwards Plateau, and the Post Oak Savannah (208). It is also a common component of mixed-brush communities in the South Texas Plains and Coastal Prairie (Fig. 2.1, areas 2–7, 10). It generally grows in association with other shrubs, especially oaks and junipers (249). Texas persimmon fruits are relished by wildlife and consumed by livestock. The seeds will not germinate until removed from the pulp of the fruit and scarified. Seedlings rapidly establish root systems, although aerial portions apparently grow very slowly during the seedling years. Leaves drop during drought but are quickly replaced following rainfall (136). Texas persimmon occurs as individual, single-stemmed trees or as multistemmed bushes in mottes. It reaches greatest stand development on shallow, rocky sites and on sandy soils (87). Although there are reports of trees to 40 feet tall (208), individual Texas persimmon plants rarely exceed 8 to 12 feet. A deterrent to effective range management in some areas, Texas persimmon is considered by many as highly desirable for wildlife food and cover. It apparently increases in abundance following most mechanical brush control methods (249).

Control. Texas persimmon sprouts readily from the stem base and from the roots. Since the roots extend laterally a great distance from the parent plant, it is resistant to most mechanical control meth-

3.42. Texas persimmon occurs as a multistemmed bush or a small tree. The fruits are relished by wildlife, and Texas persimmon is valuable for game cover, but stands may become so dense that they form a serious range management problem.

ods. Tree grubbing is not usually effective, especially where infestations occur on rocky or shallow soils (136). Broadcast aerial sprays of conventional herbicides have been ineffective, and about 3 pounds of picloram per acre as a broadcast spray were required to control half of the Texas persimmon population in one test (203). Even aerial application of 2,4,5-T plus picloram does not effectively control Texas persimmon (31). Basal bark and individual-plant foliage sprays with high rates of 2,4,5-T (16 pounds per 100 gallons of spray solution) in July, August, or early September have been most satisfactory. Individual-plant sprays (basal or foliar) of picloram, dicamba, and 2,4,5-T plus picloram and granular applications of picloram appear promising (208, 249). Picloram pellets at 0.022 ounce active ingredient per foot of canopy diameter will control Texas persimmon.

60. Texas virgin's bower; old man's beard; Drummond clematis. *Clematis drummondii* T. & G. (Ranunculaceae). Highly but delicately branched vine with twisting leaf petioles; flowers white; fruit with long (2 to 4 inches), plumose styles; achenes 0.08 to 0.125 inches long;

3.43. Texas virgin's bower is a common vine in South Texas. It may be noted growing in fences along highways or as a heavy cover over other woody plants or debris on rangeland.

leaves opposite, pinnately compound, three- to seven-foliate, leaflets 0.5 to 2 inches long, lanceolate to ovate, coarsely toothed and lobed (317) (Fig. 3.43).

Distribution and Ecology. Texas virgin's bower is conspicuous in fences along highways of much of South and West Texas (Fig. 2.1, areas 2–4, 6, 7, 10). It spreads by windblown achenes and reaches greatest proportions in lowlands, where it may grow over other woody species, forming an almost impenetrable barrier. It is palatable to sheep, goats, and deer (199).

Control. Heavy stocking of sheep and goats evidently will control this species (199).

Promising treatments. Picloram pellets at the equivalent of 1 to 2 pounds active ingredient per acre spread along fence lines is a promising control method.

61. Twisted acacia. *Acacia tortuosa* (L.) Willd. (Leguminosae). Deciduous shrub, rarely a small tree, usually less than 6 feet tall; long, slender, sharp spines at nodes; heads yellow orange, small; pods pu-

3.44. Twisted acacia is spread throughout South Texas but exerts most influence as a component of the mixed-brush complex.

bescent, slightly curved, constricted between seeds and mostly more than 2.75 inches long (Fig. 3.44).

Distribution and Ecology. The vernacular name "huischillo" is used locally, probably because of the similarities of twisted acacia to huisache. However, the legume of *A. tortuosa* is more narrow and elongate, and the plants rarely reach the proportions of huisache. Twisted acacia is spread throughout South Texas, usually in association in the mixed-brush complex as a low-growing shrub (Fig. 2.1, areas 2, 6, 7). It is highly adapted to sandy loam or clay loam soils (87). Although it is of relatively low stature, twisted acacia sometimes develops considerable canopy spread. It assumes a position in most communities similar to that of catclaw. It spreads by seed and rapidly reinfests areas following initial control efforts (87). Twisted acacia survives top removal by resprouting from the stem base (196).

Control. Twisted acacia tolerates moderate to high rates of phenoxy herbicides such as 2,4,5-T applied broadcast. Root plowing is recommended for dense stands in annual rainfall zones of 15 inches or higher, and dozing or basal application (8 pounds of 2,4,5-T per 100 gallons of oil) is used for controlling scattered plants or small stands (234). Twisted acacia has increased in abundance following burning of South Texas ranges (40), probably because of its ability to resprout. The presence of twisted acacia has been reduced by root plowing or root plowing followed by raking in the South Texas Plains (71). When the plant density is two hundred trees per acre or less, low-energy grubbing, in which the entire trunk must be removed, is an effective method of control (325).

Promising treatments. Combinations of equal amounts of 2,4,5-T and picloram (0.5 to 1 pound of total herbicide per acre) usually give fair to good control of twisted acacia top growth, but results are somewhat erratic depending on range site and season. Aerial applications of picloram pellets to shredded growth less than 3 feet tall may hold promise for twisted acacia control.

62. Vasey oak; sandpaper oak; Vasey shin oak. *Quercus pungens* var. *vaseyana* (Buckl.) C. H. Mull. (Fagaceae). Shrub or occasionally small tree rarely exceeding 5 feet tall except under most favorable conditions; flowers are catkins, male and female; fruit small brown acorns; leaves semievergreen, oblong to lanceolate, grayish green to dark green, shiny; bark grayish brown.

Distribution and Ecology. Most prominent in the Edwards Plateau, Vasey oak is occasionally referred to as "shin oak" or "little-leaf shin oak," since it closely resembles other scrub oaks. It occasionally occurs on more mesic sites of the Trans-Pecos (Fig. 2.1, areas 7, 10). Growth habit is similar to that described for sand shinnery oak. It evidently spreads from roots, with stands thickening to almost eliminate desirable forage. Vasey oak reaches its greatest development on rocky, shallow clay loam soils (87) as opposed to the association of sand shinnery oak with lighter-textured soils.

In the area of its highest adaptation, Crockett, Sutton, Kimble, Val Verde, Edwards, Real, and Kerr counties, Vasey oak serves as a browse plant for both domestic livestock and wildlife, but, like other oaks, it may be toxic during the bud stage (128). It reproduces primarily from roots or rhizomes; seedlings of Vasey oak are rare, although acorn production may be high in certain seasons. Harris (128) reported that mottes near Sonora, Texas, probably originated around the turn of the century. The species develops a heavy, matted root system which adapts it to steep, stony areas of shallow soils. It spreads by seed and persists by vegetative reproduction from a persistent crown (87). Vasey oak may replace juniper communities following fire if rangelands are overgrazed. On deeper soils it grows in association with honey mesquite and live oak. On rough terrain Vasey oak may be found in association with junipers. It affords browse for goats and deer (87).

Control. Little information is available, but chaining followed by browsing by goats is apparently an effective practice (128). Vasey oak may react like sand shinnery oak to broadcast application of herbicides. Individual-plant treatments, basal or foliage sprays with 2,4,5-T or silvex at 8 pounds per 100 gallons of spray solution, are effective but not economical for dense stands. Burning is generally ineffective for manipulating Vasey oak stands.

Promising treatments. Two successive broadcast applications of 2,4,5-T at 2 pounds per acre have provided control. Also, removal of top growth followed by treatment of regrowth in full foliage with broadcast application of 2,4,5-T at 1 pound per acre appears promising (87).

63. Water oak. *Quercus nigra* L. (Fagaceae). Tree, occasionally to 30 feet; flowers (catkins) appearing with leaves in the spring; fruit an acorn, light yellowish brown; leaves highly variable, simple, alternate and persistent but variously shaped (Fig. 3.5), typically entire, obovate or spatulate, upper surface dark green with lighter lower surface; twigs slender, reddish gray to reddish brown; bark grayish black to light brown.

Distribution and Ecology. Water oak occurs as a component of the Post Oak Savannah where overgrazing has caused formation of heavy thickets. Water oak resprouts readily from intact stem segments following top removal. It is often found in association with post oak and blackjack oaks on upland sites where, as a component of the woody-plant complex, it becomes a range management problem. The three species may be readily differentiated based on leaf morphology. Water oak is common in the entire East Texas area and is found particularly in low woods or along stream banks and swamps (Fig. 2.1, areas 1–3).

Control. Water oak is susceptible to foliar sprays of 2,4,5-T plus picloram or picloram alone at 1 pound per acre (274). Brady (41) effectively controlled water oak in Louisiana with applications of 2,4,5-T, dicamba, or paraquat at 2 pounds per acre in May.

64. Whitebrush; whitebush; bee bush. *Aloysia lycioides* Cham. (Verbenaceae). Highly branched shrub with slender, brittle stems less than 10 feet tall; flowers small, white in axillary spikes; fruit a small, dry drupe containing two nutlets; leaves aromatic, lanceolate to oblong, almost sessile (317) (Fig. 3.45).

Distribution and Ecology. Whitebrush is an aggressive invader, particularly in the Edwards Plateau and the northern portion of the South Texas Plains (Fig. 2.5). It infests over 6 million acres of Texas rangeland (286) (Fig. 2.1, areas 2, 4–8, 10). Whitebrush grows in association with other species on uplands but forms heavy, pure thickets on fertile lowland areas and is evidently a good honey plant. Whitebrush seeds are very small and difficult to germinate under controlled conditions. The seedlings are fragile, usually less than 0.5 inch tall at one week old. Upon disturbance of the top growth, whitebrush resprouts rapidly from an enlarged, buried portion of stem referred to as the "bur."

Control. Shredding and other methods of top removal offer only temporary control. Root plowing usually severs the roots from the bur, which may rapidly resprout even when dislocated for some distance. Root plowing or root plowing followed by raking has effectively controlled whitebrush on the South Texas Plains (71). Chaining is

3.45. Whitebrush is a highly branched shrub that may develop such stands as to exclude grazing by livestock. Leaves are typically lanceolate to oblong and the flowers are very small and occur as clusters.

usually not effective because of the brushy, shrubby growth of whitebrush. Chaining, especially under dry soil conditions, may simply break off the tops of the plants instead of uprooting them. Sprays of 2,4-D or 2,4,5-T are usually not effective, but foliar sprays of MCPA have given good control (206). Soil Conservation Service recommendations include (a) mowing, shredding, or chopping followed by browsing by goats; (b) grubbing or bulldozing of small areas; (c) disking of pure stands; or (d) foliage sprays with MCPA (286) for whitebrush control.

Promising treatments. Sprays of picloram of 0.5 to 1 pound per acre in September and October result in good control (207). Picloram granules applied to the base of stands also effectively control whitebrush. Aerial application of 2 pounds of active ingredient per acre of tebuthiuron has given excellent control of whitebrush at several locations in South Texas. Good results have been reported from any method that severs the plant 4 to 6 inches below the surface then

removes the plant, from disking twice (with two to six months between diskings) followed by reseeding, and from root plowing or root
raking and disking followed by reseeding (325).

65. Willow baccharis; dry-land willow. *Baccharis salicina* T. & G.
(Compositae). Shrub, 3 to 6 feet tall; weak, brittle stems; flowers
unisexual, the staminate and pistillate ones in small heads on separate
plants, whitish to yellow; fruit a flattened achene with pappus of white
bristles; leaves numerous, simple, alternate, lanceolate to oblong,
slightly dentate or in some cases almost entire (Fig. 3.46).

Distribution and Ecology. Willow baccharis is an aggressive invader of lands which are converted from cultivation to grassland

3.46. Willow baccharis, an aggressive invader of abandoned cropland
and disturbed rangeland, is characterized by a growth form similar to
that of the true willows *(Salix* spp.).

(Fig. 2.1, areas 1–9). It grows under wide extremes from association with the phreatophyte salt cedar along flood plains (46) to pure stands along roadsides, in waste areas, and on vacant lots in cities. It resembles members of the genus *Salix* (true willows). Only recently has it become recognized as a severe management problem on grazing lands. It spreads by seed but persists by sprout development after top removal (274).

Control. Plowing areas infested with willow baccharis and reseeding them with grass provides excellent control (135). Shredding offers only temporary benefits, since willow baccharis may resprout from remaining stem segments. Hand grubbing is effective for controlling a few small, scattered plants, and power grubbing is effective for removing larger plants. Broadcast foliar sprays of 2,4,5-T are not as effective as individual-plant treatments. The low-volatility ester of 2,4-D should be used at 1.5 to 2 pounds per acre for willow baccharis control. If water is used as the herbicide carrier, a wetting agent should be added. Willow baccharis is somewhat more susceptible to 2,4-D or 2,4,5-T low-volatility esters at 8 pounds per 100 gallons of diesel oil. Apply the chemical solution to the lower 12 to 18 inches of the trunk until runoff. Undiluted 2,4-D can be used as a cut stump treatment. Willow baccharis readily resprouts from the stem base, and any uninjured stem segment rapidly develops new sprouts following prescribed burns. Ground broadcast applications of picloram or 2,4,5-T plus picloram appear promising for willow baccharis control (274). My colleagues and I have obtained excellent control of willow baccharis with broadcast applications of 1–2 pounds active ingredient of picloram or tebuthiuron pellets per acre.

66. Winged elm. *Ulmus alata* Michx. (Ulmaceae). Tree occasionally attaining heights of 45 feet, with conspicuous corky wings on twigs and branches; fruit occurring before leaves form in the spring in few-flowered, drooping fascicles; fruit a samara, reddish or greenish, flat, winged; leaves simple, alternate, deciduous, ovate to oblong lanceolate; twigs reddish brown, slender; bark reddish brown to gray with flat ridges (317) (Fig. 3.47).

Distribution and Ecology. Winged elm occurs throughout eastern and into central Texas, northward to southeastern Oklahoma and Arkansas, and southward to Louisiana. It is a component of the Post Oak Savannah vegetation and often grows in conjunction with species

3.47. Winged elm is typified by conspicuous corky wings on the twigs and branches.

such as yaupon to form the primary problem for removal of the oak overstory (Fig. 2.1, areas 1–5, 7). Winged elm spreads by wind-blown seeds, which germinate under a wide range of environmental conditions (164).

Control. Winged elm is resistant to normally used rates of 2,4,5-T, which usually result only in short-term defoliation. Picloram or a combination of picloram with 2,4,5-T is effective for winged elm control. Mixtures of 2,4,5-T with ammonium thiocyanate or with amitrole also control winged elm (82). Usually at least 2 pounds per acre of 2,4,5-T are required for removal of the winged elm canopy, but the plants rapidly regrow following treatment. Retreatment within two months of the original treatment is usually required if winged elm is not controlled by initial aerial applications of herbicides.

Promising treatments. Broadcast picloram sprays at 2 pounds per acre have controlled over 80 percent of the winged elm population (274). Applications of picloram either by soil injection or as pellets have effectively controlled winged elm (82), and broadcast applications of granular picloram at 1 pound per acre have effectively controlled winged elm near College Station, Texas, at all months of the year (29). Sprays with combinations of picloram and 2,4,5-T are not as effective as picloram alone. Tebuthiuron aerially applied at 2 pounds active ingredient per acre has given excellent control of winged elm near College Station.

67. Woollybucket bumelia; chittimwood; gum bumelia; gum elastic. *Bumelia lanuginosa* (Michx.) Pers. var. *rigida* Gray (Sapotaceae). Shrub or tree to 6 feet tall; young leaves silvery pubescent on both surfaces, becoming glabrate above with age; bark of small stems dark reddish brown, older trunks grayish with dark furrows; flowers white; fruits dark blue to black (317).

Distribution and Ecology. Woollybucket bumelia is usually considered to be a minor component of the mixed-brush complex and is distributed northward to the Post Oak Savannah of Texas (317). It is a codominant with hackberry in localized South Texas communities (37) (Fig. 2.1, areas 1–3). It may commonly occur as a small tree which resprouts from the stem base upon disturbance of the top growth, forming a small shrub. Woollybucket bumelia occurs in many varieties from East and South Texas northward to Kansas and eastward to Florida. It is occasionally used as an ornamental grown from seed or cuttings. A gum exudes from the wood when it is wounded. Fruit of woollybucket bumelia is relished by birds. It occurs in rocky sites in the Edwards Plateau and is very palatable to deer and goats (199).

Control. Woollybucket bumelia is susceptible to 2,4,5-T as a ground broadcast spray (274). It is also easily controlled with foliar sprays containing 2,4,5-T plus picloram or picloram alone. Individual plants can be controlled with basal applications of 8 pounds 2,4,5-T per 100 gallons of diesel oil or kerosene (141). Trees over 5 inches in diameter should be frilled before treatment. Little data is available on response of woollybucket bumelia to mechanical methods, but simple top removal would probably be less effective than methods which uproot the plant (274). Chaining followed with browsing by goats has proven effective in the Edwards Plateau (196).

68. Yaupon. *Ilex vomitoria* Ait. (Aquifoliaceae). Evergreen, many-stemmed, thicket-forming shrub, usually less than 10 feet tall; occasionally a tree, 20 to 25 feet; fruit a shiny red drupe usually with four

3.48. Yaupon is an evergreen, thicket-forming species most commonly a problem in the Post Oak Savannah of Texas. Fruits are a conspicuous shiny red, and the leaves are oblong to ovate with crenate margins.

nutlets; leaves evergreen, simple, alternate, elliptic, oblong to oval with crenate margins; bark brownish to mottled gray, occasionally almost black, tight and smooth (Fig. 3.48) (317).

Distribution and Ecology. Yaupon is a common component of the natural vegetation from central throughout eastern Texas. It is particularly prevalent in low, moist woods along stream banks and waterways. It also occurs in southeastern Oklahoma, Arkansas, and Louisiana, but usually not in problem proportions. Infestations reach their maximum development in the East Texas woody-plant complex, where yaupon is a common understory component. When the overstory oak species are controlled in the Post Oak Savannah, yaupon may rapidly become one of the dominant species in association with other troublesome woody plants such as winged elm. It readily sprouts from the base and, in dense stands, essentially eliminates forage production (Fig. 2.1, areas 1, 2, 3, 6, 7).

Control. Frilled stump or notch treatments are effective for control of larger plants when applied from December through March or from May to August using 2,4,5-T at 8 pounds per 100 gallons of diesel oil or kerosene. Sprays are applied with knapsack or hand sprayers into the frills or notches until the herbicide bubbles out of freshly cut surfaces. Yaupon is essentially resistant to broadcast sprays of phenoxy herbicides such as 2,4,5-T at rates commonly used for range improvement. Shredding does not offer permanent control because of the potential for resprouting.

Promising treatments. Broadcast aerial sprays of picloram alone at 1 to 2 pounds per acre or in combination with 2,4,5-T at 1 pound per acre of each herbicide in early spring. Picloram alone is more effective than the herbicide combination, with control level apparently proportional to the amount of picloram in the combination with 2,4,5-T. Picloram pellets and granules have promise and, in some cases, appear superior to sprays. In other cases the application rates of pellets required for effective control on a broadcast basis have temporarily damaged desirable grass species. Paraquat combined with picloram has improved the levels of yaupon control over picloram applied alone (26, 274). Tebuthiuron pellets applied at 2 to 4 pounds per acre appear promising.

4

Mechanical Methods of Brush Management

MOST of the techniques and types of equipment for mechanical brush management have evolved from two basic approaches: removal of the aerial portion of the plant only or removal of the entire plant. In the early days, both approaches were extremely laborious and time-consuming, since they were accomplished by hand labor or with draft animals. Like other brush management techniques, mechanical methods have evolved into relatively rapid (when compared to hand labor) and in some cases sophisticated approaches since the 1950's.

Mechanical methods often present the only feasible approach to brush management and consequently are widely used, so the necessary machinery is commonly available from commercial contractors or implement companies. Innovations, some extremely effective, have been developed by landowners for specific and often unique purposes. Because energy and equipment production costs have steadily risen, use of heavy equipment has to be carefully planned in the overall management effort. The more costly mechanical methods are usually feasible for use only on range sites with high production potential. In many cases mechanical brush management techniques have been eliminated as potential range improvement methods simply because production potential will not justify the costs. However, mechanical brush management remains one of the most important range improvement practices when the total problem is considered; in some cases it is the only viable solution.

Mechanical equipment is available for a multitude of range improvement jobs. Specialized tools have been developed to meet particular land management objectives. Selection of a mechanical brush method depends primarily upon

1. *Objectives of the manager*. Is the management objective to stimulate the maximum release of native forage with minimal cost, to

alter the brush stand mechanically in preparation for the application of a secondary method, or to attain total brush removal in preparation for the establishment of tame pasture?

2. *Terrain.* Is the slope such that no soil disturbance can be tolerated? Is the land surface so rocky and rough that risk of damage to the equpiment prohibits certain approaches?

3. *Soils and site potential.* Are the soils shallow and of low fertility with a high risk that range forage production might not be economically improved? Conversely, are the soils deep and fertile with desirable water relations which will allow maximum production of species that are highly valuable for grazing when the influence of the woody plants is minimized?

4. *Growth habit and density of the primary problem species.* Is the problem composed primarily of upright trees with a low potential for resprouting, or do shrubby, multistemmed species with high regrowth potential present the primary problem?

5. *Nature of secondary species.* Are there associated woody species present, posing only a minor problem in the present brush complex, that upon removal of the primary species might be released to form a problem even more formidable than the original infestation?

The importance of plant growth habit, discussed in chapter 1 in relation to effective management, will be mentioned repeatedly in the discussion of the various mechanical brush management methods. Heavy equipment for the mechanical manipulation of woody-plant communities is generally designed either to remove the top growth of undesirable plants or to remove the plants completely by uprooting them. Mechanical methods can thus be categorized, based on function, as follows:

Simple top removal
1. Shredding
2. Roller chopping

Complete plant removal
1. Grubbing
2. Chaining
3. Cabling
4. Railing
5. Bulldozing
6. Root plowing
7. Raking (used primarily as a follow-up to other methods)

Each method has unique strengths and characteristic weaknesses that must be considered. The availability of equipment contractors and the machinery controlled or owned by the land manager must be considered in developing an efficient mechanical brush management program. In many if not most cases, mechanical brush management methods are most effective when used in conjunction with other approaches such as herbicides, prescribed burning, browsing by goats, or revegetation.

Simple Top Removal

Shredding. In general, problem woody plants are not easily controlled by simple top removal. Only a relatively few brush species are not capable of resprouting after top removal. Shredding reduces canopy cover of most species in the season of application, but new sprouts may readily develop from remaining stem segments, roots, and crowns. For example, removal of honey mesquite top growth has been shown to be more effective in North Texas in May than in other months, but even when removal was done at that time, about 25 percent of the above-ground growth had been replaced by the end of the first growing season (337).

The rate of replacement of top growth depends directly on growing conditions, especially rainfall after shredding. However, even during dry periods after shredding, many species of woody plants that are capable of taking advantage of moisture deep in the soil replace their top growth more readily than do shallow-rooted herbaceous species. For example, my colleagues and I found that twisted acacia, lotebush, and whitebrush replaced 50 percent of their original height in seven to eight months after three mixed-brush stands in South Texas were shredded. Spiny hackberry regrowth required twelve months to attain half its original height, blackbrush acacia required twenty months, and catclaw required twenty-two months. Agarito required about twenty-eight months to attain 50 percent of its height after shredding. Thus, within three or four growing seasons the woody plant stand was essentially replaced. Although regrowth was slowed during dry periods, it never completely ceased for the woody plants as it did for the herbaceous vegetation. This tolerance to top removal gives the woody plants a distinct advantage over the herbaceous forage species on the range.

Dry periods following shredding are necessary to prevent the establishment of new cactus plants from pad segments spread about by the action of the shredders. With Macartney rose, which may regenerate itself from root sprouts, crowns, or sections of the canes, shredding spreads fragments of canes which, when pressed into the moist soil surface, may take root and actually increase the plant density. Shredding induces two changes in the growth of most woody species: an increase in stem density with an ultimate increase in canopy cover, and a spreading growth form.

The principle underlying the influence of simple top removal on plants is that after removal of the stems and foliage, action of the photosynthetic apparatus is stopped for a time, forcing the plants to use energy stored in underground organs without replacement. Further, if stored food reserves are continually lowered by repeated shredding, the plants are reduced in vigor until, ultimately, they "die of starvation." In practice, top removal apparently does not adequately reduce the energy reserves of woody plants—at least those of problem species on Texas ranges—to allow their control. Repeated top removal of some woody species induces a change in growth habit but rarely reduces density. For example, repeated shredding of honey mesquite causes the number of branches to increase, and the plant tends to spread along the ground instead of growing upright. Available research information suggests that repeated top removal lowers food reserves in woody plants but that they are capable of replacing the canopy and reinstating their food production capacity in only a short time, especially under good growing conditions. Also, shredding is nonselective; the tops of desirable plants are also removed by the brush management operation. If the operation is performed repeatedly, especially during periods of stress, the vigor of desirable plants may be reduced.

On the other hand, with adequate soil moisture, removal of the woody plant cover releases herbaceous growth so that the net effect, *on the short term*, is improved range forage production. Another advantage of simple top removal is that initial reduction of the woody-plant canopy improves management efficiency by increasing visibility for the handling and care of livestock and improving the grazing distribution of livestock. Shredding also improves the browse value of many species by increasing the availability of young, succulent sprouts, a point discussed more fully in chapter 9. Removal of the woody-plant canopy releases herbaceous growth, which may afford a supply of fine fuel for maximum range improvement by prescribed burning (72). Moreover, my most recent research indicates that shredding immediately before application of dry herbicides such as picloram or tebuthiuron pellets may be beneficial, not necessarily because more woody plants are killed by the herbicide, but because no dead woody plants are left standing after the chemical treatment.

Heavy, durable shredders are required to withstand the rough rangeland terrain. Even with heavy equipment, shredding on hilly, rocky, rough terrain is not recommended. For such areas the operation is slow, and frequent equipment repairs are often costly. There is also a definite limitation on the size of woody plants that can be shredded effectively with most equipment. Most efficient shredding is usually accomplished on plants with stem diameters of less than 2.5 inches. Therefore, shredding is often used as a maintenance method after large rollers with blades (roller choppers) have removed the top growth and cut the large stem and branch sections into small pieces. However, shredders are commonly available to remove woody plants with 4-inch trunk diameters. Recently introduced heavy-duty, hydraulically operated shredders can be used in even larger brush (Fig. 4.1).

Roller chopping. Roller choppers are constructed from heavy drums or cylinders with several blades running parallel to the axis of the roller (Fig. 4.2). The welded cutting blades, with adequate weight, can penetrate the soil surface from 6 to 10 inches deep. The cylinders may be filled with water to increase their weight and improve the chopping of larger brush. Tractor-drawn roller choppers are available in single, tandem, or dual models and in a range of sizes. The roller chopper has two distinct advantages over conventional shredders. First, the added weight and durability of the roller chopper make it better adapted to rough topography and to the dense woody-plant stands normally encountered under rangeland conditions. Also, considerably larger plants can be roller chopped than can be shredded, although very large trees usually cannot be chopped effectively. The obvious disadvantage of roller choppers compared to shredders is that a large power source is required to pull and effectively operate the choppers. Roller chopping leaves a taller woody stubble than does shredding, but it is not so high that shredding usually cannot be used

4.1. Shredders have recently been introduced which can remove much larger trees than conventional drag models. (*Courtesy Hydro-Axe Corp.*)

4.2. Roller choppers, heavy drums or cylinders with several blades running the length of the rollers, are available in a wide range of sizes and weights.

as a secondary or follow-up method. Considerable time may be required for the debris left by roller chopping to decay. Where applicable, prescribed burning my hasten the removal of the debris. Also, as the roller chopper blades penetrate the soil surface, they may improve soil moisture relationships with minimal disturbance of the surface.

Complete Plant Removal

Grubbing. Grubbing is one of the oldest methods of physically removing individual plants. It was originally done by hand with shovels, axes, and the grubbing hoe (Fig. 4.3). Obviously such work was painstaking, tedious, and slow. However, hand grubbing, if the degree of brush control only is considered, has been the most effective mechanical practice, especially for crown-sprouting plants. Once the plant is removed beneath the lowermost dormant bud, its regenerative capacity is eliminated. Although there is an upper limit to the size of a plant that can be grubbed by hand, the primary requirement for its effectiveness is the availability of manpower. With high labor costs and the need to cover large areas in a relatively short time, grubbing by hand is no longer considered feasible for range improvement. Grubbing implements have been successfully mounted on crawler and wheeled tractors, with tremendous improvements in efficiency (Fig. 4.4). Yet the time required to remove woody plants from rangeland with power grubbing, also called tree dozing, varies widely, depending upon sizes of plants, stand density, type of growth, and soil texture and moisture content. For maximum efficiency the soil must be moist enough to allow a high percentage of the plants to be grubbed deeply enough to prevent regrowth. On heavy clay soils that are dry and hard, more time is required for plant removal, and many of the plants are cut off (leaving bud tissue intact) instead of being uprooted. Grubbing has not been successful on deep sands, where heavy accumulations of soil occur around the bases of the woody plants, thus increasing the effective depth requirement for grubbing, or on shallow, rocky soils.

Much has yet to be learned concerning the use of power grubbing to its full potential. Various plants react differently to grubbing mainly because of differences in their growth habits. Nonsprouting species

4.3. Complete plant removal in the early days was accomplished with the slow, laborious grubbing hoe. The task is now completed with equipment which allows relatively rapid treatment of extensive areas. (*Courtesy C. H. Meadors*)

4.4 Crawler tractors with front-mounted, U-shaped "stinger blades" are used for power grubbing. The stinger blade is placed beneath the lowermost bud and pushed forward as lift is placed on the system. (*Courtesy O. E. Sperry*)

such as Ashe juniper and many of the oaks may be removed by relatively shallow grubbing. Grubbing depth for species such as honey mesquite must be adjusted to crown depth, which is usually deeper on sandy than on clay soils, to assure removal of the lowermost dormant bud (89). Huisache, which has a growth form similar to that of honey mesquite, must be grubbed deeply enough to remove all tissue above the first lateral root. Grubbing is not feasible for vigorous root sprouters such as Texas persimmon; although the central stem is removed, viable buds along the roots some distance from the parent plant will readily sprout. Grubbing will control many species of cactus if they are stacked to ensure that the pads dry out.

The most effective control by grubbing usually occurs on sites where the woody plants are widely spaced and are large enough to be easily seen by the equipment operator. Small plants are often missed, especially when the grubbing is done while the plants are dormant. The creation of pits by grubbing is apparently of some value in improving soil moisture retention. However, attempts to control dense brush stands by grubbing greatly reduce the grass cover, leave the surface extremely rough, and are very costly.

Additional grubbings are usually necessary at regular intervals to remove small plants that were missed, new seedlings that have emerged, and plants that were not completely destroyed by the initial grubbing operation. Cost of retreatment to control small plants is often reduced substantially by the use of lighter, more mobile, and thus more economical equipment.

Chaining. The chaining operation consists of dragging a heavy-duty anchor chain, usually 150 to 300 feet long, in a loop behind two large crawler tractors (Fig. 4.5). Swath width, usually 85 to 150 feet, varies with the size of the tractors and the size and thickness of the brush. The tractors should be driven far enough apart to attain the maximum swath width but close enough together to maintain continuous forward motion. Anchor chains weighing 80 pounds or more per foot have replaced heavy cables for dragging down brush. The heavy chains are more flexible, work closer to the ground, and have less tendency to ride over dense brush than do cables. On rough terrain with permanent rock outcroppings, wear on the chain can be reduced by equipping each end with swivels which allow the chain to roll rather than drag over obstacles. Effectiveness of chaining depends

4.5. Anchor chains, usually 150 to 300 feet long and weighing 80 pounds per foot or heavier are pulled in a loop by crawler tractors to effectively knock down and uproot brush. *(Courtesy G. O. Hoffman)*

primarily on two factors: soil moisture content and size of the woody plants. In dry soil, especially where primarily small plants are present, the woody plants tend to break off rather than be uprooted.

The greatest value of chaining is the low initial cost of quickly knocking down, uprooting, and thinning out moderate to dense stands of medium to large trees. It is not effective for the control of small, many-stemmed plants that are too limber to be uprooted. Double chaining, covering the area twice in opposite directions, will usually break off nearly all the above-ground growth of woody plants and uproot from 10 to 80 percent of large trees, depending upon the soil moisture content. The need for double chaining varies with subsequent operations that are anticipated and the ultimate use of the land. However, for maximum range improvement of areas that support dense, heavy brush stands, double chaining is preferred over single chaining.

Chaining is recommended where trees do not exceed 18 inches in diameter and population density does not exceed 1,000 plants per acre. Conducted properly, however, chaining has been accomplished in all sizes of vegetation. The upper limit in size and density of trees that can be chained varies with tractor size and the width of the swath.

On an area in South Texas that supported an average of 596 woody plants per acre—mostly large honey mesquite, spiny hackberry, lime prickly ash, huisache, lotebush, and narrow-leaf forestiera—chaining one way reduced the woody-plant stands to 352 plants per acre, most of which were regrown from 3 to 6 feet tall after two years (267). Double chaining reduced the woody plant density to 305 plants per acre. In both cases the surface was littered with debris, and most of the new plants arose from stem segments of the original growth that had not detached from the soil. Soil cover with fallen debris not only prevents maximum development of range forage but also presents a problem in the handling and care of livestock, especially when the cattle must be gathered by horseback. Double chaining and then raking, stacking, and burning the debris has provided the most effective range improvement from chaining in South Texas. In one case, forage production one year after such treatment exceeded that provided by single or double chaining alone, and forage consumption by livestock, a function of availability, was improved by the increased accessibility to the area. Although burning of the stacks bared the soil for a short time, the bare areas were completely covered by common Bermudagrass in the growing season following the winter burning (267).

Chaining alone generally offers only temporary benefits. However, when used in combination with other methods such as aerial spraying, it usually reduces the overall cost of controlling troublesome species. In dense South Texas brush, chaining of areas sprayed two years before was completed in about half the time required to chain unsprayed areas. Chaining two to three years after an aerial application of herbicides has been used extensively in northwestern Texas for control of honey mesquite. The combination of aerial spraying, which is most effective on small plants, and chaining, which improves the kill by uprooting the hard-to-kill large plants, will give good control of species such as honey mesquite for ten to twenty years before retreatment is necessary (90, 197). On range sites supporting mostly old trees that are low in vigor with many dead branches, chaining followed by aerial application of herbicides to control regrowth offers a means of reducing the overall cost of control. The same general practices are occasionally used in stands of oaks. Also, as more effective herbicides are developed, the practice may have increased promise for management of South Texas mixed brush.

Chaining must be carefully applied to brush stands supporting pricklypear. High soil moisture content, conducive to effective chaining on most brush, may serve to seriously increase the pricklypear stand. Any method that breaks the pricklypear plant into individual pads and scatters the pads simply serves to transplant the species. Each pad segment has the potential to take root and establish a new plant. Therefore, where pricklypear poses a potential problem, follow-up improvement, such as railing under extremely dry conditions or herbicide application, must be considered for effective management.

Cabling. Cabling is conducted in the same general manner as is chaining except that a heavy-duty cable is employed (Fig. 4.6). Conditions for maximum effectiveness of cabling, like those for chaining, are soil moisture adequate to allow maximum uprooting of woody plants and an upright plant growth form. Growth form and woody plant size are especially critical to effective cabling. The cable, being more flexible and of lighter weight than the heavy anchor chain, has a tendency to ride up and over the woody debris during the dragging

4.6. Heavy-duty cables are used in much the same manner as chains for knocking down and uprooting brush. However, the lighter cables have a tendency to ride over brush and are especially ineffective on small brush growth. (*Courtesy O. E. Sperry*)

operation. Small, flexible brush growth may suffer peeled bark but be left intact to resprout. Cabling has been used most successfully on upright juniper growth, especially on the Edwards Plateau, where the rocky terrain is not conducive to the use of chains. Like chaining, cabling tends to spread pricklypear and other species of cacti if the soil surface is moist enough to allow the separated pads to root. However, chaining and cabling are not totally ineffective when used solely for cactus control and under the conditions described for railing (195).

Railing. Railing is a dragging operation designed primarily for the control of pricklypear and other cacti, although smaller woody-plant growth may also be controlled. The apparatus is constructed by attaching a series of sections of railroad irons, approximately 6 feet apart and usually connected with chains, behind a large crawler tractor. At least two railroad irons in tandem are needed, although three or four are often used. In contrast to soil moisture conditions optimum for the chaining or cabling of brush, *the soil surface should be extremely dry when cactus is railed.* The rails break up the pricklypear pads and distribute them over the dry soil surface, where they desiccate instead of taking root. On the South Texas Plains, chaining under conditions for maximum removal of upright woody plants more than doubled the density of pricklypear, whereas railing under dry soil conditions effectively controlled the cactus (71).

Railing for pricklypear control may be used effectively under moist conditions when it is followed by broadcast applications of 1 or 2 pounds of 2,4,5-T or silvex per acre. Bruising of the pricklypear pads by railing evidently augments the herbicide's activity, although the optimum conditions for railing (dry) are at odds with those (moist) for most effective use of herbicides.

Bulldozing. Generally the bulldozer blade is not efficient for clearing large tracts of rangeland solely for the purpose of improving native forage stands. Large trees may have to be dug out of the ground for removal, and small, limber stems may simply break off under the weight of the blade. Bulldozers, then, are most popular for the removal of large trees, especially on relatively small areas that are destined for complete conversion to tame pastures.

Restrictions on areas treated by bulldozing, especially those with dense stands, are usually based on economics instead of effectiveness when only brush removal is considered. The conventional bulldozer blade or a large V-blade is most commonly used in the bulldozing operation. Woody plants are simply uprooted, leaving large pits which may be of some benefit in trapping and holding moisture. However, bulldozing dense stands of trees drastically disturbs the soil, leaving it open to erosion unless the surface is quickly stabilized with plant cover. Unless the operator is extremely cautious, valuable topsoil may be removed and placed in mounds or windrow piles. Also, the conditions for effective bulldozing are somewhat similar to those for chaining. Adequate soil moisture is required to ensure that the trees are uprooted and not just broken off. Bulldozing is best adapted to the eastern half of Texas, where rainfall conditions are conducive to successful revegetation, where relatively small areas are cleared, and where conversion of land use to tame pastures is practiced.

Root plowing. The root plow or root cutter was developed for clearing moderate to heavy brush stands in preparation for seeding with grasses or crops. The root plow is mounted on a heavy-duty crawler tractor which pulls a 10- to 16-foot-long, V-shaped blade usually 8 to 15 inches below the soil surface (Fig. 4.7). This operation severs the plants below the root zone, preventing the regrowth of nearly all brush species except those with relatively shallow root systems such as whitebrush and pricklypear. A highly effective method, root plowing kills all sizes of woody plants (4). However, it usually destroys a high percentage of perennial grasses, so reseeding should often be planned as a follow-up measure. The method has been extremely popular in South Texas, where in the last decade hundreds of thousands of acres have been root plowed and established to buffelgrass. Ultimate success of the operation depends on rainfall following root plowing. Generally the highest survival of native and seeded grasses has resulted from root plowing and seeding during the late winter and early spring. Although it is practiced in low-rainfall areas, root plowing's highest use is restricted to sites which receive runoff water and which do not dry quickly following rainfall.

Disturbing the soil surface and underlying impermeable zones increases the moisture infiltration rate of some soils, which can be of benefit for artificial revegetation or simply for moisture storage if a good forage cover is rapidly established. Conversely, moisture loss from root-plowed areas under high temperatures may exceed losses from vegetated land (153). Therefore, it is imperative that a vegeta-

4.7. The root plow, mounted on a heavy-duty crawler tractor, is a V-shaped blade 10 to 16 feet long pulled 8 to 15 inches below the soil surface, severing woody plants below the area of greatest sprouting potential (*Courtesy C. H. Meadors*)

tive cover be established on root-plowed land in as short a time as possible if herbage production is to be maximized.

Root plowing is best applied to the deeper fertile soils where revegetation is feasible. Root plowing has been most successful on subhumid or, when carefully applied, on semiarid lands. As the rainfall potential decreases, risk of economic loss from root plowing increases.

Raking and stacking. A number of types of large brush rakes, root rakes, and stackers have been developed primarily to collect and pile debris following other mechanical operations, although they are occasionally used as the initial brush control practice. As previously mentioned, raking and stacking may be necessary to realize the full benefits from practices such as chaining, especially in heavy brush cover. Rakes are used effectively following chaining of honey mesquite (Fig. 4.8).

A brush rake, 10 to 15 feet wide and mounted on a crawler tractor, is used to rake and pile logs, branches, and other debris while

4.8. Raking after practices such as chaining aids in localizing the debris and improves accessibility to the rangeland. (*Photograph by O. E. Sperry*)

moving a minimal amount of soil. Stacker rakes are usually 15 to 25 feet long and have closely spaced tines or prongs and a 6-inch-thick steel plate welded near the base of the teeth. The steel plate shears off or pulls up small woody plants. Stackers are used as initial brush treatments where pricklypear and other small brush plants prevail. The stacker rake may also be used as an initial practice in such cases as removal of the top growth of mature Macartney rose (248). Root rakes are usually 20 to 25 feet long. They are designed to penetrate the soil 6 to 10 inches and to pull up and collect roots and stumps of woody plants following root plowing. Root raking is an excellent method of preparing a clean, firm seedbed.

5

Brush Management with Chemicals

No other area of brush management has received the research attention that has been directed toward herbicides during the past two decades. Application of herbicides to manipulate rangeland vegetation is now commonplace, and any person who contemplates involvement in brush management must be well versed in the properties and proper uses of these sophisticated chemicals. Since general understanding of the characteristics of herbicides is necessary for their proper use, the properties of herbicides mentioned in the text and their applications to brush management will be discussed in some detail. Herbicides used for range improvement represent only a fraction of those available to agriculture.

Herbicides are chemicals that kill plants or retard the rate and extent of their normal growth. Chemicals such as salts, ashes, and wastes have been used for centuries to control undesirable plant growth. Solutions of sulfuric acid, iron sulfate, copper nitrate, potassium salts, and other common chemicals were discovered to be plant control agents in the late 1800's. Before World War II, sodium chlorate was routinely used for the control of deep-rooted perennials such as field bindweed, sodium arsenate was used for industrial (nonselective) weed control, and dinitrophenols were employed for selective weed control in crops. The growth-regulating properties of 2,4-D and 2,4,5-T were reported in the early 1940's. These discoveries opened the era of selective plant control with chemicals, an era which has contributed to rapid growth of the agricultural chemical industry and has given rise to the discipline called weed science.

The new growth-regulating chemicals had three notable properties:

1. *They were highly selective.* Many herbaceous broadleaf and woody plants could be killed without damage to desirable grasses.
2. *They were systemic in action.* They were absorbed by plants and moved internally to a site of action, where they disrupted vital physiological processes.
3. *Only small amounts were required for weed control.* They were plant hormones, growth regulators in the strictest sense.

Discovery of the herbicidal properties of the phenoxyacetic acids marked the beginning of the herbicide phase of the chemical era of agriculture (121, 227). From 1941 to 1968, about 0.35 percent of the time man had worked to develop vegetation control methods, 80 percent of the progress was made (304). During that time the number of herbicides available for public use increased from fifteen to one hundred. Since discovery of phenoxyacetic acid herbicides, literally thousands of chemicals have been studied as potential herbicides.

This chapter was developed to relay the principles of proper herbicide use by discussing chemicals with applicability for brush management as examples. Before a herbicide can be offered for sale, its effectiveness for an intended use and its safety must be carefully evaluated, and it must be registered for those uses by the U.S. Environmental Protection Agency. Use of any herbicide which is not registered for that use is illegal. At the time of this writing, registration of the herbicide 2,4,5-T has been suspended for forests, rights-of-way, and pastures, and cancellation hearings are being organized to review those uses and others, including brush management on rangeland. Similar, if not simultaneous, actions are apparently being considered for the herbicide silvex. Moreover, this chapter also discusses other herbicides, such as tebuthiuron, that are not currently registered for use on rangeland or for which registration is pending.

It is not the intent of the author, the Texas A&M University Press, or the Texas A&M University System to espouse the use of any herbicide which is not approved for use by the U.S. government. Furthermore, mention of trademarks or proprietary products is for illustrative purposes only and does not constitute a guarantee or warranty, implied or otherwise, by the author, the Texas A&M University Press, or the Texas A&M University System and does not imply approval of those products to the exclusion of others that also may be suitable. The reader is also referred to the introduction of chapter 3 for additional information concerning proper selection of herbicides for specific uses.

Herbicide Nomenclature

Before pursuing a discussion of herbicides, an understanding of the standard naming system will prevent confusion. All herbicides have three types of designations (246):

1. *Trademark (trade name)* is the name under which the herbicide, as a commercial product, is advertised and sold. Trade names vary from company to company for the same basic herbicide.
2. *Chemical name* is the actual chemical designation of the herbicidal compound. Since many herbicides are rather sophisticated chemicals, chemical names are usually too cumbersome for routine use.
3. *Common name* is a short name used to facilitate referencing of herbicidal compounds. Common names of herbicides are assigned by the nomenclature committee of the Weed Science Society of America (WSSA). Table 5.1 gives the common name, chemical designations, and some of the trade names of herbicides used on rangeland. Trade names shown are for example only, since additional produtcs are continually being introduced to the market as others are being discontinued.

Once the naming system of herbicides is understood, difficulties in communicating about specific compounds are largely eliminated. For example, the land manager may want to use a herbicide called Tordon without realizing that there may be considerable differences among products with the proprietary label Tordon. The technician realizes that all products labeled Tordon have one feature in common —they contain the herbicide picloram (Table 5.1). However, picloram may be obtained alone as liquid (Tordon 22K), as a pellet (Tordon 10K), or in liquid combination with 2,4,5-T (Tordon 225) or 2,4-D (Tordon 212 and Tordon 101). Each of these products was designed for a rather specific use which the simple reference Tordon does not relate. The same relationships hold for products containing dicamba—the Banvel herbicides. The relationships must be under-

TABLE 5.1.

Designations of Commonly Used and Promising Herbicides for Brush Management (246).

Common Name	Chemical Name	Trade Name
Bromacil*	(1) 5- bromo-3-*sec*-butyl-6-methyluracil (2) 5-bromo-6-methyl-3-(1-methylpropyl)uracil	Hyvar-X; Hyvar-XL; Krovar-L; and others
Dicamba	3,6-dichloro-*o*-anisic acid	Banvel D; Banvel 2 + 2 (mixture with 2,4,5-T); Weedmaster (1:3 mixture with 2,4-D)
Hexaflurate*	potassium hexaflurate	Nopalmate
MCPA	(1) ([4-chloro-*o*-tolyl]oxy) acetic acid (2) (2-methyl-4-chlorophenoxy) acetic acid	Chiptox; Rhomene; Rhonox; Bronate (mixture with bromacil); Dow MCP Amine Weed Killer; Weedar Sodium MCP
Paraquat	1,1'-dimethyl-4,4'-bipyridinium ion	Ortho Paraquat; Gramoxone'
Picloram	4-amino-3,5,6-trichloropicolinic acid	Tordon 22K (potassium salt); Tordon 212 (mixture with 2,4-D); Tordon 225 (mixture with 2,4,5-T); Tordon 10K (pellets)
Silvex	2-(2,4,5-trichlorophenoxy) propionic acid	Kuron; Weedone 2,4,5-TP; Silvex
Tebuthiuron*	*N*-[5-(1,1-dimethylethyl)-1,3,4-thiadiazol-2-yl)]- *N*,*N*'-dimethylurea	Graslan (formerly Spike)
2,4-D	(2,4-dichlorophenoxy) acetic acid	2,4-D; Aqua Kleen; DMA-4; Dacamine; Esteron-99; Formula 40; Pennamine D; Phenox; Weedar 64; Weed-B-Gon; Weedone 638; Weedone LV4; Weed-Rhap A-4D; and many others
2,4,5-T	(2,4,5-trichlorophenoxy) acetic acid	Weedar 2,4,5-T; Weedone 2,4,5-T; Amine 4T; Lo-Vol 4T; Veon 2,4,5; Esteron 2,4,5; Brush-Rhap A-4T; Brush-Rhap LV-OXY-4T; and others

* Not registered by the Environmental Protection Agency for range use at this writing.

stood for proper herbicide use and are most effectively clarified by consulting the herbicide label. *Always read the label before using any herbicide!* The label will give the trade name, the active ingredient by chemical, and usually the common name. This point is discussed in more detail in the section on mixing sprays.

Perhaps the regulating factor in the relative availability of different herbicides for use on rangeland is the development cost in relation to the market potential for the chemical industry. Development costs of $3.4 million per compound were reported for 1967 and $5.5 million per compound for 1970 (111). From discovery to marketing of a pesticide, about sixty months were required in 1967 and seventy-seven months in 1970. About 1 percent of the chemical compounds believed to have potential use as herbicides survive initial screening processes. Only 0.025 percent, two out of eight thousand compounds, survive the development process.

The high investment in herbicide development and the relatively low amount that can be spent to improve rangeland in contrast with lands that support high-value cash crops apparently is responsible for the relatively low number of rangeland compounds on the market compared to those available for row crops. A farmer can simply afford a higher economic layout to maintain a weed-free grain sorghum or cotton field than a rancher can justify for brush management even though a single application of herbicide is expected to last for several years. For example, an expenditure of ten to twelve dollars per acre may be required each year for weed control in cotton, whereas this same expenditure may have to assure brush management effectiveness for five to seven years for profitable range improvement. However, the profitability of aerial spraying has been maintained through the availability of relatively inexpensive herbicides. Since relatively few herbicides are available for use on rangeland, scientists, applicators, and producers have continually refined the use of those available and sought methods of extending treatment life.

Herbicide Classification by Activity

Classification schemes based on chemical characteristics have considerable utility, especially when one considers the growing number of herbicides available for agricultural use. However, classifying herbicides by their general route of entry and their activity in plants is perhaps more satisfactory for organizing this discussion, since only a relatively few chemicals are used for brush management. Herbicides can be categorized as either foliage-active or soil-applied. In each general category there are both selective and nonselective chemicals (Fig. 5.1).

Foliage-active herbicides are applied directly to leaves and stems of plants and may have limited residual activity in the soil. This general group may be subdivided further into contact and translocated herbicides. Contact herbicides kill only that plant tissue directly contacted by the spray. Translocated foliage-applied herbicides penetrate the leaves and stems of plants and move through the circulation system (translocate) to the roots and other organs some distance from the point of entry.

Food materials manufactured in actively growing leaves are moved to the roots for storage through a system of living cells that also become the transport system for moving the herbicide downward. This "pipeline" is called the phloem. Herbicides such as 2,4-D are transported through the phloem to metabolically active organs, buds, young leaves, and roots so that the morphological reaction of the plants is usually first apparent at their growing tips.

Since 2,4-D and similar herbicides must move through the phloem, any factor that reduces food production also reduces herbicide movement. Rate of translocation may be altered by prolonged reductions in light, such as several overcast days. Movement may also be reduced by decreasing soil moisture or by excessive temperature. Thus, foliage-applied herbicides are most effective when applied to

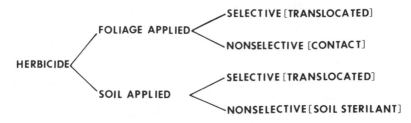

5.1. General classification scheme for herbicides based on type of activity, mode of entry, and selectivity.

actively growing plants after exposure to several bright, warm days under adequate soil moisture.

Soil-applied herbicides must be moved into the soil by rainfall, absorbed by the plant roots, and then moved upward. Upward herbicide movement occurs in the cells which pump water through the plant. This set of "pipes," constructed of nonliving cells called vessels, is the xylem. Xylem transport is favored by good soil moisture and conditions conducive to active plant growth.

Some herbicides are translocated primarily through the phloem, others move almost solely in the xylem, and others move through either or both systems (Fig. 5.2). Herbicides such as 2,4-D and 2,4,5-T move primarily through the phloem. Since picloram may be transported by either system or by both simultaneously, it may be applied as a foliar spray or as a pellet formulation depending on the most active mechanism for entering a particular species. Dicamba, a benzoic acid herbicide, is also active both through the foliage and through the soil (the degree of activity depending on particular species, rate of dicamba applied, and type of soil).

Although soil-applied herbicides may undergo degradation on the soil surface before they are activated by rainfall and may be decomposed to some extent in the soil system before they enter the roots, conditions for their application are not nearly so critical as those for optimum activity of foliage-applied herbicides. A critical requirement for the translocation of foliage-applied herbicides is absorption of the chemical by the leaf tissues.

Penetration of Foliage by Herbicides

To enter plant leaves, herbicides must first penetrate the leaf covering, or cuticle. This layer of waxy material varies in thickness from plant to plant, from leaf to leaf, or even from spot to spot on the same leaf (270). Once the cuticle has been penetrated, the herbicide must move through the walls of the epidermal cells. These stages of absorption are accomplished by diffusion, a process independent of the physiological activity of the leaves. To this point, rate of absorption depends largely on the availability of herbicide on the leaf surface and the thickness of the physical barriers—cuticle and cell walls. After the herbicide enters the cells, it must be distributed through the cells

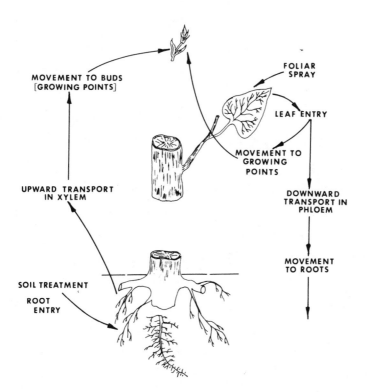

MOVEMENT TO BUDS
[GROWING POINTS]

FOLIAR
SPRAY

LEAF ENTRY

MOVEMENT TO
GROWING
POINTS

UPWARD TRANSPORT
IN XYLEM

DOWNWARD
TRANSPORT IN
PHLOEM

MOVEMENT
TO ROOTS

SOIL TREATMENT

ROOT
ENTRY

5.2. Generalized illustration of herbicide translocation.

of the inner leaf to the phloem cells in the veins for transport from the leaf. Once the herbicide is through the epidermal cell walls, absorption becomes an energy-requiring process dependent on physiological activity within the leaf tissues. Upon movement of the herbicide to the phloem, the absorption process is completed and translocation is initiated.

Simplified here for the sake of discussion, foliar absorption is a complex process. Any factor—environmental, physiological, chemical, or physical—which alters the rate and extent of foliar absorption directly affects the ultimate level of herbicide translocation. In contrast to translocated herbicides, which must be moved through the leaf tissues to the phloem, contact herbicides are moved into the leaves with destructive effects generally restricted to the leaf tissues proper.

Small pores called stomata on the leaf surfaces allow the exchange of gases between the inner leaf tissue and the atmosphere and also provide a route for herbicide entry. Stomata are usually more frequent on the lower side of leaves but may occur on both sides. Other points of foliar entry for herbicides include plant hairs (trichomes), insect punctures, and other imperfections in the cuticle.

Factors which affect herbicide penetration are related primarily to the stage of leaf development: climatic conditions as they affect growth and development and herbicide activity, specific morphological and physiological features of plants, and chemical characteristics of the herbicide, including its formulation. Plants growing under high temperatures and low relative humidity develop thicker cuticles than do plants developing under moderate conditions. Thus, cuticular entry is usually relatively slow, and total entry is limited in plants which develop under hot, dry conditions. Conversely, relatively warm, mild temperatures and high relative humidity promote herbicide penetration of foliage. High relative humidity reduces the drying rate of spray droplets on leaf surfaces, increasing the amount of time the liquid is available for penetration. As the spray droplets dry, the herbicide crystallizes on the leaf surfaces, decreasing the amount of time it is available for penetration.

Foliage-applied herbicides are usually active at relatively low application rates. Application of excessive amounts may cause a translocated herbicide to act as a contact herbicide and not penetrate to the inner leaf tissue, thus reducing its effectiveness. Care should be exercised to apply the herbicide rate suggested by the label. Exceeding the recommended application rate does not necessarily improve control level and certainly does not increase control level proportionally. That is, the level of control from 1 pound per acre will probably not be doubled by applying 2 pounds per acre. "Overdosing" is a common tendency in the use of translocated herbicides and should be avoided if for no more than economic reasons.

The stage of development may affect the plant's reaction to foliage-applied herbicides (41, 277). Herbicides, as a general rule, penetrate young leaves more readily than older foliage. For example, at germination most plants are susceptible to 2,4-D. As the seedlings are established, most grasses become tolerant of 2,4-D applied at rates normally required for range improvement. As the plants age, broadleaf species formerly killed by the herbicide may be only slightly affected. Other species may gain little or no tolerance for the herbicide with increasing age. Most broadleaf plants are easier to kill with

2,4-D and other hormone herbicides during periods of rapid growth. For many broadleaf herbaceous species such periods coincide with stem elongation; tolerance to sprays occurs after flowering. Woody plants such as honey mesquite are usually most susceptible after the leaves are fully expanded and not heavily cutinized. For honey mesquite, this time period usually corresponds with maximum trunk growth, flowering, and seed development (early May to early June, depending on the location and environmental conditions).

Most of the difference in susceptibility with seasonal development of plants can be attributed to differences in the rate and degree of penetration of the herbicide. Most leaf surfaces support small hairs and hairlike growths. A moderate density of these hairs may aid absorption by preventing the spray droplets from rolling off the leaves. However, a very dense layer of these hairs may prevent maximum contact of the spray droplets with the surface. The shape of leaf hairs, their density, and their ability to retain the spray varies with the plant species.

The general shape and angle at which leaves grow affect retention of herbicide sprays. Upright, narrow leaves intercept and retain less spray solution than do broad, flat leaves. Also of prime importance to herbicide activity within a given stage of plant development is the formulation of the herbicide.

Herbicide Formulations

Formulation is the method of preparing the herbicide so it will mix with a carrier or solvent. Herbicides may be formulated as wettable powders, granules, emulsions, or solutions. When mixed with liquid, usually water, wettable powders form a suspension which must be agitated for uniform application of the spray. Granules are formed by impregnating suitable claylike materials with herbicide. The particle sizes for dry herbicide formulations vary from finely ground particles to pellets usually 0.125 inch in diameter or larger, depending on the characteristics of the herbicide which they will carry.

Emulsions are heterogeneous mixtures formed by suspending one liquid in another without changing the basic characteristics of either. The amount of agitation needed for stability of the emulsion varies with the degree of miscibility of the two liquids. Solutions are homogeneous mixtures of two substances which do not separate and therefore require less agitation to ensure uniform dispersion.

An understanding of the role of formulation is critical, since small amounts of chemical must be uniformly applied to relatively large surface areas. Formulation also affects the rate at which the herbicide penetrates leaves. For example, two common methods of preparing 2,4-D for dispersal are by forming the amine salt or by forming the ester of the parent acid. Both preparations are sold as liquids, but they differ in that amines are highly soluble in water and esters are oillike in nature. When mixed with water, esters typically form a cloudy or milky solution, an emulsion, as opposed to the clear solution that results when amines are mixed with water. Esters are most soluble in oils, have a greater affinity for waxy plant surfaces, and therefore are usually more effective for woody plant control than are equal rates of amines except at peak periods of plant susceptibility. As noted previously, cuticle thickness may increase with plant age. Therefore, amine formulations are usually replaced with ester formulations late in the growing season, primarily because of the wetting action of esters and their ability to penetrate the leaf cuticle.

Foliar absorption occurs rapidly, and in most cases if there is no rain within six to twelve hours after spraying, a foliar herbicide application will give effective results. Ester formulations are harder to wash from plant leaves than are amines. Rainfall within fifteen minutes after the application of some ester formulations does not reduce herbicide effectiveness on succulent weeds (23). However, the same formulation may have to remain on the "tough" leaves of some woody plants for more than two hours to resist the removal of significant amounts of herbicide by washing.

The carrier used for herbicide sprays also influences plant reaction. Water is commonly used, but certain additives may enhance the penetration of herbicides. Mixing one part of diesel oil with three to four parts of water increases the effectiveness of 2,4,5-T on woody plants in some areas compared to the herbicide mixed with water only. Presumably this improvement is due to the high "penerating power" of the oil into the cuticle. For example, in one case, 43 percent more 2,4,5-T was present in foliage the day after it was sprayed in diesel oil than when water was used as the carrier (268). The effectiveness of water-based and oil-based carriers may be contrasted as follows:

Water Carriers	*Oil Carriers*
Solubilize salt and amine formutions	Solubilize ester formulations
Have high surface tension—may not wet uniformly	Have low surface tension—spread uniformly
Penetrate brush canopies well	Tend to float—may not penetrate to the understory in layered brush stands
Penetrate stomata more readily than the cuticle	Penetrate both stomata and the cuticle
Are nontoxic	Show some degree of phytotoxicity—may burn foliage
Require small cost for handling and hauling	Must be purchased, hauled, and handled

Carrier solution is usually mixed so that 1 gallon of diesel oil per acre will be applied with the emulsion. To form proper oil:water emulsions with adequate stability, an emulsifier must be used. Usually 1 to 2 ounces of emulsifier per gallon of diesel oil in the mixture adequately keeps the two liquids from separating. However, if the emulsion does not form properly, additional emulsifier may be used.

Invert emulsions are sometimes used in efforts to reduce herbicide drift (displacement of the spray from the target by wind or air currents). Whereas standard emulsions (oil in water) have the physical appearance of milk, invert emulsions (water in oil) have the consistency of mayonnaise. Special spray systems have been developed for the formation and dispensing of invert emulsions. Use of invert emulsions should not be attempted with dispensing systems not designed for thickened sprays. Standard emulsions are more widely used than are inverts for range improvement. Uniformity of coverage is more easily attained with sprays of standard emulsions than those of invert emulsions. Control with inverts may be reduced somewhat by non-uniform distribution of the spray droplets over the foliage and by low numbers of drops of spray on each leaf.

A group of additives called surfactants (*surface acting agents*) have been developed specifically to increase the length of time herbicides remain on leaves and may improve the rate of herbicide penetration. Surfactants include wetting agents, emulsifying agents, spreaders, stickers, and penetrants. Wetting agents should result in a thin, uniform layer of herbicide solution on the sprayed leaves instead of several large, individual droplets. Wetting agents increase the ability of the spray to uniformly moisten plant leaves by reducing the surface tension on the spray droplets. However, the addition of wetting agents may reduce herbicide selectivity. Plants that are uninjured by sprays without wetting agents may show herbicide symptoms or even be killed by solutions containing these surfactants.

Spreaders are essentially the same as wetting agents. The term *spreader and sticker* is often used to label surfactants. Spreaders cause the wetting action, while stickers help the sprays in adhering to plant surfaces. Some surfactants actually suppress herbicide activity, while others have no effect, depending on the particular herbicide-surfactant mixture (159). Many surfactants are inherently phytotoxic at high concentrations, and a few may stimulate growth of some species at low concentrations in the absence of herbicides. Moreover, the effects of surfactants are not necessarily the same on all species with all herbicides or levels of herbicide. Therefore, the surfactant for a particular use should be carefully selected based on recommendations of the manufacturer.

There is no need to use surfactants at concentrations which greatly exceed the amount required for the maximum reduction of surface tension (222) if plant control is not increased. The extent of improvement in brush control resulting from the addition of surfactants to herbicides varies from species to species. For example, the uptake of 2,4,5-T by detached live oak leaves was increased 7.5 times with the use of a commercial surfactant compared to uptake of water alone (182). However, the use of surfactants has generally not increased control of honey mesquite under field conditions to the extent that surfactants are considered economically feasible. This situation may change with rising cost of diesel oil.

Soil-applied Herbicides

The length of control from soil-applied herbicides, whether formulated as liquids, wettable powders, granules, or pellets, varies with the kind and application rate of the chemical, climatic factors, and the soil. Soil-applied herbicides are effective only after they move to the root zone. Thus, the length of time for a noticeable reaction to occur varies from location to location. In some cases vegetation control may improve the season after the herbicide is applied—after adequate rainfall has occurred to leach the herbicide into the root zone. The time of herbicide application is dictated by rainfall; thus, root-active herbicides should be applied just ahead of rainy periods. The amount of rainfall required for activation of soil-applied herbicides depends on soil characteristics and water solubility of the herbicide. The higher the clay and organic matter content, the more rainfall that is usually required to leach the herbicide into the root zone. In sandy soils leaching may move the herbicides that are highly water soluble below the root zone of some species, where it is unavailable for maximum root uptake (253). Since herbicides with low water solubility leach less readily than do highly soluble chemicals, herbicide solubility, soil texture, and rainfall conditions must be matched for effective results.

Although activity of soil-applied herbicides is governed by a rather specific set of conditions, root-active herbicides are not as closely tied to conditions of plant growth at the time of application as are foliage-active herbicides. For example, foliage-applied herbicides are effective for control of most oaks when applied only during a short period each spring or fall. Conversely, effective dry formulations might be applied over a much broader time period than that required for sprays. Although the timing of application would most certainly vary with species and herbicide, the only time which probably would not be considered for application of soil-active herbicides would be during the hot, dry summer period.

Dry herbicide formulations control some species not susceptible to foliar applications. For example, red-berry juniper is not satisfactorily controlled with conventional sprays of 2,4,5-T. However, picloram pellets may be applied broadcast or to individual red-berry juniper plants to achieve control (252). Whether aerial application or individual-plant treatment is used depends upon the density and extent of the red-berry juniper infestation. Broadcast applications of picloram pellets at 2 pounds per acre may control 70 percent or more of the red-berry juniper and increase range forage production significantly by one year after treatment (235). Moreover, a higher proportion of the range forage produced was of fair to good value where the picloram pellets were applied to field research plots compared to untreated areas (235).

Texas persimmon is another species which is not controlled by conventional, broadcast sprays but may be controlled with picloram pellets (249). Although individual-plant sprays will control Texas persimmon, equivalent control can be achieved with pellet applications in a shorter time and with less equipment. Whereas Texas persimmon plants defoliated by sprays may resprout, plants controlled by the pellets usually do not regrow (249). Broadcast applications of picloram pellets are highly effective for control of pricklypear and look promising for control of other species such as blackbrush acacia and spiny hackberry. However, there is still much to be learned concerning the most effective use of pellets, and some species, such as honey mesquite, which are susceptible to sprays are not controlled by most soil-applied herbicides. With other species, higher rates of pelleted herbicide are required for control than are needed when the same herbicide is applied as a spray. For example, 2 pounds of picloram pellets or granules per acre may be required to equal the level of sand shinnery oak control that is achieved from 0.5 pound of picloram per acre as a spray (251, 253). Sand shinnery oak typically infests light-textured soils, and picloram is highly water soluble. Therefore, aside from innate resistance of sand shinnery oak to soil-applied picloram, there is potential for movement of the herbicide to depths beyond the most active roots, especially by heavy rains (253). The length of vegetation control from soil-applied herbicides can be best regulated by taking advantage of the chemical characteristic of a herbicide and understanding the relationship of herbicide activity to environmental variables.

Herbicide Characteristics

PHENOXY HERBICIDES

The activity of hormone herbicides was discovered by scientists whose original interest evidently was in studying naturally occurring growth regulators called auxins. These chemicals are synthesized in certain tissues of the plant such as the buds and young leaves. Auxins play a role in the elongation phase of plant growth and are translocated in plants. Auxins promote growth when applied in low concentrations to plant shoots which do not have direct access to these inherent growth-promoting compounds. By this definition, phenoxy herbicides are like auxins in their activity.

Early researchers found that certain auxins would control the growth of broadleaved species in cereals. This discovery certainly must have sharpened the scientists' interest in synthetically producing the auxins. In their attempts they found that 2,4-D and another compound called MCPA were much more effective as herbicides than were other compounds under study. Reports of the discovery of the herbicidal activity of these chemicals were published in the mid-1940's by workers from several countries, mass production was started almost immediately, and the herbicides were readily available by the late 1940's and early 1950's.

The most common phenoxyacetic acid herbicide is 2,4-D. Produced as a white crystalline acid, it is relatively noncorrosive to metals, readily translocated in plants, and generally considered safe under normal use to humans. The acid form of 2,4-D (and of other phenoxy herbicides) has relatively low solubility in water. Therefore, special solvents are needed to dissolve it, and it is rarely dispensed in the acid form. Rather, several formulations are manufactured for dispensing in various carriers (Table 5.2).

Salts of 2,4-D, because of their high solubility in water, are sprayed as aqueous solutions. Salts are formed by replacing the hydrogen of the carboxyl (-COOH) group usually with sodium, an ammonium radical, or an amine group. Amine salts, formed by reacting the acid with amines, are most soluble in water and therefore are sold as liquids.

TABLE 5.2.
Properties of 2,4-D Acid and Two Common Formulations
for Agricultural Use.

Formulation	Molecular Weight	Melting Point	Solubility (g/100 g)	
			Water (20°–23° C)	Organic Solvents
Acid	221.0	135°–138° C	0.06–0.07	0.10–0.35 (diesel oil or kerosene)
Dimethylamine salt	266.1	85°–87° C	300	Insoluble
2-(butoxy)ethyl ester	321.2	—	Insoluble	300

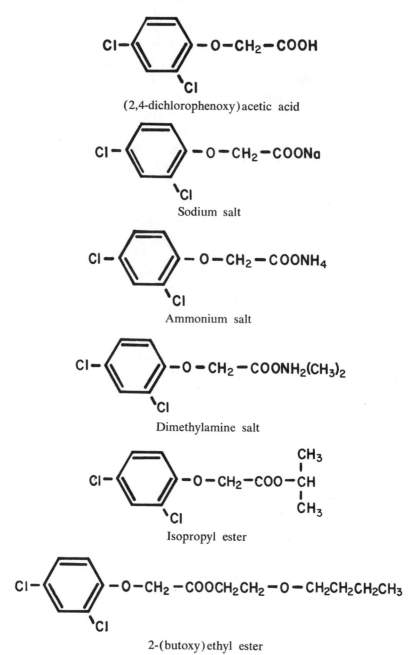

(2,4-dichlorophenoxy)acetic acid

Sodium salt

Ammonium salt

Dimethylamine salt

Isopropyl ester

2-(butoxy)ethyl ester

2,4-D and Related Formulations

Some of the most popular formulations of 2,4-D and related compounds for range and pasture work are the various esters. Formed by reacting alcohols with the 2,4-D acid, they are sold as liquids dissolved in oil and form emulsions when mixed with water. They are most soluble in petroleum oils, so an emulsifying agent usually must be added to form a stable emulsion when oil:water carriers are used.

Most workers now agree that phenoxy herbicides affect a multitude of metabolic processes, any one of which eventually may lead to death of the plant (224). Effects of 2,4-D include changes in the composition of carbohydrates, lipids, organic acids, ethylene alkaloids, steroids, aromatics, vitamins, pigments, minerals, water, auxins, nucleic acids, and enzymes. Changes in nitrogen metabolism, respiration, photosynthesis, and nucleic acid metabolism have been observed. The physiological effects of herbicides such as 2,4-D are so complex that their exact mode of action is virtually impossible to ascertain. However, the general observable effect of phenoxy herbicides is their stimulation of meristematic activity in plants, giving rise to the popular explanation of their action as "causing plants to grow themselves to death." Abnormal, tumorous growth as a result of prolonged meristematic activity results in the twisting and curling of stems and morphological changes such as the crushing and plugging of vascular tissues.

Manifestations of disruption by phenoxy herbicides include:

1. *Effects on respiration.* Specific effects evidently depend on the susceptibility of the species and the application rates. High application rates of phenoxy herbicides tend to suppress respiration, whereas low concentrations tend to increase the rate of respiration.

2. *Effects on synthesis and use of phytosynthates.* These effects are not completely understood, but applications of 2,4-D evidently cause an imbalance between the use and the synthesis of plant food.

3. *Disruption of metabolism and enzyme activity.*

4. *Increase of turgor pressure within the plant.* Treated herbaceous plants become extremely turgid and brittle.

Increased turgidity, brittleness, and epinasty, which is the twisting, bending, and curving of the stems, are the most obvious changes in treated plants. Leaves become strap-shaped, with veins closer to each other than those in normal leaves. These effects are evidently the result of differential turgor pressures and differential rates of cell division in various parts of the plant.

2,4-D. Probably the herbicide most commonly used for range improvement, 2,4-D is most effective for control of herbaceous, broad-leaved plants. Susceptibility to it may vary among ecotypes within species (184).

From 0.5 to 2 pounds of 2,4-D per acre are usually applied for broad-leaved weed control with either ground or aerial equipment (167). Excellent control of western ragweed, common broomweed, heath aster, and other weeds common to Texas can be obtained with 1 pound of 2,4-D per acre formulated as an amine salt or as various esters (83). Top growth of many species of perennial weeds such as western ironweed may be controlled by 2,4-D without controlling the underground vegetative parts (185, 186, 188). Yields of weeds may be reduced from 75 to 95 percent with 1 to 2 pounds of 2,4-D per acre, resulting in increased yields of forage by 0.8 to 1 pound for each pound of weeds controlled (226).

Although used primarily for herbaceous weed control, 2,4-D effectively controls some woody species. Excellent control of western snowberry results from application of 1 to 2 pounds of the isopropyl ester of 2,4-D per acre (183). When 2,4-D is used to control Macartney rose, a troublesome woody plant of the Texas Coastal Prairie, the benefits are increased carrying capacity of the land for livestock, better use of available rainfall, and higher net return to the ranching enterprise (138). Willow baccharis may be effectively controlled by spraying the foliage of individual plants with 2,4-D (274). The herbicide has also been used for control of sand shinnery oak and several other woody species (251).

One of the primary problems with the use of 2,4-D and other hormone herbicides is the response of susceptible crops such as cotton to minute amounts of the sprays. Much of the spraying for pasture weed control and range improvement is done in areas adjacent to such susceptible crops. Less than 1 pound per acre of ester formulations of 2,4-D, 2,4,5-T, MCPA, and silvex may eliminate cotton crops (211). Foliar applications of only 0.001 pound per acre of cotton in the early square stage may cause leaf malformations, including strapping and cupping, epinasty, and proliferation of callous tissue in the root-stem transition zone (Fig. 5.3). Greater damage to cotton may be caused

5.3. Extremely small amounts of phenoxy herbicide such as from spray drift or from contaminated equipment will cause leaf malformations including strapping, cupping and epinasty in susceptible crops such as cotton. (*Courtesy R. Palmer*)

by 2,4-D than by 2,4,5-T or silvex (211). However, there is essentially no difference in the morphological malformations exhibited by cotton exposed to the various herbicides.

Cotton plants treated with low rates of 2,4-D may produce seed of inferior quality, which is shown particularly by its decreased and delayed germination. Although 2,4-D applied at extremely low rates (about 0.001 pound per acre) may not affect fiber quality, fiber quality may be reduced by foliar applications of 2,4-D at 0.1 pound per acre (211).

MCPA. This herbicide is identical to 2,4-D except that a methyl (CH_3) group replaces chlorine in the number two position on the benzene ring.

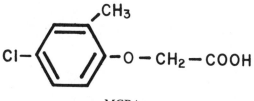

MCPA
[(4-chloro-*o*-tolyl)oxy]acetic acid

MCPA and 2,4-D were discovered almost simultaneously, and their herbicidal properties, available formulations, and phytotoxicity are very similar. MCPA is more expensive than 2,4-D, and usually higher rates are required for equivalent levels of brush control. MCPA has shown promise for control of whitebrush; however, with the advent of more effective herbicides such as picloram and tebuthiuron, that use may be greatly reduced (206, 207).

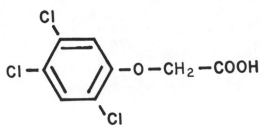

2,4,5-T
(2,4,5-trichlorophenoxy) acetic acid

2,4,5-T. The chemical structure and properties of 2,4,5-T are also very similar to those of 2,4-D. A chlorine ion added to the number five position on the benzene ring of 2,4-D results in 2,4,5-T. Yet 2,4,5-T is effective on many woody plants that are not susceptible to 2,4-D, and it is less effective on some herbaceous species. It is the herbicide used most widely for control of undesirable woody plants on grazing lands. Generally it is more expensive than 2,4-D. Mixtures of 2,4-D and 2,4,5-T are sold for the control of mixtures of woody plants, especially hardwoods, in the eastern United States. Rates of application for woody-plant control range from 0.5 to 2 pounds per acre. Recommended uses of 2,4,5-T for brush control in Texas indicate the broad spectrum of species that are susceptible to it and the various methods of application and rates of application. Recommendations for 2,4,5-T in individual-plant treatments are given in Table 5.3.

Influence of environmental factors on the action of 2,4,5-T will be discussed in a later section. However, the influence of several critical variables studied is noteworthy here. In the laboratory there were no significant differences in the amounts of 2,4,5-T absorbed at air temperatures of 70° and 80° F, but an increase in absorption occurred at 100° F after seventy-two hours (213). Only slight differences in absorption occurred at different relative humidity levels. Translocation was primarily basipetal (toward the plant base) from the point of application at 70° F, both acropetal (toward the apex) and basipetal at 85° F, and acropetal only a short distance at 100° F. The quantity of 2,4,5-T translocated into untreated honey mesquite tissue at 100° F was less than amounts moved at 70° to 85° F. Thus, the physiological reason for application of 2,4,5-T under mild to moderate rather than extremely high temperatures becomes evident. Although absorption may be increased, translocation is greatly reduced under high air temperatures.

Highest concentration of 2,4,5-T following foliar application occurs in tissues of honey mesquite with the highest soluble sugar concentration (213). Approximately 80 percent of 2,4,5-T absorbed by mesquite leaves may be metabolized after twenty-four hours (213). Metabolism of 2,4,5-T was completely inhibited at 50° F, and a lower rate of metabolism was noted at 100° F than at 70° or 85° F.

Phenoxypropionic acids. Closely related to 2,4,5-T, silvex (2,4,5-TP) is formulated like the various salts and esters of 2,4-D. It is usually more expensive than 2,4-D or 2,4,5-T, but it controls some species not effectively controlled by the other compounds. Some lawn and aquatic weeds are more susceptible to silvex than to the phenoxyacetic acids.

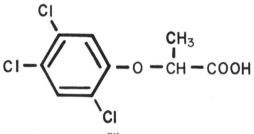

Silvex
(2,4,5-trichlorophenoxy)propionic acid

Silvex has also demonstrated a rather high specificity for control of oaks. For example, silvex was found to be the most effective herbicide among several tested, including 2,4,5-T, 2,4-D, and picloram, for reducing the density of sand shinnery oak and increasing grass production in the Rolling Plains of Texas (251, 254). Silvex at 0.5 pound per acre is more effective than lower rates of 0.25 or 0.125 pound per

TABLE 5.3.
Recommended Uses of 2,4,5-T for Individual-Plant Treatments (141).*

Kind of Brush	Size of Brush	Method of Application	Season of Application	Chemical Mixture (lb./100 gal.) †
Sprouts and seedlings	Sprouts at least four years old and six feet tall	Foliage spray—complete wetting of foliage	April, May, June with adequate soil moisture for active growth	3 plus 2–8 oz. of wetting agent‡
Elms; water oak	All sizes	Frill; stump	December–March; May–August	16
Blackjack oak; post oak	Trees to five inches in diameter	Trunk base	December–March; May–August; any time of year	16
	Trees over five inches in diameter	Frill; stump		
Willow baccharis; hackberry; woollybucket bumelia; honey locust; lime prickly ash; retama; sumacs	Trees to five inches in diameter	Trunk base	December–March; May–August; any time of year	8
	Trees over five inches in diameter	Frill; stump		

Kind of Brush	Size of Brush	Method of Application	Season of Application	Chemical Mixture (lb./100 gal.) †
Live oak; yaupon	All sizes	Frill; stump; notch	December–March; May–August	8
Honey mesquite; huisache; lotebush; catclaw (acacia); agarito; elbowbush	Trees to 5 inches in diameter	Trunk base	Any time when soil is dry and not fused to tree trunk	8
	Trees over 5 inches in diameter	Frill; stump	Any time of year	
Cactus (pricklypear, tasajillo, cholla)	All sizes	Foliage spray—thorough coverage of pads, stems, and trunks to point of slight runoff	Any time when air temperatures are above 60° F	8
Yucca	All sizes	Crown bud spray—thorough coverage until solution runs to ground line	Any time of year	8

* 2,4,5–T herbicide rates based on 4 lb. acid equivalent per gal.
† Except where noted, carrier is diesel oil or kerosene.
‡ Applied in water.

acre (254), but 1 pound per acre may not significantly improve sand shinnery oak control.

BENZOIC ACIDS

Several benzoic acid derivatives have herbicidal properties. However, the chemical representative of this group with the most utility for the control of herbaceous and woody plants on grazing lands is dicamba.

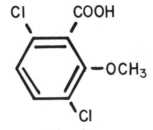

Dicamba
3,6-dichloro-*o*-anisic acid

The acid form of dicamba is white, crystalline, and odorless, and the compound has molecular weight of 221.0. Its pattern of use is comparable to those of both 2,4-D and 2,4,5-T since it is effective on herbaceous as well as some woody species. It is more active than 2,4-D as a preemergence application for controlling broadleaf weeds, and it is effective for controlling some grassy weeds.

Dicamba is formulated as the dimethylamine salt in liquid form and as granules. It is also commercially available in combination with 2,4,5-T or with 2,4-D. At 0.5 pound per acre, control of honey mesquite with dicamba is equivalent to that from the same rate of 2,4,5-T (258). In most cases, weed and woody plant control with dicamba has been roughly equivalent to that expected from the phenoxy herbicides 2,4-D and 2,4,5-T on susceptible species. However, dicamba may broaden the spectrum of species controlled compared to either of the phenoxy herbicides alone. Also, with some herbaceous, perennial species, dicamba has improved control over the same rate of 2,4-D.

Dicamba at 1 pound per acre has given fair control of western whorled milkweed, whereas the same rate of 2,4-D has not controlled the species (188). Roughly equivalent control of western ironweed was obtained with 1 pound per acre of both 2,4-D and dicamba (185).

Results were only slightly better with dicamba than with 2,4-D for control of western ragweed, but the control from dicamba was highly erratic (184). Control of common broomweed was improved with application of 0.5 to 1 pound of dicamba per acre as opposed to the same rates of 2,4-D (277). Improved control of common broomweed was attributed to the activity of dicamba as a soil application. Dicamba is readily absorbed by the leaves of most species and in lethal quantities by the roots of some plants, but granules appear to be somewhat less effective than the liquid formulations for control of most species (252, 253). For some unknown reason, activity of dicamba seems to increase in the western portion of Texas as compared to the eastern part of the state. Control of honey mesquite, for example, in the Trans-Pecos and in New Mexico is consistently greater than from the same application rate in East Texas.

Like that of phenoxy herbicides, the exact mode of action of dicamba has not been well defined, since a complex of physiological expressions of phytotoxicity occur. Benzoic acids such as dicamba cause reactions in plants similar to those caused by the phenoxy herbicides. They reportedly disrupt nucleic acid metabolism and interfere with photosynthesis.

PICOLINIC ACID

Picloram, introduced in 1963 (120), has proven to be one of the most effective herbicides available for the control of a broad spectrum of herbaceous and woody plants on rangeland. It is formulated as a liquid (potassium salt) alone and in combination (triethanolamine salt) with 2,4,5-T or with 2,4-D. It is also formulated as beads or pellets.

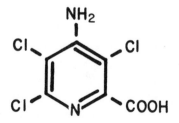

Picloram
4-amino-3,5,6-trichloropicolinic acid

Picloram is absorbed by the leaves and roots of most broadleaf species and moves readily via either the phloem or the xylem (198). It is absorbed by both upper and lower leaf surfaces.

Although many species are controlled by either foliar or soil applications of picloram, honey mesquite is a notable exception. Honey mesquite is not susceptible to soil treatment with picloram. The pellet formulation applied at 2 or 4 pounds per acre has not resulted in control. In contrast, 0.25 to 0.5 pound per acre of picloram in combination with equal amounts of 2,4,5-T will effectively control honey mesquite. Honey mesquite roots may absorb picloram, but it is redistributed and eventually lost back into the soil (15). However, most broadleaf species, especially certain crops, are highly sensitive to picloram in the soil. Symptoms like those produced by auxins may occur with crops such as common cucumber following application of only 0.01 part per million of picloram to the roots (180).

Picloram is most widely used on rangeland as a commercial combination with 2,4,5-T for brush control. The combination of 2,4,5-T and picloram is synergistic for control of honey mesquite—that is, a higher level of control occurs from the combination than from the same rate of either herbicide alone. Honey mesquite is the primary species for which the synergism has been documented, but research continues into the potential of improving brush control levels by combining picloram with other herbicides. The uptake and translocation of picloram alone and in combination with the contact herbicide paraquat has been studied with honey mesquite, huisache, yaupon, and field beans. Combination with paraquat increases the uptake of picloram by yaupon but does not affect translocation. In field studies, the advantages of mixing paraquat and picloram for control of the other woody plants have not been demonstrated.

Like phenoxy herbicides, picloram affects a multitude of vital processes, so it is difficult to attribute its biological activity to disruption of any given process (23). Most of the symptoms of phytotoxicity are similar to those discussed for phenoxy herbicides. Typical malformations, such as twisting of the stems, death of growing points, and occurrence of callous growth of susceptible broadleaf seedlings, occur after treatment with picloram (53). Low levels of picloram promote the growth of some species and inhibit that of others depending on species, stage of plant growth, herbicide concentration, and the specific tissue to which it is applied (23, 216, 270). Nucleic acid metabolism and various enzyme systems are disrupted by picloram. Application of picloram to honey mesquite and huisache roots stimulates ethylene production, a plant response that has been noted with several growth regulators (14).

In general, broadleaf species are much more susceptible to picloram than are grasses. However, young grasses may be damaged by the herbicide. It prevents germination of sideoats grama, big bluestem, and blue grama when applied before emergence (9). Application of picloram to established native range typically does not reduce forage production of desirable plants or frequency of some forbs. Applications of picloram have not affected the seed production of grasses such as creeping bentgrass, colonial bentgrass, Italian ryegrass, or tall fescue (172). However, germination of creeping red fescue seed from plants treated with picloram at rates of two pounds per acre was significantly reduced. Picloram is taken up by the roots of smooth bromegrass (316), so it has been proposed that the herbicide be used to remove bromegrass from established stands of other grasses. The susceptibility of smooth bromegrass, a cool-season species, to picloram varies with the time of application, with the likelihood of damage being greater from fall treatments than from spring applications (187). Some warm-season species also apparently take picloram up via the roots. For example, root production and top growth of switchgrass were reduced by one to 2 parts per million of picloram in the soil, whereas stimulation of growth occurred with sideoats grama exposed to the same herbicide concentration (262).

Picloram is highly effective for control of broadleaf herbaceous species on rangeland. It is more effective than 2,4-D or dicamba for control of goldenrod (226), western ironweed (185), western ragweed (particularly ecotypes resistant to 2,4-D) (184), and other species resistant to 2,4-D, such as western whorled milkweed (188). It is also extremely effective for control of common broomweed (277).

A number of woody species occurring in Texas that are not controlled or are only partially controlled by phenoxy herbicides are susceptible to picloram (24) (Table 5.4), and control of many species susceptible to phenoxies may be improved with picloram. Many species are susceptible to picloram pellets, though some of them are not controlled by picloram sprays. Bovey and his fellow researchers (32)

evaluated ten soil-active herbicides for control of brush in South Texas
and found that picloram was among the most effective. Granular picloram effectively controls live oak, huisache, and yaupon (29). Red-
berry juniper is effectively controlled with relatively low application
rates of picloram pellets but is not controlled by granules of dicamba
or monuron [3-(p-chlorophenyl)-1,1-dimethylurea] (252). Redberry
juniper is also susceptible to aerial applications of picloram pellets,
whereas standard 2,4,5-T sprays are ineffective (235). Lotebush and
Texas persimmon, extremely difficult to control with most herbicides,
can be controlled with individual-plant treatments of picloram (249,
271).

TABLE 5.4.
Responses of Problem Woody Species to Picloram, 2,4,5-T,
and Picloram Plus 2,4,5-T (adapted from 24).

| Species | Controlled by single spray application of | | |
	Picloram	2,4,5-T	Picloram plus 2,4,5-T
Honey mesquite	partial	yes	yes
Live Oak	yes	no	yes
Post oak, blackjack oak	yes	yes	yes
Macartney rose	yes	no	yes
Winged elm	yes	partial	yes
Cactus (pricklypear and tasajillo)	yes	partial	yes
Yaupon	yes	no	yes
Whitebrush	yes	no	partial
Blackbrush acacia	yes	partial	yes
Huisache	yes	no	yes
Mixed hardwoods	yes	yes	yes
Texas persimmon	yes	no	partial
Spiny hackberry	yes	no	yes
Twisted acacia	yes	no	yes
Lotebush	yes	no	partial
Catclaw	yes	no	yes
Agarito	no	no	no
Lime prickly ash	no	no	no
Yucca	no	yes	no
Red-berry juniper*	yes	no	partial

* Added to original table.

The potassium salt of picloram is more effective than the phenoxy herbicides 2,4-D or MCPA for controlling whitebrush (207). September and October applications of picloram are more effective than spring (May) applications for whitebrush control. Aerial applications of picloram in the early spring or in the fall will effectively control Macartney rose (174); however, one year after fall treatment with 1 or 2 pounds per acre, Macartney rose may regrow to such an extent that retreatment is required. Control of Macartney rose with commercial mixtures of 2,4,5-T and picloram is roughly equivalent to the amount of picloram in the mixture (248). Excellent control of pricklypear may be obtained with either sprays or beads at rates of 1, 2, or 3 pounds per acre (137).

Addition of picloram to phenoxy herbicides broadens the spectrum of species controlled. Control with picloram in the mixture of underbrush species not susceptible to 2,4,5-T alone may result in excellent forage release (Fig. 5.4). Excellent response of Post Oak Savannah vegetation may occur following application of picloram with ground equipment to woody-plant regrowth (274). Picloram sprays at 2

5.4. Aerial spraying of South Texas mixed brush with 2,4,5-T plus picloram resulted in dramatic release of range forages.

pounds per acre are more effective in reducing plant densities of the mixture of woody species and increasing production of desirable species than is either 2,4,5-T or 2,4,5-T plus picloram at the same rate. Picloram effectively controls winged elm and yaupon, which are essentially resistant to 2,4,5-T.

BIPYRIDINIUMS

Paraquat, a general contact herbicide, a chemical which kills only the tissues with which it comes into physical contact, is a representative bipyridinium.

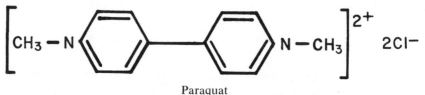

Paraquat
1,1'-dimethyl-4,4'-bipyridinium ion, as dichloride salts

Paraquat is tightly bound to soil particles, so it is not effective when applied to the soil and must be applied directly to the foliage of plants. It causes rapid dessication of the foliage by destroying the cellular membranes. In susceptible plants, which include most species, free radicals are formed by reduction of the original ions in the presence of light, oxygen, and chlorophyll. Hydrogen peroxide (H_2O_2) is formed during oxidation reactions and is probably the primary toxicant (10).

Paraquat may be transported in the xylem system in the dark when the stomata are closed, but translocation under those conditions is greatly reduced and distribution is mainly confined to the treated area of the leaf (12). The rate of leaf necrosis in woody plants after treatment with paraquat is directly related to air temperature (25). At low temperatures leaf necrosis may be delayed for at least forty-eight hours after treatment. The chlorophyll content of leaves also directly affects the rate of activity of paraquat on them (25), with the rate increasing as chlorophyll content increases. This dependency on chlorophyll content may determine the different susceptibilities of various plants to paraquat.

The primary use of paraquat for range improvement has been

for revegetation. This chemical is used effectively for the control of annual grasses (85) and has been especially effective for killing strips of vegetation left standing as buffers against environmental extremes so that desirable grasses may be seeded directly into the treated strips.

OTHER HERBICIDES

AMS. An effective herbicide for control of woody plants, especially where other growth regulators such as phenoxy herbicides pose a hazard, AMS is used primarily as a stump or trunk treatment, although foliage sprays are especially effective on poison ivy and poison oak. It is sold as a yellow powder and is highly soluble in water. The usual carrier is water containing surfactant or an oil:water emulsion.

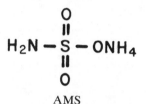

AMS
ammonium sulfamate

Hexaflurate. This herbicide is selective for the control of prickly-pear, dog cactus, tasajillo, and other cacti on rangeland. Hexaflurate applied at 2 pounds per acre in water at 2 to 5 gallons per acre for aerial application and at 10 to 40 gallons per acre with ground equipment has effectively controlled several species of cactus. It is absorbed by the roots and may be applied at any time during the year. It leaches slowly but is not susceptible to microbial decomposition or photodecomposition, so it may persist for one to four years after application.

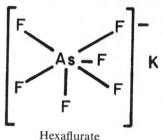

Hexaflurate
potassium hexafluoroarsenate

Hexaflurate, at this writing, has not been cleared by the Environmental Protection Agency for use on rangeland.

Tebuthiuron. Another promising experimental herbicide, tebuthiuron has been used primarily as a nonselective herbicide for total vegetation control. At the time of this writing, registration of tubuthiuron by the U.S. Environmental Protection Agency for use on rangeland is pending.

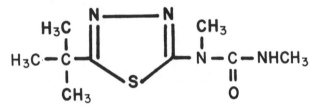

Tebuthiuron
N-[5-(1,1-dimethylethyl)-1,3,4-thiadiazol-2-yl]-*N*,*N'*-dimethylurea

At 1 pound per acre or less active ingredient, tebuthiuron has given excellent control of sand shinnery oak. One to 2 pounds per acre effectively controls whitebrush and willow baccharis, and 2 pounds per acre controls post oak, blackjack oak, live oak, winged elm, blackbrush acacia, spiny hackberry, yaupon, and woollybucket bumelia (267a). On loams and sandy loams huisache may be controlled with 2 pounds per acre, but 4 pounds per acre are apparently required on clay soils. Also controlled by 2 to 4 pounds per acre of tebuthiuron are Macartney rose, American beautyberry, coralberry, lotebush, wolfberry, twisted acacia, guajillo, cenizo, Texas colubrina, javelina brush, guayacan, desert yaupon and several other species. Rates of 3 to 4 pounds per acre only partially control honey mesquite, and tebuthiuron has not been effective for control of lime prickly ash, Texas persimmon, pricklypear, tasajillo, or saw greenbrier. Control of eastern red cedar has been erratic and generally not considered promising.

Grass damage may occur in the growing season after application of 2 pounds or more of tebuthiuron per acre. The possibility of damage to grasses is apparently increased when tebuthiuron is applied during a relatively dry winter followed by a wet spring and a dry summer. However, aerial applications of 2 pounds active ingredient tebuthiuron per acre to mixed brush and whitebrush-dominated stands on the South Texas Plains significantly increased grass yields one, two, and three years after treatment (266*a*). Higher rates did not significantly increase grass production over that from 2 pounds per acre, and lower rates did not cause grass production to be any higher than on brushy areas at two of three locations. The genus *Chloris* appears to be particularly tolerant of tebuthiuron, with species such as four-flowered false chloris, hooded windmillgrass, and Bell Rhodesgrass increasing after treatment. By two to three years after application of herbicide, the overall grazing value of grass stands had improved for cattle where at least 2 pounds per acre were applied.

Forb production and diversity were decreased where 1 pound per acre or more tebuthiuron was applied, and the detrimental effect on forbs increased as the herbicide rate was increased. Forb production was nearly eliminated for two years following application of 4 pounds per acre on the South Texas Plains, but recovery of the population was evident after three years, regardless of rate of application.

Aerial applications of 4 pounds active ingredient of tebuthiuron per acre seriously damaged grass production on the Post Oak Savannah near College Station for at least two growing seasons. However, at one year after application of 2 pounds per acre and under closely supervised grazing of cattle, grass cover increased, with a trend toward a grass stand of higher grazing value than on brushy areas. The desirable species, little bluestem, silver bluestem, Florida paspalum, and sideoats grama, increased in presence after tebuthiuron application. Although much is yet to be learned about tebuthiuron and its most effective use, it appears to hold great promise as a brush management tool for range improvement.

Herbicide Combinations and Split Applications

Herbicides may be combined by (1) applying two or more herbicides in a single application or by (2) applying two or more herbicides separately, or split application. Split application may be advisable when two or more different herbicides are required at different times to improve the spectrum of species controlled and when two or more applications are required for effective control of a particular species. Thus, split applications are usually completed in different growing seasons.

When two or more herbicides are combined and the results are equal to the same rate of either herbicide applied alone, the herbicide combination is said to be additive (110). Additivity is really the expected control level from herbicide mixtures. When a greater level of control occurs than is expected, the combination is said to be synergistic, that is, a complementary mixture. When less control occurs than would be expected from either herbicide used alone, the herbicide combination is said to be antagonistic.

Most herbicide combinations used for brush control are additive. However, picloram and phenoxy herbicides perform synergistically on some species. For example, combinations of silvex with picloram and 2,4,5-T with picloram are synergistic for sand shinnery oak control (251). However, picloram plus 2,4-D, 2,4,5-T plus dicamba, and silvex plus dicamba are usually additive.

Picloram combined with 2,4,5-T is usually synergistic for honey mesquite control (64), but 2,4,5-T plus dicamba is additive (258). In both mixtures, 1:1 ratios of the herbicides are usually used, and additivity or synergism may not result when the ratio of herbicides in combination is varied.

Split application of herbicides is used particularly in thick, heavy brush with stratified or layered vegetation. For example, in the mixed brush of South Texas where large honey mesquite trees form the overstory and the understory is composed of hard-to-kill species such as whitebrush, blackbrush, spiny hackberry, pricklypear, and other troublesome species, the top layer may be effectively controlled with herbicides such as 2,4,5-T. After removal of the top layer, usually one or two growing seasons after the initial treatment, a second application of herbicide such as one containing picloram may be applied to control the hard-to-kill understory species.

Two applications of 2,4,5-T at 1 to 2 pounds per acre each are usually required for control of post and blackjack oaks. The applications may be made in successive years or separated by one or two years depending on control achieved with the original treatment. Also, where phenoxy-tolerant species such as winged elm or yaupon exist, it may be advisable to use a herbicide containing picloram for the second application.

Several successive applications of 2,4-D are required for control of Macartney rose. Usually the initial treatment consists of 2 pounds per acre followed by two or three successive annual applications of 1 pound per acre. Two successive annual applications of 2,4,5-T plus picloram in the fall have also been used effectively. Such repeated herbicide applications may seriously reduce the population of desirable broadleaf plants on rangeland, so alternative practices such as prescribed burning may be advisable at least on a periodic basis (248).

Methods of Herbicide Application

There are several ways in which herbicides may be applied to undesirable plants on rangeland. For ease of presentation, the methods will be classified into two categories: broadcast methods and individual-plant treatments.

BROADCAST METHODS

Aerial application. This is probably the single most important technique for successful use of herbicides on rangeland. The method is rapid (most aircraft cover at least a 40-foot-wide swath at 90 to 120 miles per hour), unaffected by terrain, and economical (Fig. 5.5).

5.5. Aerial application is the most efficient method of treating large acreages of woody plants with herbicides. It is unaffected by terrain and brush growth type and can be accomplished with 5 gallons per acre or less of carrier fluid.

It is especially useful in thick, heavy brush where other methods are not feasible. Herbicide may be applied as spray, usually in 3 to 5 gallons per acre of water or oil:water emulsion, or as a dry formulation such as pellets.

Ground application. Ground sprayers are less adapted to rangeland conditions than is aerial equipment, but they are used a good deal in thin stands of brush or for herbaceous plant control in pastures. Booms may be attached to the spray tanks, but use of cluster nozzles decreases the risk of equipment damage. Herbicide sprays are usually applied in 10 to 40 gallons of carrier solution per acre.

Application of dry herbicides may be accomplished with conventional ground equipment such as spreaders for fertilizer or seeds. Good results have been achieved by the author using the type of speader which attaches to the three-point hitch and is driven by the power take-off of a rubber-wheeled tractor. Swath width can be regulated somewhat by varying height of the spreader, but effective swaths wider than 20 feet have been difficult to achieve.

INDIVIDUAL-PLANT TREATMENTS

Foliage sprays. Sprays to the foliage of individual plants are often used to selectively thin woody plants. They are also used in thin stands where broadcast application is not feasible. Hand-operated or power sprayers are used, and the foliage is wet thoroughly.

Basal sprays. Herbicide is sometimes applied, usually in fuel oil or an oil:water emulsion, to the lower 18 to 24 inches of the tree trunk until the liquid runs off.

Frill application. In this method a ring is cut through the bark around the tree at the base, and herbicide solution is applied directly in the cut. Enough herbicide is applied to make the solution bubble out of the frill.

Notch application. This method is similar to frill application. Overlapping downward ax cuts are made about 3 inches apart around the base of the tree. The chips are knocked out, and herbicide is applied in the cuts.

Injector method. In this technique an injection tool with a sharp bit is used to cut into the tree, and the chemical is then released from the reservoir through the injector bit.

Stump treatment. In some cases woody plants are cut off and the

5.6. In stump treatment the herbicide spray is applied directly to the freshly cut stump surface. (*Photograph by O. E. Sperry*)

herbicide spray or crystals may be applied to the cut surface (Fig. 5.6).

Pellets, granules, beads. Pellets and similar formulations may be applied by hand to the soil at the base of the tree to be removed. Depending on the specific situation, the dry herbicide may be applied in a ring, 6 inches wide or less, around the trunk base, but usually it is applied uniformly to cover the soil under the entirety of the tree's canopy. Dosage may be based on trunk diameter (ounces of herbicide per inch of trunk diameter) for single-stemmed plants or may be based on canopy diameter (ounces active herbicide per foot of canopy diameter) for multistemmed plants and vines.

Application Equipment

Just as important as a working knowledge of herbicides and their properties is a thorough understanding of application equipment. Ineffective or faulty equipment, poor application techniques, or miscalibration may negate the beneficial effects of herbicides.

AERIAL SPRAY EQUIPMENT

The primary equipment factors that must be considered in aerial application are the type of aircraft and characteristics of the spray dispensing system (326). Aerial spraying systems vary, since aerial applicators usually have equipment adapted for the most effective spray application under conditions they are most likely to confront. Aerial spray equipment usually consists of a propeller-driven pump, a pressure regulation system, a spray boom, and nozzles. Several types of these components are combined in various ways by commercial applicators. Generally, spray booms are positioned behind and immediately below the trailing edge of the wing, in view of the pilot during flight and accessible for repairs and maintenance.

Hydraulic pressure nozzles and various spinning brushes, disks, and screens are popular for aerial application. The Zeigler nozzle system is relatively trouble-free, has a manually operated control cap for positive shutoff, and is usually operated at low pressure. The nozzle tip simply consists of a hole, sized according to the desired delivery rate, drilled into a brass plug (Fig. 5.7). The open hole delivers a solid stream which strikes the flat cap of the system and breaks up into a spray. Another popular system is the diaphragm system (Fig. 5.8), in which nozzle tips with various orifice sizes are available to allow much variation in the flow rate of the spray pattern. The diaphragm nozzle system operates on the tension of a spring, which closes a check valve when the spray pressure drops below about 7 to 12 pounds per square inch. This system assures positive shutoff but limits the applicator if low-volume–low-pressure systems with pressures below 7 to 12 pounds per square inch are required. The diaphragms must be properly maintained, since they are susceptible to leaking and clogging.

Both fixed- and rotary-winged aircraft are used to apply herbicides for range improvement. Fixed-wing aircraft may be monoplanes or biplanes. A fairly wide range of horsepowers are available in spray planes. The combination of aircraft design and horsepower influences spray patterns and methods of using the aircraft. Monowing, low-horsepower aircraft generally apply herbicides in swaths from 35 to 40 feet wide. This swath width is comparable to that of standard rotary-winged aircraft. Biwing, low-horsepower aircraft generally apply swaths from 40 to 45 feet wide. High-horsepower aircraft, either

5.7. The Zeigler nozzle system is relatively trouble free and operates by manually controlled caps for positive shutoff. *(Courtesy C. E. Fisher)*

5.8. The diaphragm system operates based on spring tension which shuts off the spray when line pressure falls below 7 to 12 psi. (*Courtesy H. T. Wiedemann*)

monowing or biwing, may apply swaths from 40 to 50 feet wide without affecting spray pattern. In general, the spray swath should not exceed the width of the wingspan plus 10 percent. When volumes of 2 gallons per acre or less are used, spray swath probably should not exceed the width of the wingspan. However, there is no set rule, and swath width should be determined based on aircraft characteristics and necessary swath overlap for an effective job.

Some workers feel that the additional turbulence generated by larger aircraft with higher horsepower may provide more uniform coverage of the spray to understory brush. Presumably this additional turbulence assures contact of both upper and lower leaf surfaces by the spray. Large planes of high horsepower usually provide greater payload capacities, which, combined with the wider swaths and somewhat greater airspeeds, allow treatment of a larger area per unit of time than do smaller aircraft. However, the maneuverability of smaller aircraft is certainly an important consideration.

One of the most important factors in effective aerial application is the development of a uniform aerial spray pattern. This uniformity is sometimes difficult to achieve because of undesirable air currents produced by the aircraft itself. The movements of air currents about the propeller and the wing tips are the primary sources of distortion to the spray pattern (Fig. 5.9). Vortex action, the movement of air currents which carries the spray from the lower side to the upper side of the wing, not only distorts the spray pattern but increases the probability of herbicide drift, the lateral displacement of spray particles from the intended point of application.

Vortex action is basic to both fixed-wing aircraft and helicopters (326). The effect of vortex on spray pattern may be reduced by placing the spray boom so that it does not extend to the tips of the wings. Helicopters produce a downwash which, presumably, forces the spray pattern directly downward. However, helicopters do not have much greater downwash at forward speeds above 15 to 25 miles per hour than do fixed-wing aircraft (326).

Propeller wake, the movement of air currents as a result of the direction and speed of the propeller, may cause excessive movement of the spray pattern to the left-hand side of the aircraft. Also, propeller wake may produce a distinct opening in the center of the spray pattern. Detrimental effects of propeller wake and vortex on the spray

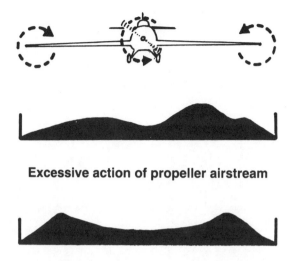

Excessive action of propeller airstream

Excessive action of wing-tip vortices

5.9. Generalized effects of wing-tip vortices and propeller wake on spray patterns. (*Adapted from Weidemann et al., 326*).

pattern can be reduced by proper placement of the boom nozzle and proper boom length in relationship to wingspan.

GROUND SPRAY EQUIPMENT

Several types of ground spray equipment are available for range weed and brush control, and excellent sprayers can be constructed from materials readily available to the ranch. As previously noted, ground spray equipment can be designed either with booms (Fig. 5.10) or without (Fig. 5.11). In general, booms are not constructed to withstand continual abuse from spraying rangeland with rough terrain. They have the advantage on smooth, level terrain of producing a more uniform pattern than that of boomless sprayers, but excessive maintenance costs usually reduce their overall utility. Several types of boomless sprayers have been developed and used for spraying limited acreages of weeds and brush. The most common type employs a cluster of flat spray nozzles mounted in an assembly to produce a relatively uniform spray distribution pattern.

Swath width is dependent on spraying pressure and nozzle orientation and generally should not exceed 30 feet wide with boomless sprayers. It is critical that the nozzles are mounted high enough for the spray to completely cover the vegetation canopy. In general, drift

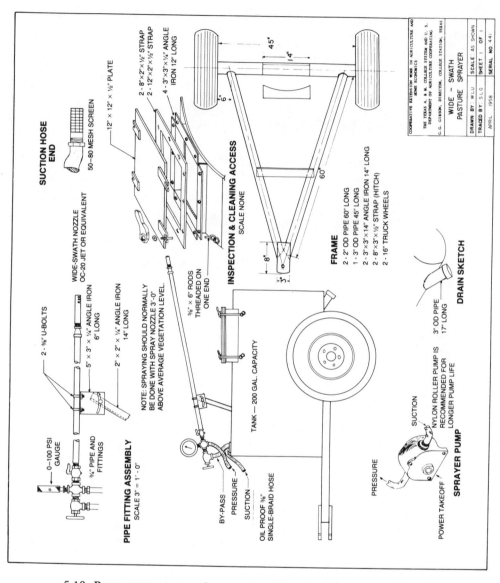

5.10. Boom sprayers may be constructed so that the booms swing back over the sprayer and lock into place for transport. (*Courtesy Texas Agricultural Extension Service*)

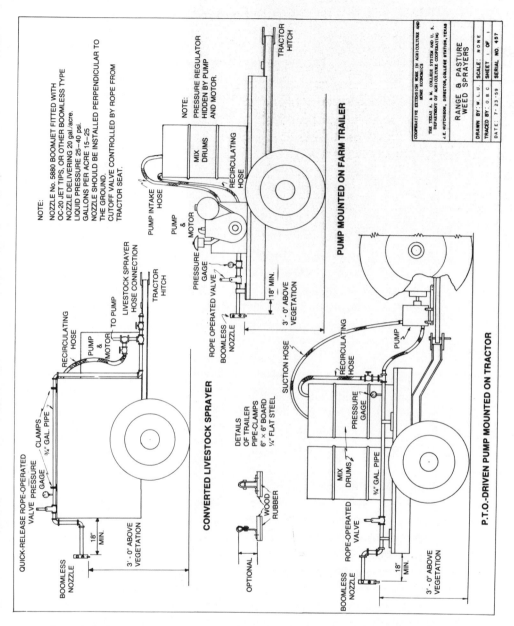

NOTE:

NOZZLE No. 5880 BOOMJET FITTED WITH
OC-20 JET TIPS, OR OTHER BOOMLESS TYPE
NOZZLE DELIVERING 20 gal./acre.
LIQUID PRESSURE 25–40 psi.
GALLONS PER ACRE 15–25
NOZZLE SHOULD BE INSTALLED PERPENDICULAR TO
THE GROUND.
CUTOFF VALVE CONTROLLED BY ROPE FROM
TRACTOR SEAT.

NOTE:
PRESSURE REGULATOR
HIDDEN BY PUMP
AND MOTOR.

TRACTOR
HITCH

PUMP MOUNTED ON FARM TRAILER

MIX
DRUMS

RECIRCULATING
HOSE

PUMP INTAKE
HOSE

PUMP
&
MOTOR

PRESSURE
GAGE

ROPE OPERATED VALVE

BOOMLESS
NOZZLE

18" MIN.

3'–0" ABOVE
VEGETATION

QUICK-RELEASE ROPE-OPERATED
VALVE PRESSURE
GAGE   CLAMPS
¾" GAL. PIPE

RECIRCULATING
HOSE

PUMP
&
MOTOR

TO PUMP

LIVESTOCK SPRAYER
HOSE CONNECTION

TRACTOR
HITCH

BOOMLESS
NOZZLE

18"
MIN.

3'–0" ABOVE
VEGETATION

CONVERTED LIVESTOCK SPRAYER

DETAILS
OF TRAILER
PIPE-CLAMPS
6" × 6" BOARD
¼" FLAT STEEL

WOOD
RUBBER

OPTIONAL

RECIRCULATING
HOSE

SUCTION HOSE

PUMP

PRESSURE
GAGE

MIX
DRUMS

¾" GAL. PIPE

ROPE-OPERATED
VALVE

BOOMLESS
NOZZLE

18"
MIN.

3'–0" ABOVE
VEGETATION

P.T.O.-DRIVEN PUMP MOUNTED ON TRACTOR

COOPERATIVE EXTENSION WORK IN AGRICULTURE AND
HOME ECONOMICS

THE TEXAS A. & M. COLLEGE SYSTEM AND U. S.
DEPARTMENT OF AGRICULTURE COOPERATING
J.E. HUTCHISON, DIRECTOR, COLLEGE STATION, TEXAS

RANGE & PASTURE
WEED SPRAYERS

SCALE: NONE	
SHEET I OF I	
SERIAL NO. 457	

DRAWN BY: W. L. U.
TRACED BY: O. B. G.
DATE: 7-23-'59

5.11. Suitable ground sprayers may be constructed from materials available to the ranch or by converting livestock sprayers. (*Courtesy Texas Agricultural Extension Service*) potential is reduced at lower sprayer pressures. Satisfactory results have been achieved with spraying pressures as low as 20 pounds per square inch using ground equipment. At that pressure, depending on nozzle orifice size, 10 gallons per acre or higher delivery rates (generally required to provide adequate foliage coverage) can be achieved with boomless sprayers.

Air-carrier sprayers or mist blowers, adapted to range weed and brush control, have several nozzles placed in a high-speed blast of air. Their advantages are that they produce wider swaths and more uniform foliar coverage with lower spray volumes than do other types of sprayers. However, they usually require a higher initial investment for equipment than is necessary for other types of sprayers, and their potential for spray drift is greatly increased. Spray discharge is horizontal or directed slightly downward by air directional vanes positioned directly in front of the air blower. Mist blowers will produce a swath width of 40 feet, which can be used to effectively control brush from 3 to 6 feet tall (326).

SPRAYER CALIBRATION

Proper calibration is of utmost importance for effective, economical, and safe herbicide application. Miscalibration may result in reduced levels of brush control from application of too little herbicide, in an improper spray pattern, or in increased costs because of the application of excessive herbicide. Whether calibrating hand sprayers or any of the various ground or aerial sprayers, the speed, flow rate, and swath width must be determined.

Flow rate, usually expressed as gallons per minute, is a direct function of spraying pressure and nozzle orifice size. Swath width should be measured under the field conditions for which the calibration is being made. Sprayer speed, especially if ground equipment is being used, should also be determined on the area to be treated. Aircraft speed varies little from place to place but should be checked before making final calculations. Final calculations of airspeed should be an average of calibration flights in both directions over the area to be sprayed unless the spray is to be applied with the aircraft flying one direction, either with the wind or into the wind, only. This averaging is especially important if the wind direction is exactly parallel to the flight lines. It allows calculation of the actual ground speed by averaging speed into the wind and speed with a tailwind.

Sprayer speed can be determined by timing the ground sprayer over a known distance while operating at the selected gear and engine speed required for proper spray pump operation and then using the simple formula

$$\text{Speed (miles per hour)} = \frac{\text{distance traveled (feet)}}{\text{time (seconds)}} \times 0.682.$$

Once the speed is determined, flow rate must be checked. The spray system should be filled with the carrier solution to be used and operated at a pressure which will assure proper functioning of all nozzles. When the nozzles are operated properly at the selected pressure, discharge from all the nozzles should be collected for at least 1 minute. Different spray solutions—for example, water compared to an oil: water emulsion—have different flow properties.

Effective swath width is the actual swath width minus enough overlap to give uniform coverage of the vegetation. After determining effective swath width, the number of acres sprayed per hour may be determined by the formula

Acres per hour = speed (miles per hour) × swath width (feet) × 0.121.

Then carrier rate in gallons per acre can be calculated:

$$\text{Gallons per acre} = \frac{\text{flow rate (gallons per minute)} \times 60}{\text{acres per hour}}.$$

Two general methods may be used to calibrate ground sprayers. The difference method involves filling the spray tank with a known amount of carrier solution and then actually spraying a predetermined distance at the desired speed and pressure. The area (acres) covered by the trial run is calculated as

$$\text{Acres covered} = \frac{\text{swath width (feet)} \times \text{distance (feet)}}{43,560}.$$

The amount of carrier fluid required to refill the spray tank represents the number of gallons delivered to the area covered by the trial run and is calculated by

$$\text{Gallons per acre} = \frac{\text{gallons delivered}}{\text{acres covered}}.$$

When the desired delivery is achieved, at least three trial runs should be used to verify delivery rate before the herbicide is actually applied.

Ground equipment may also be calibrated by the stationary delivery method. After the speed and swath width are determined, the number of acres which can be covered during each minute of operation is calculated as

$$\text{Acres per minute} = \frac{\text{swath width (feet)} \times \text{speed (feet per minute)}}{43,560}.$$

The average delivery rate (gallons per minute) per nozzle must be determined by collecting the fluid for a given length of time. The average delivery per nozzle times the number of nozzles equals the flow rate per unit time:

$$\text{Gallons per acre} = \frac{\text{flow rate (gallons per minute)}}{\text{acres per minute}}.$$

As examples of determining delivery rates, consider the following situations:

Example 1. It has been decided to use the difference method to calibrate an aircraft with a 250-gallon hopper capacity. A 42-foot-wide swath is covered over a 0.25-mile calibration distance. The calibration flight is completed, and 6.35 gallons of water are required to refill the hopper. Delivery rate is calculated as follows:

$$\text{Acres covered} = \frac{\text{swath width (feet)} \times \text{flight distance (feet)}}{43,560}.$$

$$= \frac{42 \times 1,320}{43,560} = 1.27.$$

$$\text{Delivery rate (gallons per minute)} = \frac{\text{gallons delivered}}{\text{acres delivered}}$$

$$= \frac{6.35}{1.27} = 5.$$

Example 2. A drag-type boom sprayer will be used to spray woody sprouts. The sprayer delivers a 20-foot-wide swath, and after a few trial runs it is determined that the sprayer can safely travel at 5 miles per hour over the pasture. Therefore:

$$\text{Acres covered per minute} = \frac{\text{swath width (feet)} \times \text{speed (feet per min.)}}{43,560}$$

$$= \frac{20 \times 440}{43,560} = 0.20.$$

At twenty-five pounds per square inch, each of the ten nozzles on the boom is checked for delivery for one minute. On the average, the nozzles delivered 0.4 gallon each for the one-minute check period. The delivery rate (total gallons per minute) equals the average delivery per nozzle (gallons per minute) times the number of nozzles, or $0.4 \times 10 = 4$. Therefore:

$$\text{Delivery (gallons per acre)} = \frac{\text{delivery rate (gallons per minute)}}{\text{acres per minute}}$$

$$= \frac{4}{0.2} = 20.$$

Mixing the spray. Before mixing the herbicide into the carrier solution, read the label on the herbicide container in detail. Herbicide labels are made up of several component parts. In the center, usually in large, striking letters, is the trade name of the herbicide. Beneath the trade name, generally in smaller letters, is a listing of the chemistry and concentration of the active ingredients (a.i.). The active ingredients of liquid herbicide may be expressed as acid equivalent (percentage) or by weight (pounds of active herbicide per gallon of formulated material). Most calibrations give the weight instead of the percentage of acid equivalent. A caution statement, which should be read carefully, occurs below the description of active ingredients. The directions for use of the herbicide must be listed on the side of the container before the manufacturer can merchandise the product. These use directions should be followed closely. They provide information on the uses for which the herbicide is registered and valuable information about application rates, recommended carriers, mixing instructions, and necessary application conditions for the most effective results. After the delivery (gallons per acre) and the herbicide application rate (pounds per acre, a.i.) have been determined, the amount of formulated herbicide required can be calculated. One approach is to first determine the acres that can be covered with a tank of spray solution using the formula

$$\text{Acres per tank} = \frac{\text{tank capacity (gallons)}}{\text{gallons per acre}}.$$

Then:

Herbicide required (gals. per tank) =
$$\frac{\text{acres per tank} \times \text{application rate (pounds per acre)}}{\text{herbicide concentration (pounds per gallon)}}.$$

For example, a 100-gallon spray tank calibrated to deliver 10 gallons per acre will cover 10 acres per tank of spray mixture. If 1 pound per acre is desired for the application rate, 10 pounds of herbicide (a.i.) will be required for each tank of spray mixture. If the herbicide contains 4 pounds (a.i.) per gallon of formulated material, then 2.5 gallons (10 ÷ 4) of the formulated herbicide will be required. Total spray mixture would consist of 2.5 gallons of herbicide and 97.5 gallons of water if a straight aqueous spray is to be used.

When oil:water carriers are used, the calculations become a bit more complicated. For example, consider the use of a 250-gallon tank in an aircraft which has been calibrated to deliver 5 gallons per acre. One hopper load will spray 50 acres. Oil:water emulsions are usually mixed on the basis of delivering 1 gallon of diesel oil per treated acre. Therefore, if a 1:4 oil:water emulsion is selected, 1 gallon of oil per acre plus 4 gallons of water per acre will compose the spray carrier. When the overall spray mix is considered, herbicide should be added so that it becomes a part of the proper phase in the overall carrier. If an amine salt formulation(water soluble) is to be used, it should be considered in the calculations as a part of the water phase in the carrier. If an ester (oil soluble) is to be used, it should be considered as a part of the oil phase. For example, with the aircraft calibrated as described above, consider the application of 0.5 pound per acre of a herbicide formulation containing 4 pounds per gallon of an ester. To treat 50 acres, 25 pounds will be required. Using a formulation containing 4 pounds of active herbicide per gallon 6.25 gallons (25 ÷ 4) of formulated herbicide will be required for the spray mixture. At 1 gallon of diesel oil per acre, 50 gallons of oil will be required per tank load. However, if the amount of diesel oil is reduced by the amount of formulated ester required for the tank of spray, then the oil phase will consist of 43.75 gallons of diesel oil and 6.25 gallons of the formulated herbicide. Commercial emulsifier will be required to form a stable emulsion in the spray tank. The amount of emulsifier required is about 1 ounce per gallon of diesel oil in the spray mixture, although more may be required to form a stable emulsion. To simplify calculations, we will use 1 ounce of emulsifier per gallon of the oil phase. Fifty ounces of emulsifier is roughly 0.4 gallon (50 ÷ 128 = 0.39). The emulsifier may be considered to be a part of the aqueous phase, so the total spray mixture will consist of 43.75 gallons of diesel oil, 6.25 gallons of the formulated ester, 0.4 gallon of emulsifier, and 199.6 gallons of water.

If an amine salt is used, the herbicide should be considered part of the aqueous phase. Using the same herbicide rate and concentration (4 pounds per gallon), the tank mixture would consist of 50 gallons of diesel oil, 6.25 gallons of herbicide, 0.4 gallon of emulsifier, and 193.35 gallons of water.

To properly mix the spray components, a small amount of water is usually added to the mixing vat followed by the necessary amount of diesel oil and emulsifier. The spray tank should have constant agitation during the mixing. The herbicide is then added as the remainder of the water is being pumped into the mixing vat to assure a thorough tank mix.

Active ingredient content of dry formulations such as wettable powders is generally expressed as a percentage. Generally, aqueous carriers containing the necessary amount of surfactant are used for wettable powder formulations. To apply 1 pound per acre (a.i.) of an 80 percent wettable powder, 1.25 pounds per acre (1 ÷ 0.8) of formulated herbicide will be required. If a ground sprayer with a 100-gallon tank has been calibrated to deliver 10 gallons per acre (10 acres per tank), then 12.5 pounds (10 × 1.25) of formulated herbicide per tank would be required. Amount of surfactant required is generally calculated on percentage by volume of the total spray solution. If 0.5 percent (by volume) of surfactant is required, 0.5 gallon will be mixed in each 100 gallons of spray. Since wettable powders vary somewhat in bulk, the recommended mixing procedure to achieve the proper tank mix is to first add a small amount of water to the mixing tank, followed by the proper amount of formulated wettable powder. As with the previous example, the mixing vat should be under constant agitation. After the dry herbicide has formed a uniform slurry in the initial amount of water, the remainder of the water and the necessary amount of surfactant should be added to bring the batch to the total volume required for the spray job.

Spray carrier volume. The Zeigler system has been used to develop low-volume–low-pressure spraying systems which reduce the amount of carrier volume required for herbicide application to rangeland. Three, 4, or 5 gallons of an oil:water emulsion per acre have been widely accepted for range improvement work. However, recent research has shown that cost of herbicide application for control of species such as honey mesquite may be significantly reduced when a carrier volume of 1 gallon per acre is used (91).

Assuming brush control level can be maintained, there are several advantages to the use of lower volumes. For example, with a 250-gallon tank, 250 acres of rangeland may be treated at 1 gallon of carrier volume per acre, compared to only 50 acres at 5 gallons per acre, before the applicator must return to the mixing location and refill with spray solution. Average payload carried by an airplane while in flight is reduced when low carrier volumes are used, thus reducing both gasoline consumption by the aircraft and the amount of diesel oil required for emulsion carriers. With rising energy costs, these reductions represent notable savings. Equally important, there is a reduction in "down time" for the applicator, thus increasing the number of acres that can be sprayed in a given amount of time. Consequently, more area may be treated when wind and environmental conditions are correct for spraying. The equipment required for hauling and mixing the carrier solution may be reduced by premixing the spray and pumping it directly into the aircraft.

Original low-volume work was conducted with biplanes of 450 to 650 horsepower (91). Evaluations of efficiency of applying 1 and 5 gallons per acre with 650-horsepower monowing aircraft (259) were comparable to those for biwing aircraft (91).

SPRAYER CARE

Proper cleaning, storage, and maintenance of sprayers is of utmost importance, especially following application of growth-regulator herbicides. Phenoxy herbicides such as 2,4-D are extremely difficult to remove from sprayer parts. Thorough cleaning of sprayers after each use of such herbicides will prevent possible injury to susceptible crops when the sprayer is next used on them. Some crops are so sensitive to 2,4-D that it is advisable to use a different sprayer for such herbicides than is used for application of other pesticides. For short-term storage the tank should be emptied and rinsed with water immediately after spraying. If the sprayer is not to be used for a considerable time, it should be rinsed with kerosene or fuel oil to protect moving parts from corrosion.

Water-soluble formulations of phenoxy herbicides are more easily removed from spray equipment than are esters. Amine salts may be removed with a mild solution of household ammonia followed by several water rinses for final decontamination. Esters are most effectively removed with organic solvents such as acetone. However, such solvents are expensive, and most of the ester residue may be removed with ammonia-water solution. Rinsing with water containing a detergent will help remove remaining oil particles. Several final rinses with water will remove excess detergent and aid in decontamination of the sprayer. The spray tank should be filled with ammonia-water (1 quart of household ammonia in 25 gallons of water) and enough of the solution pumped through the hoses and nozzles to fill all the sprayer parts completely. The full tank should then be closed and left for twenty-four hours before being rinsed thoroughly with water. The day before the sprayer is used again, the tank should be flushed with water. If available, activated charcoal may be used after the preliminary rinsing to further decontaminate the sprayer. A 0.3 percent suspension of activated charcoal immediately absorbs most of the 2,4-D residue from the sprayer. The suspension should be agitated for twenty to thirty minutes and then drained, and the sprayer should be rinsed thoroughly with clean water before it is used again.

Dry Herbicide Application

Application of dry herbicides formulated as large particles may be accomplished with spreaders used for aerial seeding or for the application of fertilizer (Fig. 5.12). The difference method described for liquids is also generally used to calibrate aerial equipment for the application of pellets. Herbicide manufacturers usually provide blank

5.12. Aerial application of pellet herbicide formulations is performed with spreader attachments generally used for the application of fertilizers and seeds.

pellets or granules for the necessary calibration work. With a known amount of blank pellets or granules in the hopper, a calibration trial run over a known distance should be flown and the swath width determined. The blank material remaining in the hopper after the trial run can then be weighed. The difference in the amount loaded and the amount returned divided by the area covered is the application rate (pounds per acre) of formulated herbicide. The amount of formulated herbicide applied must be adjusted for the percentage of active ingredient. For example, if in a calibration run 20 pounds of pellets containing 10 percent active ingredient were applied to 2 acres, then 1 pound of active ingredient per acre would be the application rate.

Timing Herbicide Applications

Woody perennials are generally more sensitive to the timing of herbicide applications than are herbaceous perennials. Leaves must be fully formed but not so mature that a heavy cuticle will limit herbicide absorption. The canopy should be uniformly developed—that is, be formed as nearly as possible of leaves of the same age. The plant system must be physiologically active in order to expedite absorption and translocation of the herbicide. Although research has long sought a reliable indicator of herbicide susceptibility, choice of proper time of herbicide application remains a judgment decision. The calendar serves only as a general indicator for the timing of sprays, and the condition of the plant is most indicative of its potential response to herbicides.

There is some general difference in the timing of herbicide applications for the control of evergreen species such as Macartney rose, live oak, and yaupon compared to that for deciduous species. The influence of spray date on the response of those species varies somewhat with herbicide (117). For example, picloram at 0.5 pound per acre is more effective than 2,4-D at 2 pounds per acre for control of Macartney rose regardless of application date. Picloram has been most effective in April and May, whereas 2,4-D is most effective in May and early June (117). Combinations of picloram and 2,4-D have been effective when applied from April to late June. Macartney rose may be effectively controlled in the fall with picloram at 1 pound per acre (117) or with 2,4,5-T plus picloram at 1 pound per acre (248). Yaupon is more sensitive to herbicidal sprays as growth is actively renewed in early spring (April) than at other dates (30). Picloram is the most effective treatment for yaupon, and granular forms are more effective than sprays regardless of the date of application. Live oak may be controlled by either fall or spring applications of picloram (28). Phenoxy herbicides are ineffective on live oak regardless of the date of application.

The optimum spray date for the application of herbicides such as 2,4,5-T, dicamba, or picloram to woody plants correlates well with times for maximum herbicide absorption and translocation (41). These times of maximum growth are strongly responsive to environmental conditions such as rainfall, moisture availability, and temperature (178). For example, picloram is most toxic to whitebrush when applied in cooler months, especially when application is followed by rainfall (207). The effectiveness of picloram granules for whitebrush control suggests that root uptake is the most effective mode of the herbicide's entry into whitebrush. Applications of picloram in the fall are more effective than applications in the spring for whitebrush control (206). Broadcast applications of relatively high rates of 2,4,5-T effectively control huisache in the spring and early summer (31); picloram is effective in late spring, early summer, or fall; and mixtures of the two herbicides are effective in both spring and fall.

Environmental factors greatly influence the reactions of honey mesquite when the stage of its growth is optimum for treatment with 2,4,5-T (89). The intricate interrelationships among environmental and physiological factors preclude isolating a single factor that limits plant growth or the absorption and movement of 2,4,5-T. Although any single factor may limit honey mesquite growth and influence herbicide effectiveness, research suggests that final control always depends on the interplay among many environmental and plant growth factors.

Honey mesquite is usually most susceptible to herbicides fifty to ninety days after "bud burst" in the spring. This time period usually extends from May 15 to the first week in July and correlates with the greatest 2,4,5-T movement in honey mesquite (88). Spraying before the leaves are fully developed in late summer results in only partially defoliated trees with flagging and death in only the younger stems and twigs. Maximum herbicide translocation usually occurs about thirty days after the honey mesquite is in full leaf, from late May to late June in northwest Texas. This is usually about twenty days after the leaves change from a light olive to a deep green color. Factors such as cool weather, drought, and insect damage may delay this development. Applications of 2,4,5-T are not effective on honey mesquite during dormancy, before full leaf development, or during the fall months (88). Growth factors apparently associated with herbicide effectiveness on honey mesquite are cessation of stem elongation, a thickening of tissue for translocation of the herbicide, radial enlargement of the new wood ring, and a lowering of total available carbohydrates (205).

Another consideration in developing a spray program is the type of brush growth—whether original or regrowth. Regrowth of perennial species, both herbaceous and woody, is generally more difficult to control with translocated herbicides than is the original growth. Honey mesquite is a good example of a plant which shows this differential reaction. The difficulty in controlling regrowth may be because of reduced foliar area in relation to root volume. The level of control of honey mesquite seedlings with 2,4,5-T has been directly correlated with foliar area (279). The greater the foliar area, the greater the level of control.

Environmental variables such as air temperature, relative humidity, soil temperature, and soil moisture have been directly correlated with herbicide susceptibility. However, as previously noted, there is no single environmental factor that can be isolated as a primary regulator of herbicide susceptibility in plants. The critical soil temperature for control of honey mesquite is apparently about 80° F at 18 inches deep (59). Although there is no doubt that such a relationship exists, other limiting factors such as reduction in canopy due to drought or insect damage, excessive air temperatures, or low relative humidity will offset the influence of soil temperature on the ultimate level of control.

Susceptibility of honey mesquite to foliage-applied herbicides is best correlated with the combined effects of air and soil temperature, percentage of relative humidity, and percentage of soil moisture availability. Soil water content is probably one of the more important factors. Under soil moisture conditions conducive to rapid growth, honey mesquite control with 2,4,5-T has averaged 60 percent based on long-term observations (89). Under dry conditions about 20 percent of the plants have been controlled. Thus, variation in soil moisture probably accounts, to a large extent, for much of the variation in the control of honey mesquite with 2,4,5-T, even among sites within a pasture. Unusually high levels of control of honey mesquite occur in wet years following dry years, probably because of the stimulation of growth and rapid assimilation of food materials by honey mesquite after experiencing a prolonged stress period.

The role of moisture is probably directly related to canopy development and herbicide translocation (63) as they vary with available soil moisture. Honey mesquite and other brush species adapt to varying availability of water by varying foliar density. Development of the canopy and of the individual leaves is a good indicator of the relative level of susceptibility of honey mesquite to foliage-applied herbicides. Plants easiest to kill are those having fully developed canopies of dark green foliage and mature legumes (59).

Variation in soil texture has also been investigated with respect to control of species such as honey mesquite, but only generalizations about edaphic effects are possible. Generally, honey mesquite control is better on upland and sandy soils than on clay soils (59, 89). This is probably because of the effects of soil texture on soil temperature, moisture availability, and other factors. Clay soils apparently warm more slowly in the spring than sandy soils, especially to depths of 6 inches or more. Moreover, soil water is more tightly held by clay particles than by sandy soils, where much of the water is free.

Thus far the discussion has centered around the use of foliar sprays relative to the stage of plant growth most susceptible to herbicides. The optimum stage of plant growth for chemical treatment varies with the application method and the chemical formulation. Frill or stump sprays can be completed at any time of the year (189). Trunk base sprays should be applied from the time of full foliage development to the first fall rains. These sprays should not be applied when growth is renewed in the early fall following late rainfall, but treatment can be resumed in late fall and completed throughout the winter dormancy of the undesirable woody plants. Soil injection treatments are usually most effective during the spring.

Pellet treatments may be applied anytime except during the summer dry period with potential for good results. Pellets and other soil-active formulations are usually most effective when applied just ahead of rainy periods which precede periods of maximum growth of the woody plants. The rainfall serves to dissolve the herbicide and move it into the soil, where it will be available for root uptake with soil water. Thus, herbicides such as picloram or tebuthiuron in dry form may be most effective when applied in late winter to take advantage of spring rains and renewed spring growth of woody plants or if applied in early fall ahead of the fall flush of growth activity.

Foliage sprays are the most restricted, relative to the best time for application, of all the treatment methods. For example, a six- to eight-week period in the spring from about April 15 to June 10 is the longest period of susceptibility that can be expected for species such as honey mesquite. Since these applications are governed by foliage development, only a four-week period is available for treatment in some years.

6

Herbicides and the Rangeland Environment

THE complexity of the rangeland ecosystem and the sophistication of agricultural chemicals used today make interactions of herbicides with the environment a basic immediate concern. That concern over the fate of agricultural chemicals in the environment has long provided the impetus for careful study of chemical residues, their persistence, and the forces which determine the rates and routes of their dissipation.

Considering all the uses of chemicals in agriculture, herbicide residues on rangeland received relatively little interest before the 1960's. Apparently there were three primary reasons for the general lack of research activity on herbicide residues. First, most research effort was directed toward study of the fate of pesticides used on food crops which are directly ingested by man. Since vegetation of rangeland must be converted to protein by grazing animals, human contact with the treated vegetation is minimal. Second, the common attitude among the public was that rangeland, like most natural resources, was wild land to be tended by the relatively few who resided upon it. Although federal agencies such as the Soil Conservation Service had long worked with landowners to properly manage and conserve rangeland, the attitude of responsibility for stewardship of our natural resources had yet to become a prime concern of the average citizen (a notable exception being awareness of the need to prevent uncontrolled burning of our forests). Finally, broad-scale herbicide use on rangeland was restricted almost solely to 2,4-D and 2,4,5-T. Those herbicides had a long record of safe use and were not considered a threat to environmental quality.

However, in the last ten years considerable attention has been focused directly on the fate of herbicides applied to rangeland. As public interest in the destiny of our natural resources has intensified, the use and treatment of those resources has begun to be scrutinized more closely. During the mid-1960's additional herbicides with potential for range improvement began to appear as candidates for registration and future broad-scale use. These new herbicides were more effective than conventional materials, but they also appeared to be somewhat more persistent in the environment. The proximity to rangeland of row crops that were sensitive to hormone herbicides emphasized the need for detailed research on the residual properties of any herbicide applied to rangeland ecosystems.

This chapter will center primarily on the reactions that result from the aerial application of herbicide sprays to rangeland. However, many of the principles discussed also apply to dry herbicides. Since dry formulations appear to hold potential for range improvement, their activity in the ecosystem will be noted occasionally.

The rangeland ecosystem is conceptualized, for this discussion of herbicide residues, as being made up of four interrelated components (Fig. 6.1). Each of those environmental components—atmosphere, soil, vegetation, and water—will be discussed separately. However, it must be understood that the environment cannot be compartmentalized in the strictest sense. The environment is an open system, and reactions taking place in each segment of the ecological system affect all other parts (245).

Atmospheric Effects

Immediately upon its release from the nozzle, herbicide spray is subject to drift, the movement of airborne spray particles away from the intended target. The action of air currents is primarily responsible for displacement of the spray droplets. Under high wind a significant portion of the spray may be blown away from the intended target. Factors influencing spray drift are droplet size, wind direction and velocity, and the height above the target at which the spray is released.

The size of droplets generated by sprayers is affected by spraying pressure, the type of carrier (generally whether an oil or water base), and the nozzle orifice size. In general, low spraying pressures and large nozzle orifices produce large droplets. As the spraying pressure is increased and/or nozzle orifice size is decreased, the spray is broken up

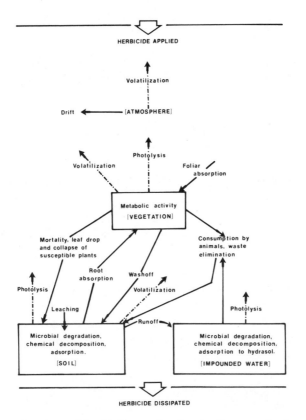

HERBICIDE APPLIED

Volatilization

Drift ← [ATMOSPHERE]

Photolysis

Volatilization | Foliar absorption

Metabolic activity
[VEGETATION]

Mortality, leaf drop and collapse of susceptible plants | Consumption by animals, waste elimination

Photolysis | Root absorption | Washoff | Volatilization | Photolysis

Leaching | Runoff

Microbial degradation, chemical decomposition, adsorption.
[SOIL]

Microbial degradation, chemical decomposition, adsorption to hydrasol.
[IMPOUNDED WATER]

HERBICIDE DISSIPATED

6.1. From the time of herbicide application to the rangeland ecosystem until it is dissipated, it is subjected to a great number of reactions and environmental forces (244).

into smaller and smaller particles which are increasingly susceptible to drift.

As spray droplets fall through the atmosphere, they become increasingly smaller until they contact a plant or soil surface or until they are completely evaporated. Thus, the height above ground at which sprays are released is extremely important in determining spray displacement. Obviously the potential for spray drift is greater from aerial application than from ground spraying under the same environmental conditions. In still air at 68° F and 80 percent relative humidity, a water droplet 50 microns[3] in diameter has a lifetime of 12.5 seconds and a potential fall distance of 5 inches (326). The same

[3] A table for conversion from metric to English units is given in Appendix B.

droplet subjected to 86° F and 50 percent relative humidity has a lifetime of only 3.5 seconds and a fall distance of only 1.25 inches. As droplet size increases, so does lifetime and potential fall distance in the atmosphere. In contrast to the smaller drop, a water drop 200 microns in diameter may last for 200 seconds and fall 268 feet through still air at 68° F and 80 percent relative humidity. Increasing the air temperature to 86° F and reducing the relative humidity to 50 percent decreases the lifetime of the 200-micron droplet to 56 seconds and the fall distance to 69 feet.

Extent of displacement is a function of droplet size and wind speed. A 400-micron droplet (coarse) has potential for lateral displacement of 8.5 feet while dropping 10 feet in a 3-mile-per-hour wind (326). Under the same conditions, a 50-micron droplet may be moved laterally 178 feet, while a 10-micron drop may be displaced as much as 0.84 mile. Obviously, as wind speed is increased, the potential for lateral displacement increases, and since sprays are composed of a broad spectrum of drop sizes, from very small to coarse, some displacement will occur even under low wind speeds.

Safe conditions for spraying have been determined based on the long-term experience of applicators and researchers. In general, 10-mile-per-hour winds at ground level are considered maximum for the aerial application of sprays. Susceptible species such as cotton, vegetables, and certain ornamentals respond to small quantities of hormone herbicides (Fig. 6.2). Sprays should not be applied when the air temperature is 90° F or higher, wind speed is 10 miles per hour or more, and relative humidity is 30 percent or less. The safe distance of crops from spray operations using hormone herbicides is assessed by considering herbicide formulation, air temperature, and wind and then exercising common sense. As a general rule, when the wind velocity is 0 to 3 miles per hour, susceptible crops should be no closer to the spray operation than 1 mile downwind and 0.5 mile upwind. When the wind speed is 4 to 6 miles per hour, susceptible crops should be no closer than 2 miles downwind and 0.2 mile upwind from the spray operation. When spraying in a 7- to 10-mile-per-hour wind, the crops should be no closer than 4 miles downwind and 250 feet upwind of the chemical application.

As the herbicide travels through the atmosphere, and as it is exposed to the air after deposition on environmental surfaces, it is

6.2. Symptoms of 2,4-D damage on tomatoes at various distances (feet) away from a sprayer applying 1 pound per acre of the herbicide in a 3- to 5-mile-per-hour wind.

subject to volatilization. Volatilization is the tendency of a liquid to vaporize or turn to a gas. This tendency is directly related to the vapor pressure of a chemical—that pressure exerted when a solid or liquid is in equilibrium with its own vapor—a function of the substance and of the temperature. Herbicide vapors may escape the target area and damage susceptible crops (damage from vapors can actually exceed that from physical drift) or simply reduce herbicide effectiveness by reducing the amount of chemical at the target area. According to the Weed Science Society, a volatile herbicide is one "having sufficiently high vapor pressure that, when applied at normal rates and normal temperatures, its vapors may cause serious irreversible injury to desirable plants away from the site of application" (133). Vapor injury and injury from herbicide spray drift are often impossible to differentiate.

A herbicide's formulation strongly affects its volatility. The acid and salt formulations have very little tendency to volatilize (acids are generally more volatile than salts) whereas certain esters are highly volatile. Generally in esters the longer the carbon side chain, the lower the volatility. Esters with five carbon atoms or fewer in the side chain are highly volatile. The isopropyl ester (see chapter 5) and the butyl ester of 2,4-D are in this category. Low-volatility esters include the 2-(butoxy)ethyl esters (see chapter 5), the propylene glycol butyl ether esters, and similar structures with long side chains.

Ester formulations of hormone herbicides should not be applied when the air temperature is 90° F or higher. Aerosal particles (droplets 2 microns in diameter) can be displaced 29 miles while falling only 10 feet in a 3-mile-per-hour wind (326), so the potential movement of herbicide vapors is tremendous.

Specific chemical activity also greatly affects the extent of damage from volatilization and may override the influence of formulation. For example, although salts do not volatilize readily (in fact, they are considered nonvolatile by many), small amounts of vapors from the potassium salt of picloram, because of its increased properties of growth regulation, are more toxic to susceptible broad-leaved plants than are the greater amounts of vapors from the propylene glycol butyl ether esters of 2,4-D or the dimethylamine salt of dicamba (100).

The potential overall atmospheric levels of herbicides and their broad-scale effects on various ecosystems are not well defined. However, air samples obtained near Pullman, Washington, over a 106-day period (May–August) contained detectable and identifiable 2,4-D esters on more than 80 percent of the days sampled. The concentrations ranged from 0.001 to 0.28 milligrams per cubic meter of air during the sampling period (1).

Loss by Photodecomposition

Once the herbicide has traveled through the atmosphere, it must come into contact with, and remain for some time on, surfaces in the ecosystem—plants, soils, water, and animals. After coming to rest on those surfaces, some herbicides are susceptible to photolysis—decomposition by light (photodecomposition).

Picloram is highly susceptible to photodecomposition. The picloram molecule is rapidly broken down by ultraviolet light, which releases two chlorine ions and cleaves the ring structure, eliminating the molecule's phytotoxicity (119). Breakdown is slower by sunlight than by continuous ultraviolet light, but photolysis is an important means of picloram loss in natural systems.

Photodecomposition of phenoxy herbicides is probably a minor means of their loss from range ecosystems. Although photolysis occurs on phenoxy herbicides, it is much less important than other forces of degradation such as microbial decomposition. Photodecomposition of dicamba is also considered to be a relatively minor source of loss, although it has been noted in experimental systems (282). The rate of loss of dicamba from water was increased by a factor of 2.3 when exposed to artificial lighting plus the natural light that penetrated a greenhouse compared to the amount degraded in the dark. The loss was interrelated with microbial breakdown, which could have been enforced by the introduction of pond sediment.

The role of light in the loss of AMS is considered minor. However, paraquat, thought to have only a short-term residual life, is susceptible to photodecomposition.

Herbicide Persistence in Plants

Once absorbed by plants, herbicides applied for range improvement persist for varying lengths of time depending on species and weather (growth) conditions. There is some concern about the persistence of herbicides in forage and their possible transfer through grazing animals to man. Within 30 minutes after the application of 2,4-D esters at 2 pounds per acre, most 2,4-D in or on the forage is hydrolyzed from the butyl esters to the acid form (166). In one study, milk from cows grazing on treated pastures contained from 0.01 to 0.09 parts per million of 2,4-D the second day after the pastures were sprayed. By four days after spraying, residues in milk were below the limits of the detection method used. On native range the esters of 2,4-D, 2,4,5-T, and dicamba in silver beardgrass, little bluestem, Dallisgrass, and sideoats grama are rapidly hydrolyzed to the acid by the grasses (214). The apparent average half-life of various herbicides in the grasses is about two weeks. However, disappearance of the three compounds is slower in sideoats grama than in the other species. Rainfall is important in accelerating dissipation of the herbicides from native forages. This dissipation can be attributed to leaching of the herbicides from dry forages and metabolic activity from renewed growth in established grasses (Fig. 6.1).

Loss rates of picloram from grasses following application of 0.25 pound per acre to northwestern Texas rangeland may be 2.5 to 3 percent per day for thirty days (278). On the average, nearly 90 percent of the herbicide may be dissipated from the range grasses by ten to thirteen days after application. Initial rate of loss varies somewhat among locations, but the amount detected from twenty-three to seventy-two days after application is usually less than 5 percent of the initial concentration. By four months after application, over 99 percent of the picloram may be dissipated from the grass tissues. After application of 0.5 to 2 pounds per acre, picloram may persist in grass tissues for eight to sixteen weeks (101). In general, picloram is considerably more persistent in forage than is 2,4-D, 2,4,5-T, or dicamba.

Residues of picloram in native grasses following application of the pellet formulation follow a different pattern from that of sprays. The pellets must be dissolved, moved into the soil solution, and taken up by the grasses before detectable amounts occur in the foliage. For example, the highest concentrations of picloram from high rates of sprays (4 pounds per acre) may occur in grass foliage within two weeks after treatment (181). In contrast, the highest concentrations of residues in the grass foliage following application of the same rate of picloram pellets may not occur for eight weeks or longer after application of the herbicide and may be half the maximum amount detected after application of the sprays. Typically, there are no residues detected in grass tissues until the first rainfall following application of the pellets. Residue concentration then gradually increases to maximum in the foliage, followed by a gradual decline, with the maximum concentration attained depending on application rate (181). The extent of the time lag from application to uptake is evidently dependent upon timeliness of rainfall and soil characteristics, and the total amount of picloram taken up by grasses from pellet applications is probably dependent on the amount of rainfall received. When rainfall is received within two weeks after application of the pellets, the concentration after sixteen weeks may be reduced to 2 parts per million or less, a level comparable to that resulting from application of the same rate of the spray.

Herbicide Persistence in Soil

Too often the wrong connotation is attached to the term *residue*. The misconception that residues are solely detrimental has become widespread among the general public. Without the presence of active herbicide in the soil, preemergence applications of herbicides would not provide weed control. Therefore, soil residues of certain herbicides are necessary for weed control in row crops. Residues of herbicides are also considered beneficial in certain instances for brush management. There must be residual activity of pelleted herbicides for root uptake and ultimate control of the woody plants. Ideally, the herbicides would persist long enough to control the target species, then dissipate completely and quickly. Besides photodecomposition, discussed above, primary factors which affect the length of residual activity of herbicides in soil are (1) microbial decomposition, (2) chemical decomposition, (3) adsorption on the soil colloids, (4) leaching, (5) volatility, and (6) surface movement or runoff.

MICROBIAL DECOMPOSITION

There are no documented cases of herbicides, at normal rates under field conditions, significantly reducing microbial growth. On the contrary, detoxification of herbicides by microorganisms is a method of regulating the persistence of many herbicides in the soil (Table 6.1). Herbicides such as 2,4-D which are susceptible to microbial decomposition would be unlikely to persist into the succeeding year even at extremely high rates, 10 pounds per acre or higher (314). Other herbicides such as picloram, which is degraded only slowly by microorganisms, may persist for a year after application rates of 1 pound per acre (depending on weather and soil conditions).

Soil factors critical to the rate of microbial activity are usually temperature, moisture content, and acidity or alkalinity (pH). The generalized optimum temperature for microbial activity is 80° to 90° F. Optimum soil moisture content for degradation of herbicide by microbes is 50 to 100 percent of field capacity (300). Effect of soil acidity or alkalinity depends on the particular herbicides and microbes involved, and the soil reaction regulates the type of microorganisms present. Bacteria and actinomycetes are favored by medium to high pH (alkaline soil), whereas fungi tolerate a range in soil pH.

There are some indications that microbial populations "adapt" to certain herbicides (314). This adaptation occurs evidently through changes in enzymatic constituents of the microbes or through mutation. There are also indications that populations of microbes attack certain herbicide molecules and use the carbon as their energy source,

TABLE 6.1.
Microbial Degradation of Herbicides (adapted from 133).

Herbicide	Mode of Microbial Degradation
Amitrole	Microbially degraded in two to three weeks in moist, warm soil.
AMS	Strains of *Aureobasidium pullulans, Aphalosporium acremonium,* and two unidentified *Achromobacter* and *Flavobacterium* species used sulfamic acid as a nitrogen source. After application of 3 pounds of herbicide per 1,000 square feet, phytoxicity disappeared in six to eight weeks.
Dicamba	Most evidence suggests microbial degradation.*
MCPA	Microbial detoxification probably via hydroxylation; persists up to one month under moist conditions, up to six months under drier conditions.
Paraquat	Rapidly and completely inactivated by complexing with clay fraction; may be subject to attack by microorganisms which are capable of extracting tightly bound elements from soil.
Picloram	Degradation by soil microorganisms proceeds slowly; rate of disappearance depends on conditions (most rapid under warm, moist conditions).
Silvex	Microbial degradation proceeds somewhat more slowly than for 2,4-D, but no buildup occurs from annual applications.
2,4-D	Microbially degraded; generally persists for one to four weeks in warm, moist soil.
2,4,5-T	Same as for silvex.

* Data from Scifres and Allen (281).

a concept that has been substantiated by growth curves of microbial populations in herbicide-treated soils. Any factor that restricts growth of microbial populations retards breakdown of the herbicides. Cool, dry, poorly aerated soils are more likely to retain herbicide levels longer than those under more temperate conditions.

Adaptive microbial decomposition of herbicides follows a characteristic pattern. The curve is composed of three distinct phases—a lag phase, a rapid decomposition phase, and a slow decomposition phase. During the lag phase the populations of microbes capable of decomposing the herbicide increase in numbers. This phase is completed nearly twenty times more rapidly for 2,4-D than for 2,4,5-T, accounting for the longer residual time of the latter. The rapid decomposition phase reflects activity of the increased population of microbes capable of degrading the herbicides. Whereas the lag phase for 2,4-D may require ten to fifteen days, the rapid decomposition phase may be completed in a relatively short time, a matter of hours. During the slow decomposition phase, a reduced amount of herbicide is available to the microbial population compared to earlier phases of decomposition. The slow decomposition phase lasts until the herbicide is depleted as a carbon source for the microorganisms. Not all herbicides degraded by microorganisms require an "adapted" population. In these cases there is no lag phase, and degradation proceeds at a rate depending on relative availability of the herbicide to the microbial population and relative activity of the microorganisms.

Dicamba, although more persistent than phenoxy herbicides, is evidently also degraded by microorganisms (Table 6.1). Apparently the triphasic or adaptive pattern is not applicable to degradation of dicamba.

Susceptible species, especially seedlings, may be damaged by only small amounts of hormone herbicides in soils. Field beans, soybeans, sunflowers, and cucumbers may show symptoms of phytoxicity from 5 parts per billion or less of picloram in soils (280). Typical symptoms of such crops when 5 parts per billion or less of picloram are present in the soil include curvature of true-leaf petioles, epinastic cotyledons, and slight curvature of hypocotyls and epicotyls. At 10 parts per billion of picloram in the soil, susceptible crops may demonstrate severe epinasty, leaf cupping, chlorosis, unexpanded or barely exserted true leaves, severe thickening of all plant parts, and severe height reduction (280). When 100 parts per billion of picloram are present in the soil, seedling emergence may be greatly reduced or delayed, emerged organs may be severely thickened and extremely turgid, and some plant parts may be necrotic.

ADSORPTION

Adsorption, which is the attachment of the herbicide molecule to clay particles or organic matter, is related to the potential for herbicide leaching and is influential in determining the herbicide rate required for brush control, especially with soil-active herbicides. Much literature is available relating sophisticated studies of adsorption phenomena, but for the purposes of this discussion, the importance of the process, without detailed discussion of the mechanics, is of main interest.

Most herbicides, if not all, are subject to deactivation (tie-up) by being adsorbed by clay particles, but the relative importance of such tie-up varies among herbicides. Paraquat, an example of one extreme, is such a strong cation that it is immediately and totally deactivated upon contact with the soil. The paraquat ions are held so tightly that they cannot be extracted by plant roots. Conversely, picloram sorption by soils may be more closely related to organic matter in the soils, pH as it affects ionic form (acid or salt), and the presence of hydrated metal oxides than to clay content. Substituted urea herbicide activity, on the other hand, can usually be directly related to clay content of soils. However, the following generalization is possible.

The greater the clay and organic matter content of soils, the shorter the residual life of detectable amounts of most herbicides (obviously, microbial activity is also enhanced in soils containing relatively high amounts of clay as opposed to sands, which may enhance rate of dissipation). Because of this relationship, application rates of soil-applied herbicides for equivalent levels of brush control usually must be higher on clays than on sandy soils (see also discussion of tebuthiuron activity, chapter 5).

LEACHING

Once the herbicide falls on the soil surface, it may be dissipated before entering the soil or it may be leached into the soil by rainfall. Movement into the soil is more likely to occur than complete degradation on the soil surface. The rate of leaching depends on soil texture, herbicide solubility, and the relative affinity of the herbicide for the soil complex.

Water solubility is probably the most influential factor regulating potential infiltration of the soil. The degree of water solubility depends to a great extent on the formulations of herbicide applied (Table 6.2). Picloram as the salt formulation is highly soluble in water (40 parts per 100 parts of water, by weight) and can be expected to move with the wetting front in soils. The degree and rate of movement are dictated by explicit characteristics of the vegetation and soil and the rate of picloram applied. Generally, when 0.5 pound per acre or less is applied to rangeland, especially rangeland with heavy-textured soils,

TABLE 6.2.

Water Solubility of Several Herbicides Used for Brush Management
(adapted from 133).

Herbicide	Temperature (°F)	Solubility (parts per 100 parts water, by weight)
AMS	77	68.40
Dicamba dimethylamine salt	—	72.00
MCPA acid*	—	essentially insoluble
Paraquat	68	completely soluble
Picloram acid*	77	0.043
Silvex acid*	77	0.018
2,4-D acid	77	0.09
2,4-D dimethylamine salt	68	300.00·
2,4-D 2-(butoxy)ethyl ester	—	essentially insoluble
2,4,5-T acid*	77	0.0238

* As illustrated for 2,4-D, amines and salts are water soluble and esters are essentially insoluble.

downward movement of the herbicide is much less than that which occurs where higher rates are applied to highly permeable sandy soils (273). In fine sandy soils, detectable residues are rarely moved deeper than 12 inches following the application of only 0.25 pound per acre to rangeland in North and West Texas (276). Subsurface lateral movement is also dependent on the direction and rate of soil water flow. Subsurface lateral movement, however, is apparently of less importance than vertical mobility in the soil profile. Once picloram is moved to the cool lower portion of the soil where it is protected from light, degradation proceeds at a relatively slow rate.

Dicamba is more readily adsorbed by clay than by sands (45), and it dissipates more rapidly from acidic than from basic soils (56). Dicamba phytoxicity in soil is less at temperatures of 70° F than at 80° or 90° F (45). Based on experimental results over an eight-week period at 95° F and 0, 33, 75, and 100 percent relative humidity, very little dicamba is lost to volatilization (45). Dicamba dissipates more rapidly as soil temperature is increased from 60° to 95° F (118).

Extent of dicamba leaching within a given soil is highly dependent on the length of time from application to first rainfall (97). The herbicide movement with the wetting front in the soil includes an upward movement with subirrigation (124). Dicamba is more persistent than 2,4-D in soil, but general conditions of degradation are evidently similar for the two herbicides (281). For example, in loams and sandy loams, 1 pound per acre of 2,4-D may dissipate after two weeks, whereas dicamba at 0.5 pound per acre may persist for six to eight weeks. Dicamba phytotoxicity is rapidly reduced in soils with a high content of organic matter compared to sandy soils (73).

Dissipation of dicamba is complete by one month after application of 0.25 pound per acre, and within two months after 0.5 pound per acre is sprayed on grassland soils of Texas (281). Dicamba residues in the soil are usually no deeper than 48 inches and only rarely deeper than 60 inches regardless of the time from application of the sprays to the recovery of soil samples. However, dicamba residues at 12 to 28 inches deep may persist a year after application of granules at 1.75 to 2 pounds per acre to semiarid grasslands. Dicamba sprays are usually applied at 1 pound per acre or less for grassland restoration in Texas. Thus, it is unlikely that residues will persist in the soil for the duration of the growing season after spring application.

Because of their high water solubility, salts of phenoxy herbicides leach readily through porous, sandy soils. In soils with high organic content, most phenoxy herbicides are rapidly adsorbed, thus reducing movement through the soil. The tendency of ester formulations to leach through soil is reduced by their lower water solubility. Once phenoxy herbicides are adsorbed by soils, they resist leaching and usually degrade completely without further vertical movement.

Movement of phenoxy herbicides also varies among the chemicals. After application of the herbicides to silty clay loam and the addition of enough water to move the wetting front 22 inches deep, an amine salt of 2,4-D was leached to 15 inches, and amine salts of 2,4,5-T and silvex leached to approximately 9 inches (327). Esters of 2,4-D, 2,4,5-T, and silvex remained in the top 3 inches of soil.

SURFACE MOVEMENT

After contacting plant and soil surfaces, any free herbicide, depending on its solubility in water, may move from the soil surface to impounded water supplies. Amine formulations of 2,4-D are usually moved into the soil with first moisture contact (13). The ester formulation will be washed off the soil surface in greater quantities than will the amine, especially if the soil receives a large amount of rainfall immediately following application. Probability of runoff depends on the time between herbicide application and the first rainfall, the intensity of rainfall, the slope of the land, the soil texture, the herbicide rate applied, and the extent of vegetation cover. Since these factors occur in virtually all possible combinations, probabilities of herbicide runoff must be considered case by case.

Unless rainfall occurs almost immediately after the application of picloram, appreciable quantities will not be washed from rangeland. For example, in one experiment in the Rolling Plains, rainfall the first few days following application of the herbicide at 0.5 pound per acre resulted in only 17 parts per billion of detectable residue of picloram in surface runoff from a 3 percent slope with a good cover of native grasses (278). Rainfall after twenty or thirty days resulted in less than 1 part per billion of picloram residue in the runoff water. Presumably more picloram was available on the soil surface soon after treatment than at later dates because of losses to photodecomposition.

In another study, picloram loss in runoff water from small plots within twenty-four hours after application was greater from sod than from fallow plots. Four months after application, picloram losses averaged less than 1 percent of that lost twenty-four hours after application. The maximum loss of picloram, dicamba, or 2,4,5-T in runoff was 5.5 percent of the amount applied, and the average was approximately 3 percent (305).

Available evidence suggests that the probability of surface movement after the application of a pellet formulation may be somewhat higher than after application of equivalent rates of sprays. Monitoring of picloram residues in soils after the application of 2 or 4 pounds of pellets per acre to a 3 to 4 percent slope near Mertzon, Texas, indicated that the residue tended to accumulate at the lower end of the slope. The surface was sparsely vegetated, and gravel outcrops were common. It is suspected that most of the downslope movement was in the form of dissolved herbicide rather than from physical movement of the pellets (24). Most pellets tend to immediately dissolve at first contact with moisture, reducing the probability of movement of the pellets.

After use of sprays, no significant increases in picloram concentrations usually occur at the lower ends of slopes of less than 3 percent when no more than 0.25 pound of the herbicide is applied per acre (24). As the slope is increased to greater than 3 percent, and if 0.5 pound or more of herbicide per acre is applied, the probability of detectable herbicide residues in runoff is increased.

Herbicide Persistence in Impounded Range Water

There is little probability of significant amounts of herbicide being washed into impounded water after standard spraying operations. However, the cumulative amounts of herbicide in range water from overspray and from minor amounts of runoff can result in detectable amounts of residues in ponds. In general, the forces operable in the degradation of herbicides in soils, especially microbial degradation, also function in impounded water. Also, photolysis is important in the loss of some herbicides from surface water.

Generally, phenoxy herbicides dissipate relatively rapidly from impounded water. For example, silvex residues were not detectable three weeks after ponds were sprayed with the equivalent of 8 pounds per acre of the herbicide (11). Based on relative persistence in soil, 2,4-D or 2,4,5-T applied at the same rate would probably be eliminated from pond water more rapidly than silvex.

Picloram is usually dissipated from impounded natural water sources within one month to six weeks after its introduction (116). However, low concentrations, 1 or 2 parts per billion, may be detectable a year after application of 1 pound per acre to pond surfaces. Undoubtedly photolysis is a most important factor in the dissipation of picloram from impounded water. In the photolysis process, certain light energy levels are required for the degradation of each picloram molecule. Since light energy is randomly dispersed, the interception of a photon of light by a picloram molecule would be a random occurrence. Therefore, degradation of picloram proceeds rapidly shortly after its introduction and slows as the concentration in the water is reduced. Such a system is said to be concentration-dependent—the dissipation rate depends on the herbicide concentration. Residue levels of herbicides which dissipate in such a manner vary considerably in ponds as water level fluctuates. As the water level lowers, the herbicide is concentrated; as the level rises, it is diluted.

Dicamba is highly susceptible to microbial degradation in ponds (281). Pond sediment evidently contains microbial populations capable of degrading dicamba at a rate which depends on temperature. Under the warm conditions of late spring and summer, dicamba dissipates from ponds of East Texas within forty days, even after the equivalent of roughly 4 pounds per acre is applied to the pond surfaces (281). The rate of loss is the same whether dicamba is sprayed into a clear, vegetated pond or into a new, turbid body of water. Under laboratory conditions, exposure of simulated ponds to light increased the rate of loss compared to dark conditions. Whether or not extent of light penetration into the water influences degradation is unknown. Perhaps the influence of photolysis is exerted primarily at the immediate water surface and depends on continual turnover to maintain some herbicide in the surface water. Most rapid degradation of dicamba depends on microbe-rich sediment and light.

Herbicide Toxicology and Safety Factors

The expanding use of all agricultural chemicals has stimulated an awareness of the need for an adequate safety margin in the broad-scale application of herbicides. Thus, herbicides must not only be tested for effectiveness but must be established as safe for broadscale use. Increasing emphasis is being placed on the use of chemicals with short residual lives, especially those which are biodegraded. As a group, herbicides have relatively low toxicities to mammals (Table 6.3). However, this does not mean that persons who handle herbicides should be any less careful than when working with other pesticides. Moreover, toxicological data are developed from tests on laboratory animals and it cannot necessarily be assumed that humans would not be more sensitive to the chemical than the test animals. Perhaps the safest assumption is that the herbicides are *at least if not more toxic* to man as to the test animals.

The Swedish veterinarian Erne studied distribution of 2,4-D as the soluble salts after administering single oral doses of 50 to 100 milligrams per kilogram of body weight to calves, pigs, rats, and chickens. The herbicide concentrations in the plasma rose to a peak within two to seven hours and then declined to insignificant levels over a few days. The half-lives of 2,4-D in the plasma ranged between three and

TABLE 6.3.
Acute Oral Toxicity of Several Herbicides (adapted from 133).

Herbicide	Acute oral toxicity	
	Lethal dose (LD_{50}, mg/kg)	Test animals
AMS	3,900	Rats
Dicamba	2900 ± 800	Rats
MCPA	700	Rats
Paraquat	120	Rats
Picloram	8,200	Rats
Silvex	650	Rats
2,4-D	100–300	Rats, guinea pigs, rabbits
2,4,5-T	100	Dogs

twelve hours, depending on species. The 2,4-D was distributed fairly evenly through the body water, the highest levels being in the ovaries, adrenals, and lungs, with relatively low levels in the brain. The average half-lives of 2,4-D in the tissues ranged between five and thirty hours. Repeated administration of subtoxic doses did not lead to excessive accumulation of phenoxy acids in the tissues studied (84). The major pathway of elimination of 2,4-D is excretion through the kidneys. Steers fed 2,4-D eliminated the herbicide as the intact compound in the urine (179). The following was the opinion of Leng (177) concerning residues of 2,4-D, 2,4,5-T, silvex, and MCPA:

Residues of phenoxy compounds and of their respective phenolic moieties are not likely to occur in milk, meat, fat, or meat by-products of cattle and sheep from agricultural use of these herbicides. Such residues would occur only under the unlikely circumstances when the animals are milked or slaughtered while actually ingesting freshly treated forage in pasture or rangeland treated at high rates of application. This conclusion is based on practical consideration of treatment rates, of dissipation of residues in forage and tissues, and/or grazing restrictions on current labeling for these herbicides.

No harmful effect is likely to occur in livestock grazing areas treated with phenoxy herbicides, even at exaggerated rates of application.

As pointed out previously, formulation completely changes the physical properties of herbicides such as 2,4-D. Also, toxicological reactions vary with species. Therefore, only generalizations concerning toxicological reactions are possible. As body tolerances for these materials vary, so do the symptoms from various dosages. For example, Erne (84) detected no clinical changes in rats fed from 100 to 200 milligrams per kilogram of various 2,4-D formulations. On the other hand, calves fed the same levels showed such clinical effects as transient dysphagia (difficulty in swallowing), bloating, thirst, and muscular weakness.

Research has shown that 2,4,5-T ingested by livestock is excreted in the urine, usually within seven days. Palmer and Radeleff (221) concluded that application rates of 2,4,5-T commonly used (0.5 to 4.5 pounds per acre) would not be hazardous to cattle, sheep, or chickens. This report was consistent with the conclusions of Rowe and Hymas (237) that 2,4-D and 2,4,5-T have low chronic toxicity and of others (212, 218) that the present patterns of use of conventional herbicides do not present an environmental hazard.

The discussion of herbicide toxicology is based on my interpretation of research which presumably dealt with pure active ingredient. At the time of this writing, there is intense public controversy concerning the safety of herbicides 2,4,5-T and silvex, with the possibility that registration for some or all of their current uses may be cancelled. Although the active ingredients of these compounds are being closely scrutinized, greatest concern is focused on contamination of the formulated chemicals by a representative of a family of chemicals called dioxins. Dioxin is apparently an inevitable by-product of the manufacturing process of 2,4,5-T and silvex, and it is highly toxic. However, there is a line of argument that contends that the level of dioxin in commercial 2,4,5-T and silvex is so low that it does not pose a hazard to man and other animals in the ecosystem under normal patterns of use. Regardless of the final resolution of this controversy, its existence emphasizes that public attitudes concerning herbicide safety are changing as additional research information is being accrued, and that common sense and routine safety precautions should be exercised in the use and handling of herbicides as with any agricultural chemical.

Another herbicide that has raised concern is paraquat. In the case of paraquat, however, the concern is about the active ingredient rather than a contaminant, as is the case with the phenoxy herbicides.

7

Brush Management by Burning

IT is generally accepted as basic to the art and science of range management that climax vegetation is the result of a given environment and that vegetation of any given area is in approximate balance with the soil, weather, and biological factors (including man during the last few thousand years). The influence of rainfall, temperature, and edaphic factors and their interrelationships with biological factors such as grazing animals are invariably considered in developing the management logic for any given unit of rangeland. In short, natural vegetation is managed on the premise that the roles of all the natural factors which contribute to its form and function are understood. From that premise is developed the goal of manipulating certain of those factors to assure maximum productivity. But fire, a natural factor of critical influence, has been either ignored or largely overlooked as having been associated with the development and maintenance of natural grasslands (229). Instead of acknowledging the potential of fire in the improvement of rangelands, man has worked zealously to develop substitutes for the role of fire with only partial success.

Grasslands of the world have evolved under the influence of fire (239). Lightning is a universal cause of range fires, and early man's use of fire on rangeland as a tool for the manipulation of both domesticated animals and wildlife as they responded to desirable changes in the rangeland after burning is well documented (156). Since fire was an integral part of pristine ecosystems, the distribution of most of present-day native range plants has been influenced by fire.

Repeated burnings have perpetuated fire-modified vegetation types dominated by grasses and called fire climaxes. These grasslands, responding to the influence of fire, have been maintained over long periods at the expense of forests (62). Indeed, one line of thought proposes that fire is more important even than climate in maintaining grasslands (129) on the basis that repeated burnings for tens of thousands of years have resulted in "fire-dependent" plant communities (215). Moreover, according to this theory, elimination of fire has been responsible for the establishment of forests and woodlands in the place of grasslands. This theory is commonly espoused by those who believe that the reduced role of fire on Texas grasslands is one of the primary factors accounting for the increase in the density and stature of brush. Evidence continues to accumulate that bestows a great deal of credence to this point of view (17). In the absence of fire, and under continual overgrazing, woody plants have spread from the draws and waterways to the uplands (35), converting open grasslands and savannahs to shrublands and thickets.

Most of the activities of agriculture, industry, and commerce by necessity upset natural laws (50). Initial disturbance of the natural balance in the ecosystem occurred with settlement, and this disturbance has continually expanded as man has become dominant in the world ecosystem. Many changes in the natural balance were necessary for man's success, and with the proper application of knowledge natural laws can be violated to the benefit of man on a long-term basis. However, complete disregard for natural laws can result in major undesirable short- and long-term changes and waste of great proportions. Such disregard has been shown in the elimination of the influence of fire, largely because of fear and misunderstanding.

In this country at about the turn of the century an attitude of "good conservation" caused condemnation of fire by many agriculturalists, and that attitude was readily accepted by the general public (62). Thus, whereas early in man's history fire was used to sustain life, there has recently been a brief period in which its influence has been limited, ostensibly for the same reason. This paradox has emerged as a result of the obvious—the disastrous effects of uncontrollable wildfires on our ever-dwindling natural resources. Coupled with the cessation of natural burning, the disturbance or misuse of the existing native vegetation has allowed extensive deterioration of grassland communties. The desirable species are either absent, have been replaced by undesirable species, or have been seriously reduced.

Studies in the Southwest have shown that when burning is artificially returned to the ecosystem and coupled with sound grazing management, the desirable range species return more rapidly than when either procedure is applied alone. The influence of the grazing animal on grassland is natural, and the prolonged absence of grazing is as unnatural as the omission of fire. Obviously both must be carefully manipulated to reinstate and maintain the integrity of rangeland.

Fire was considered a potentially effective tool for natural resource management by the late 1960's (215), and this renewed interest in the beneficial uses of fire has spurred considerable research activity during the last decade. For example, the Tall Timbers Research Station at Tallahassee, Florida, sponsored the first Tall Timbers Fire Ecology Conference in 1962 at Florida State University. That conference has been held annually since then as a professional forum for the role of fire in the management of forests, rangelands, and associated wildlife habitat.

Much is still to be learned concerning the proper application of burning for range improvement, but recent study has shown the general benefits of fire as a grassland management tool. Increased herbage yields, improved forage use (especially increased grazing of the less palatable grasses) by range animals, increased availability of forage, improved wildlife habitat, control of undesirable shrubs, formation of a mineral seedbed, and control of various parasites such as liver flukes (*Fasciola hepatica* and *F. magna*) have been cited as general advantages of burning (334). Removal of accumulated litter, promotion of wood borer activity on honey mesquite, control of cactus, and control of some less desirable broadleaf species such as common broomweed are specific benefits of burning (334). Consequently, the potential use of burning is becoming more widely recognized by Texas rangemen, and the application of fire is gradually being accepted by land managers as an integral part of their range management plans.

However, this shift in attitude from attacking and suppressing fire to one in which burning is viewed as necessary and desirable is not without resistance from the public. As G. H. Stankey has said, "The fear of fire is deep and not easily lost" (296). Many landowners still do not favor range burning because they identify any sort of fire with catastrophic wildfires. Such an attitude may be changed by the understanding that range fires may be effectively controlled and that the risk of their becoming wildfires can be virtually eliminated if they are properly applied.

Wildfires, normally originating by accident or by lightning, usually occur in dry years, but fires for range improvement are usually applied in wet years (334). Wildfires generally magnify drought conditions, but burnings for management are beneficial, since soil moisture conditions are adequate for the immediate initiation of plant growth. Wildfires generally occur after excessive amounts of highly combustible materials have accumulated; they are extremely difficult to control and are generally detrimental to the ecosystem, whereas properly applied burning usually results in relatively little, if any, permanent environmental damage. Wildfires may occur during the growing season when desirable range plants are susceptible to fire damage. Burning for range improvement may be scheduled for dormant periods to remove old, rough top growth which is of little value to grazing animals. Other benefits, such as promotion of nitrification, may result if fire is applied at the appropriate time. Thus, range burning may be approached logically so that the results are desirable and, in most cases, predictable.

Approaches to Range Burning

With increased knowledge of the behavior of fire and its proper application, range burning is emerging from a relatively haphazard affair requiring only fuel, wind, and a match to the careful application of fire on a prescribed basis. Fire applied for range improvement can be classified into three general approaches (315):

1. *Convenience burning.* Since only the time and place of the burn are considered in convenience burning, this is the worst possible approach to the use of fire for range improvement. An area is selected as "needing a good burn," and the fire is set. Unfortunately, the results of this approach too often persuade the landowner that burning is generally detrimental. Convenience burning increases the risk of wildfire, since control methods have been slighted, or it results in an ineffective, spotty burn, since weather and fuel conditions are inappropriate.
2. *Controlled burning.* In this approach, the application and confinement of the fire are carefully planned. Time, place, and fire control methods are considered. Although this method is more desirable than simple convenience burning, the potential maximum

benefits of fire from controlled burnings may not be achieved, since long-range objectives for the management unit may not be considered.

3. *Prescribed burning.* This application of fire is the most effective, since the burnings are systematically planned, with consideration given to periods when weather and vegetation favor particular methods of burning. All required fire control methods are employed in a well-designed fire plan. The application of fire is designed to maximize the benefits of other management practices such as the grazing system and brush control methods in an overall long-range management plan.

Range fires may be set as *headfires* or *backfires*. Simply compared, headfires spread with the wind, and backfires spread against the wind. Environmental conditions being equal, headfires move much more rapidly and generate more heat than do backfires. Flame heights from headfires are elevated, whereas backfires move close to the soil surface.

The strip headfire is a modification that is satisfactorily employed in areas where fuel is heavy or where an extreme fire hazard exists and the probability of losing control of the fire is significantly greater than it would be under optimum burning conditions. Strip firing allows a relatively large area to be burned in a continual series of small fires. As the name indicates, a series of headfires is spaced at regular intervals the length of the area to be burned. The spacing between fire lines varies from 20 to 120 feet, depending upon the wind and fuel conditions. Thus, a series of areas generally less than 120 feet wide is burned instead of the entire area at once. After the preceding headfire burns out, it leaves a backfire to burn into the next headfire.

A backfire is usually considered to be a safe fire once it has moved away from the point of ignition. It develops a relatively slow-moving fire front which is easy to control. However, an adequate fire barrier is required at the ignition line so that the vegetation downwind does not ignite and create a headfire. Also, it is advisable that well-developed fire guards be maintained around the periphery of the area to be burned with a backfire, since a shift in wind direction can create a headfire.

All other conditions considered equal, headfires are usually more damaging to broad-leaved herbaceous and woody plants than are backfires. Headfires are fanned by the wind, causing fuel to ignite well ahead of the fire front (123). The maximum temperature of a headfire occurs along the vertical profile of the fire front and more completely damages the aerial plant parts than does a backfire. Since the hottest part of the fire front is elevated well above the perennating buds of grass plants, desirable grasses are preserved and growth of many species of undesirable broad-leaved plants is suppressed by headfires.

Center firing is another burning technique used in most regions where burning is prominent. The fire is ignited in the center of the area to be burned. Once it has spread and generated adequate heat to ensure its momentum, other fires are ignited further away from the center. These fires are drawn toward the center by an indraft of air to the original fire. The center fire will seldom run toward the edge, because the high heat it generates, with the resulting indraft, acts as a stabilizer. Wind speeds of 8 to 10 miles per hour from all sides toward the center have been measured with center fires in California (8).

Generally a combined headfire and backfire are used for range burning in Texas. The entire periphery of the area is ignited at the same time, or nearly so, depending on the fire plan. This procedure, properly applied, creates safe burning conditions. Shortly after ignition, the fire is big enough to pull air from all sides toward the center and heat the standing fuel well ahead of the fire front.

Most burning is done during the daytime. However, night burning may be appropriate when cool fires are desired, and more particularly when hazardous amounts of fuel have accumulated. A suitable night would be characterized by clouds, relatively stable air temperature, a persistent wind, a relatively stable humidity, and the lack of dew formation (55).

Fuel Characteristics

The physical nature of grass fires can be characterized as a rather narrow zone of flames advancing across a finely divided and rather homogeneously dispersed fuel (62). Rate of spread of a grass fire quickly reaches maximum velocity. In the early stages of fire development, the weather, including surface and wind velocity, air temperature, and relative humidity, is the most influential factor in determining the direction and rate of spread. However, the amount and rate of heat generated by a fire also depend upon fuel characteristics, namely kind, amount, moisture content, coarseness, position, and arrangement.

The kind of fuel, volatile or nonvolatile, is critical in determining the characteristics of the fire (62). Volatile fuels contain relatively high amounts of ether extractives such as waxes, oils, terpenes, and fats (334). Grasses are generally considered nonvolatile (species such as Gulf cordgrass may be the exceptions [219]) whereas junipers, Macartney rose, and sagebrush are examples of volatile fuels, explosive by nature, which must be burned with a somewhat different fire plan than that used for nonvolatile fuels.

Size and arrangement of the fuel contributes directly to the nature of the fire. Fuel may be positioned on the ground or be aerial. In either position, coarseness, composition, and uniformity of distribution are important in regulating rate of fire spread, heat intensity, and heat duration. Within a given set of weather conditions, most rapidly moving fire fronts generally develop when large volumes of standing fine fuel, loosely arranged and continuous in distribution, are available. Oxygen and heat are necessary for fuel combustion. If the fuel is compacted and oxygen is limited, combustion will not occur readily. Temperature of ignition varies considerably with fuel size. Consequently, loosely arranged grass (fine fuel) is more easily ignited than coarse fuel (logs, limbs, and so on) which is tightly arranged.

Obviously, loosely arranged fuel must be continuous for spontaneous ignition to occur, so loose arrangement certainly should not be interpreted as scattered fuel. In certain cases, fuel too loosely arranged—aerial woody material, for example—can be compacted somewhat by crushing or mashing it to improve its continuity and facilitate a hot, even burn.

The moisture content of fuel influences the ignition temperature, the rate of burning, and the generation of heat during the fire. Within a given set of environmental parameters, rate of burning is usually inversely related to moisture content. Relative dryness of fine fuel is related to the ratio of green to dead plant material and to atmospheric moisture levels (108). In mature brush stands, rate of spread of the fire and its intensity depend primarily on the relative proportions of live and dead material (322). Relative humidity is important in regulating the moisture content of fuel, especially the dead, fine fuel (62). However, fine fuels may dry within a few hours after a shower, and effective burnings have been conducted in the Coastal Prairie over standing water after the standing dead fuel has dried (248).

The time required for fuel to come into equilibrium with environmental moisture varies with fuel particle size. Very fine fuels are essentially in constant equilibrium with the environment, whereas large particles require varying lengths of time to equilibrate with ambient moisture. The moisture content of green herbaceous (fine) fuels depends on their stage of growth, time into the growing season, and the availability of soil moisture as well as environmental parameters such as relative humidity (93). Above a certain critical level, moisture content delays the ignition time of fuels and may prevent effective burning. Once the fire front is moving at maximum speed, fuel particles well ahead of the fire front are heated, increasing their internal energy and aiding in ignition (94). A relative wide range of fuel moisture levels has been used in range burning, depending on other fuel characteristics, the weather, and the reason for the burning. In the Coastal Prairie, fuel moisture contents of 15 to 30 percent have been used successfully with wind speeds of 12 to 15 miles per hour (108). Other workers have reported a range of from 3 to 18 percent with an optimum of about 8 percent (55). In other cases, fuel moisture contents to 20 percent have been recommended (285).

Fuel load, as it functions to determine the rate and intensity of the fire, is important in determining the response of plants to burning. On the Coastal Prairie, fine fuel (defined in this case as those fuels with diameter less than or equal to 0.125 inch) load was more closely related to rate and intensity of burning than was the amount of coarse (diameter greater than 0.125 inch), widely spaced fuel (108). The minimal fuel load required for effective burning varies with location, the character of the fuel, and weather conditions. Generally at least 2,500 pounds of air-dried fine fuel per acre, evenly distributed, are required for maximum burning effectiveness on most Texas rangelands. Generation of an effective fire can be accomplished with lighter fuel loads by compensating with increased wind speed, reduced relative humidity, and increased air temperature. Maximum soil surface temperatures in fires in the Rolling and High Plains of Texas varied from 182° to 1,260° F for fuel loads that varied from 1,546 to 7,025 pounds per acre (298). Fires generating surface soil temperatures above 1,000° F apparently have potential for killing woody species such as honey mesquite (298). As the fuel load increases, a proportional increase in maximum temperature and duration of the maximum temperature above 150° F occurs. Maximum temperatures of 256° to 468° F have been predicted for the first 1,000 pounds of fine fuel per acre, with a 73° to 85° F increase per 1,000 pounds of additional fuel per acre (298). Thus, a fuel load of 5,000 pounds per acre may result in maximum temperatures of 550° to 806° F. Duration of temperatures above 150° F averages from about one minute for thin, light fuels such as buffalograss to five minutes for heavier fuels such as tobosa.

In a study on the Coastal Prairie, soil surface temperatures during burning ranged from 386° to 581° F with 2,860 to 3,125 pounds of relatively moist fine fuel per acre. At 6 inches above the soil, maximum temperatures ranged from 1,075° to 1,160° F. In this case a high percentage of the fine fuel load was afforded by species, such as little bluestem, which burn readily (248).

There is no quick and easy way to estimate fine fuel load. The most accurate approach is to actually cut and weigh samples from the area to be burned. Sampling frames, for example 2 feet square, can be constructed from relatively small rod (0.25 inch in diameter may be satisfactory). At regular intervals across the area to be burned the frame is dropped and all herbaceous vegetation within it is clipped to the ground. Care should be taken to obtain a representative sample; that is, all sites in the management unit to be burned should be sampled in proportion to the area they occupy within that unit. The samples should be air-dried for at least ninety-six hours and then weighed. Based on average sample weight, fuel load per acre can be estimated. The accuracy of the estimate increases as the number of samples is increased. With experience, the manager will be able to visually assess the fuel load, but there is no substitute for careful inspection of the area to be burned before implementing the fire plan.

In some cases fine fuel must be prepared, even generated, for an effective fire. In South Texas where the vegetation is shredded, roller chopped, root plowed, or root plowed and raked two years before the installation of burnings, canopy reduction of woody plants by fire is increased, compared to the reduction from burning alone (39). The increased effectiveness can be attributed to the uniform hot fires that occur following the mechanical treatments that release fuel to carry the fire. After the initial burning, subsequent characteristics of the rangeland for burning are related primarily to the donors of fine fuel— grasses and forbs. Where no mechanical pretreatment is used, low quantities of fuel and discontinuities in fuel load prevent a uniform hot fire (39).

Planning a Burning Program

Before planning a burning program, the land manager must answer four basic questions: Why burn? What to burn? When to burn? How to burn? By answering these questions, the use of burning can be justified based on consideration of alternative methods, and the areas, times, and methods of burning can be carefully selected.

PURPOSE OF BURNING

Since motive determines the approach, the land manager should have a well-defined reason for selecting fire as a management tool. Burning is not necessarily selected only for brush management. Even in areas where undesirable brush is not a problem and a good cover of grass exists, burning may be of benefit in livestock production. Fire may be used to stimulate early spring growth of grasses and remove the old growth. The blackened landscape allows sunlight to be directed to the plant crowns and the soil, warming the burned habitat earlier than unburned areas. Fire also removes rough plants, providing grazing animals with uniform early spring growth.

In considering burning an area infested with undesirable woody species, one must decide if burning will effectively control the undesirable species or if a better alternative is available. It may be that aerial spraying, a mechanical method, or a practice such as browsing with goats would be the first logical step to brush management, with burning applied as a subsequent practice.

The decision to burn for brush management may be based on the need for land reclamation or for the maintenance of improved range. A reclamation fire is an intense fire used to reclaim brush-infested areas. Such a fire is considered to be the most damaging and the hardest to control because, of necessity, it must be intensely hot.

The primary purpose of reclamation burning is to destroy or retard the growth of undesirable species which are usually present in large quantities. Certain detrimental effects on the desirable species may also be associated with this intensity of burning. A reclamation burning is relatively dangerous since it is the initial fire on an area, and accumulated fuel, control lines, and "hot spots" may be misjudged. In general, results from the first reclamation burning only partially achieve the potential response of the herbaceous vegetation. The first fire functions primarily to open the brush canopy, allowing development of more uniform fuel in adequate amounts for subsequent fires. Maximum benefits from reclamation burning are usually not achieved until after the second and perhaps even the third fire. In heavy South Texas mixed brush, at least three burnings have been required for reclamation. The burnings are usually not applied in consecutive years unless moisture conditions are highly favorable.

In contrast to reclamation burning, maintenance fires are "cool" fires used to maintain a desirable balance in the vegetation. Such a fire will generate sufficient heat to kill most undesirable hardwood seedlings. Since a maintenance burning follows reclamation burning, fire control problems are considerably less. Fire guards have already been established, tested, and corrected, and the accumulation of fuel is uniform and may be purposely damp. Maintenance burning is used to a certain extent in South Texas to suppress invasion of woody sprouts in fields of intensively managed grasses such as Bermudagrass or buffelgrass. The fire serves not only to reduce the influence of woody plants but also to rejuvenate the grass stands.

WHAT TO BURN

The area selected for burning must be a natural unit—an area of such size and shape that fire can be directed over it to remove the maximum amount of undesirable vegetation but where the fire can be controlled with minimum effort. Such an area is determined largely by the nature and combination of fuel types, prevailing local winds, topography, and natural barriers (8). Also, the area should be of sufficient size to discourage the congregation of wildlife and domestic livestock. Burning of relatively small areas of large management units invariably results in localized overgrazing. Burning is most effective when entire pastures are burned at such a time that grazing deferment can be easily scheduled into the management plan.

In selecting an area to burn, the present vegetation, the use of the area, the time required to obtain a protective cover, and the quantity and size of the undesirable species must be considered. On areas supporting heavy grass cover and scattered but relatively large undesirable woody species, the beneficial effects of burning might be outweighed by its detrimental effects if the goal is to kill the large trees. In general, the larger the woody plant, the higher the temperature needed for its control, and at some point the fire intensity required may be so great that the risk of bad effects on some of the desirable species will eliminate burning from the management plan.

The head of an arroyo on a steep slope heavily infested with brush may, at first consideration, meet the requirements for burning. However, the short-term results of removing the aerial portions of the undesirable species and the ground cover afforded by the herbaceous plants might introduce the risk of accelerated erosion of the arroyo.

Many natural grassland areas, however, are infested with brush that a fire may effectively suppress. Areas on which the brush cover is not so heavy that it would prevent adequate accumulation of fine fuel and the brush plants are not so large that they would be highly tolerant of the fire are ideal candidates for improvement by burning. Such areas are generally characterized by deep soils of moderate to high fertility and desirable water relationships. Areas of level to gently sloping topography which are not highly susceptible to water erosion are most desirable.

Physical features such as topography and slope exposure have a pronounced influence on fire behavior. In general, considering constant fuel loads, fires move faster upslope than on level ground because fuels just ahead of the fire front, at a higher level, are heated by convection to the ignition temperature. Fires move up a 10 percent slope about twice as fast as on the level, and they progress up a 20 percent slope about four times faster than on the level (62). They move most slowly downslope. The actual speed at which fire moves also depends on fuel coarseness. The slowest fires, theoretically, occur on the downslope with coarse fuels, and the most rapid upslope movement occurs when fine fuels are uniformly distributed in the path of the fire front.

The effects of slope exposure on the rate and direction of spread of a fire are manifested primarily by influencing fuel characteristics. Slope exposure functions in determining fuel moisture content and coarseness by determining species composition of the standing crop, origin of the fuel load, and mulch cover. The greater the mulch cover, the greater the level of heating during the burn. Slope exposure also influences soil temperature, soil moisture, and other factors which directly affect fire behavior and vegetation responses after burning.

WHEN TO BURN

In addition to fuel, three general criteria—the weather (before and during the burning), the season, and the time of day—must be evaluated in determining when to burn. Influence of each of these factors will vary depending upon the purpose of the fire.

Atmospheric conditions that must be considered when planning a fire include air temperature, wind direction and speed, and relative humidity and precipitation. These three facets of the weather regulate the "combustibility" of any given kind and amount of fuel.

Air temperature. High air temperature favors a high fire temperature and reduces the increase in temperature needed to reach the point of ignition, that temperature at which combustion takes place and burning proceeds without the addition of heat from an outside source. At high temperatures on a bright day the heat of radiation increases the fuel temperature. Hot, dry winds decrease fuel moisture content and, in conjunction with the heat of radiation, facilitate ignition. An air temperature of approximately 90° F is generally required for a reclamation burning which requires temperatures that will kill woody plants. This requirement can be compensated for, to some extent, by other factors such as soil and mulch moisture content. High air temperatures can result in a crown fire which, in turn, facilitates killing a higher percentage of the woody plants. Thus, summer burnings have been used more successfully as reclamation fires in South Texas mixed brush than have burnings at other seasons.

About 140° to 150° F (60° to 66° C) is usually considered the threshold temperature at which leaf tissue is killed. However, the critical temperature depends, in large part, on factors such as species, time of year, and weather (12). In calculating the intensity of fire required to damage a plant, threshold heating level for tissue damage is less important than the amount of heat required to raise the leaf temperature to the threshold temperature. For example, if the temperature of a leaf exposed to summer sun is about 95° F, then an increase of only 45° to 55° F is required to bring the tissue to the threshold level. The difference in initial temperatures probably partially explains why hot summer fires are more detrimental to vegetation than fires during cooler periods (123).

Low air temperatures are usually desirable for maintenance burning, since the purpose is to destroy seedlings and rough vegetation. Air temperatures ranging from 40° to 70° F have been adequate in several regions for maintenance burning.

Wind. The importance of wind speed with respect to fire control is obvious; wind is necessary to install an adequate burn. However, wind is the most treacherous environmental variable that must be considered in developing burning plans. Generally, the wind speed should be between 4 and 15 miles per hour, and it probably should never exceed 20 miles per hour. If wind speeds of about 4 miles per hour move a backfire about 1.5 feet per minute, the headfire may move about 17 feet per minute (66). Speed of the fire front increases as the wind velocity increases, fuel conditions being equal. For example, in one experiment with annual grasses furnishing the fuel, winds of 15 miles per hour moved headfires at 80 feet per minute and moved backfires at 6 feet per minute. At a wind velocity of 5 miles per hour, the speeds were 20 feet per minute and 1.2 feet per minute, respectively (191).

Specific wind velocity needed to satisfy the need for burning depends upon the purpose of the fire and other environmental conditions during it. Factors which often offset or compensate for each other in their effects on the properties of fire are important. For example, high wind velocity, by supplying oxygen to the fire, may compensate somewhat for an increased fuel moisture content, but it may also have a general cooling effect on the fire.

The higher the fuel moisture content, the greater the wind velocity that is required to drive the fire. For example, on the Coastal Prairie with wind speeds of 8 to 10 miles per hour, headfires moved at an average of 47 feet per minute when the relative humidity was 57 percent and the fuel moisture content was 13 percent. In the same area but with a relative humidity of 70 percent and fuel moisture content of 30 percent, the fire front moved about 25 feet per minute with a wind speed of 15 miles per hour (108).

Wind direction and its persistence from a particular direction are of utmost importance in burning. If a wind persists from a given direction for an eight-hour period or longer, burning is facilitated. However, variable and shifting winds, particularly those that shift ninety degrees or more in a matter of hours, complicate the burning effort. A simple shift in wind direction can change an easily controlled, cool fire into an uncontrollable hot fire that can cause great damage.

Obviously, wind activity is difficult to predict. However, certain general judgments are possible based on wind records from local weather stations. These records should indicate the most persistent wind direction for each month or season of the year. Before a fire is ignited, frequent contacts with the local weather station to ascertain the wind conditions will help project their persistence. Checks during the burning may also be of benefit if adverse conditions are predicted.

Even if persistent winds are available, a whirlwind, a common sight on hot summer days, can create problems. A whirlwind running either through the fire front or just behind it can scatter sparks and firebrands for some distance and result in spot wildfires in adjacent vegetation.

Moisture. Relative humidity and its interaction with fuel moisture is one of the most important weather elements to consider when conducting prescribed burning. The relative humidity range considered satisfactory for burning is between 30 and 60 percent, with the optimum around 40 percent (55). Although this range is thought to be best suited for burning in most regions of the United States, there are exceptions. With a reclamation burning, 30 percent relative humidity may be the maximum desired because of the need for fuel consumption and high lethal temperatures. Conversely, relative humidities as high as 90 percent may be desired in some vegetation types for maintenance burning.

Precipitation is seldom desirable before the installation of reclamation fires. However, sufficient precipitation to wet the mulch and the upper surface of the mineral soil may be desirable before ignition of a maintenance fire. The amount needed depends upon the vegetation type and the mulch conditions. As little as 0.25 inch may be sufficient for light standing fuel and mulch, while 0.75 inch may be required for heavy standing fuel and mulch. This wetting of the mulch and surface soil tends to reduce the amount of mulch consumed as well as the maximum heat intensity attained during the fire.

Moisture evidently has a compensating effect on the penetration of heat into soil. Moisture conducts heat, but it also has a strong cooling effect. Therefore, surface temperature during a grass fire is generally higher for dry soil than for moist soil. However, low soil content reduces the downward penetration of heat (62). Only the upper 0.125–0.25 inch of the surface soil is usually significantly increased in temperature by range fires (334).

Combustibility increases as temperature and wind velocity increase and as relative humidity and mulch moisture content decrease. Generally, the time for initiating the burning should coincide with peak temperature and minimum relative humidity for the day. This condition is usually attained between 2 and 4 P.M. Later in the day combustibility decreases, since temperature normally decreases and relative humidity increases, a condition which may be desirable to facilitate fire control.

Installing Fires

Preparing for the burning. There are several practices and safeguards to consider when a prescribed burning is planned. In constructing fire guards, both natural and artificial features, including ravines, gulleys, access strips, fence lines, and roadways, should be considered. Firebreaks may have already been constructed to prevent wildfires. These structures are important, for they not only slow or prevent the spread of wildfires but also serve as fire guards for prescribed burnings. They should always be burned, preferably with a backfire, or their mineral soil should be exposed on the surface before the prescribed fire is installed.

In some cases it may be necessary to prepare the fuel (particularly brush) for burning by crushing or mashing it (108, 315). This procedure compacts the fuel, facilitates ignition, makes the fire easier to manage, and may actually control some brush before the fire. Aerial spraying with herbicides has proven effective in preparing for prescribed burning on the Coastal Prairie (248). Spraying causes the woody fuel component to dry and releases fine fuel, resulting in increased temperatures near ground level during the burnings. Where heavy brush cover exists, a method such as aerial spraying may have to be employed to assure a uniform, effective fire. Otherwise, several years and attempts at burning may be necessary before a uniform burning is possible.

The fire plan. The firing of land for range improvement should follow a systematic, highly methodical plan. By following proper procedures, the risk of a prescribed fire turning into a wildfire is greatly reduced. Wright (334) has described effective fire plans for volatile and nonvolatile fuels under semiarid conditions (Table 7.1). The plan for nonvolatile fuels is ideal for areas supporting 4,000 pounds or more of fine fuels, especially tobosa, per acre. If fine fuel load is less than 2,000 pounds per acre and the management objective is to kill woody plants or burn logs, a wind in excess of 8 miles per hour will be required (334). As a note of caution, wind speeds should be measured in the actual area to be burned instead of adjacent open areas. When burning volatile fuels, as following the bulldozing of junipers, the piles of volatile fuel should be burned before the overall burning (334) and at least one day following a rain. Heavy grazing before burning the juniper piles reduces the fire hazard. However,

TABLE 7.1.

Weather Conditions and Fire Guard Construction (adapted from 334).

Conditions		Fuel Type	
		Nonvolatile	Volatile
Perimeter fire guard width (feet)			
Upwind side		10	10
Downwind side		10	15
Width of backfire (feet)		100	400
Fire guard for backfire			
(width, feet)		10	10
Wind speed (mph)	backfire	8	8*
	headfire	8–15	8–15
Relative humidity (percent)	backfire	50–60	50–60*
	headfire	25–40	25–40
Air temperature at			
headfire set (°F)		60	65–75

    * Burn in wind of less than 8 miles per hour and when relative humidity is 50 to 60 percent if grass fuel is more than 2,000 pounds per acre. If grass fuel is less than 2,000 pounds per acre, burn when wind is less than 8 miles per hour but when relative humidity is 25 to 40 percent.

grazing deferment after burning the juniper piles to accumulate fine fuel for broadcast burning the following winter is recommended.

Range burning in South and East Texas, especially on the Coastal Prairie, presents somewhat different problems than those encountered in the drier western and northern portions of the state. During the winter dormancy period in the coastal zone, relatively few dry, clear, bright days occur. The relative humidity is consistently high, increasing the moisture of the fine fuel above that considered optimum for burning (248). However, experimental fires have been conducted successfully over pools of standing water and a saturated soil surface. Although this procedure is not suggested, it serves to illustrate compensation for moisture content by wind speed and fuel load. Wind speeds of 12 to 15 miles per hour during bright sunny conditions have been most effective for burning on the Coastal Prairie, and winds of at least 8 to 10 miles per hour are required. Under these conditions, and with a fine fuel load exceeding 2,500 pounds per acre, the fire front effectively consumes essentially all the standing vegetation. Within a given wind speed, fine fuel load and fuel moisture content are the primary factors that regulate the duration and intensity of the fire.

Groundwork should constitute the majority of the time invested in developing a prescribed burning, and proper site preparation is the key to success. Potential hazards such as heavy fuel accumulations and potential routes for the fire to escape must be carefully considered.

The fire torch is an effective device for igniting the vegetation uniformly. A mixture of gasoline and diesel oil (1:3) or kerosene and diesel oil (2:3) is placed in the sealed aluminum reservoir of the torch.

Before installation of the fire, local weather reports should be consulted. Weather instruments on the site should include at least a sling psychrometer (wet- and dry-bulb thermometer) for monitoring relative humidity and obtaining air temperature and a wind velocity gauge.

A mobile water supply should be strategically located near the area to be burned. Too often fires which escape could have been controlled easily if adequate water supplies had been properly located.

Disked alleys at least 15 feet wide surrounding each area to be burned have been used effectively as fire guards on the Coastal Prairie (108). To successfully contain the fire, the firebreak must be disturbed until adequate amounts of mineral soil are mixed with the vegetation. Corners should be checked carefully for bridges of vegetation. The local fire department should be notified several days before burning.

Burning. Backfiring preferably should be accomplished in the fall when green fuel is sufficient to assure fire control. However, backfiring in the fall is not always possible on the Coastal Prairie. Backfiring has been effectively accomplished immediately before setting of the headfire. When vegetation is predominantly nonvolatile (mostly grass, with only a low to medium density of species such as Macartney rose), the headfire may be ignited after the backfire has burned into the area about 50 to 60 feet (Fig. 7.1). In areas supporting a high density of Macartney rose, especially where the plants have undergone no previous improvement practices, it may be advisable to let the backfire burn for 100 feet before lighting the headfire. Since backfiring is burning against the wind, these fires are slow, and the flame height is characteristically low.

The simultaneous use of headfires and backfires presents some hazard of developing firewhirls (fire storms). Firewhirls are generated by wind shears that result when a fire moves upslope into a wind or when a headfire runs into a backfire. Wright (334) cites personal accounts of firewhirls that developed when headfires and backfires met in 10- to 15-mile-per-hour winds as well as under light and variable wind conditions. Firewhirls may loft firebrands and sparks and may move for at least several hundred feet from the point of generation. For that reason it may be advisable to complete backfiring before installing the headfires whenever possible.

After the backfire has been ignited, the entire fire line should be checked to ensure uniform burning before authorization is given to light the headfire. Discontinuities in fuel load, such as cattle trails, are sometimes difficult to backfire and may have to be reignited to achieve a uniform burning.

When the wind is perpendicular to the intended direction of movement of the fire front, one side can be ignited for an adequate headfire (Fig. 7.1). Personnel should begin at the center of the windward side of the area and work toward the corners. However, when the wind is moving at a diagonal to the fire guards, personnel should begin backfiring at the leeward corner and work down each of the

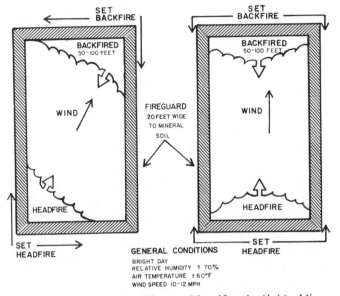

7.1. Procedures for igniting backfires and headfires in (*left*) oblique winds and in (*right*) direct winds.

two adjacent sides; fire should be started similarly along the windward sides to assure an even flame front.

As a general rule, burnings should be patrolled for twenty-four hours after they burn out. Stumps, manure, and bases of bunch grasses that continue to burn should be broken up to reduce fuel density. Herbaceous vegetation, such as bunch-grass stubble, can be best extinguished by spraying the area with water from a mist nozzle. Special care should be taken to extinguish fires in root systems of large woody plants.

There are indirect costs that should be considered in the use of prescribed burning for range improvement. For example, it may be necessary to defer use of the rangeland after burning. However, proper deferment following burning is as crucial to successful improvement as are the effects of the fire itself. Usually it is necessary to defer the area from grazing until the grass plants develop six to eight true leaves. If only a portion of a fenced area is burned, the stocking rate should be adjusted to that area, not the entire pasture. Systematic burning must be part of the management plan so that adjustments in grazing

can be smoothly incorporated into the overall ranch operation to reduce or eliminate deferment costs.

Responses of Plants to Fire

Plant responses to fire vary with their morphology and with their
phenological stages of development at the time of the burning. Plants
of the same species but in different phenological stages may differ considerably in their morphology and, consequently, respond somewhat
differently to fire.

Plant morphology. The physical features of plants, including
growth form, are largely responsible for their relative susceptibility to
fire. Perennial grasses are generally more tolerant of fire than other
plant life forms, primarily because their perennating buds, located at
or near the ground line, are relatively well protected from fire damage
(Fig. 7.2). Usually only the surface 0.125 to 0.25 inch of mineral soil
is increased in temperature during burning, and then for only a few
minutes. Soil temperature increases are usually negligible below a
depth of 0.25 inch even during relatively hot surface fires (334). Although grasses are highly adapted to fire, their susceptibility varies

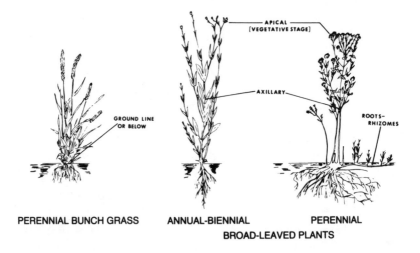

PERENNIAL BUNCH GRASS   ANNUAL-BIENNIAL   PERENNIAL
                               BROAD-LEAVED PLANTS

7.2. The perennating buds of grasses are located at ground line or below,
which affords them more protection from fire damage compared to annual or biennial broad-leaved plants.

somewhat among species. This variation has been attributed to differences in characteristics of top growth as they relate to the intensity and duration of the heat generated. For example, there is considerable difference in the response of the bunch grasses squirreltail and needle-and-thread to burning with a given set of fire characteristics (335). Squirreltail plants burn quickly, minimizing heat penetration to the buds because there is usually a low density of dead plant material in the individual bunches. Bunches of needle-and-thread typically contain higher amounts of dead material, so they burn at higher temperatures for a longer time. Thus, needle-and-thread is more likely to be damaged by any given fire than is squirreltail, since degree of fire damage is a function of both intensity and duration of exposure to the heat.

Fire may alter the growth form of some grasses such as Gulf cordgrass, a robust species of low, wet areas in the Coastal Prairie. Bunches of mature Gulf cordgrass are characterized by rings of live tissues surrounding accumulations of dead material. Gulf cordgrass ignites easily, and burning usually removes all its top growth, but the live outer ring grows and expands. If the original outer ring of tissues is not continuous, several small clumps of live tissue, which apparently function as individual plants, may remain. The result of the replacement of a single large plant with several smaller clumps is usually increased foliar cover and, ultimately, a higher density of plants which are somewhat smaller than the original plants. In this case, burning serves to rejuvenate grass stands which have otherwise become almost stagnant.

Annual grasses are typically more susceptible to fire damage than are perennial grasses since the annuals do not possess perennating buds. Although cool fires early in the season may allow regrowth of annuals, hot fires after floral initiation will remove them. Annual broad-leaved plants have well-elevated buds, which increases their susceptibility to burning. Consequently, prescribed burning may be used to reduce the influence of annual herbs, both grasses and broad-leaved plants, in the ecosystem not only by removal of the top growth but also by reduction of the number of viable seeds produced each year. Fire damage to desirable annual forbs can be alleviated by burning before the plants emerge. Also, burning can be delayed until after the forbs mature, when their grazing value is extremely low.

Perennial herbaceous broad-leaved plants which resprout from roots and rhizomes and woody plants which regenerate from a crown are protected by a layer of soil. The effects of fire on perennial broad-leaved plants may be likened to the results of any method of simple top removal such as mowing or shredding. The tops are removed or damaged by the fire, releasing the underground buds from apical dominance.

Since the apical buds of woody plants are relatively unprotected, and protection is limited for the tissues responsible for radial expansion (cambium) and the phloem, extensive damage to aerial parts may result from burning. If the woody plant is not capable of regenerating itself from below-ground buds, fire is an effective means of total removal. Following burning, those species which possess an underground bud system may be drastically altered in growth form, much as regrowth is altered when it is allowed to develop after shredding. This change in growth form is of some advantage in that the area affected by the woody-plant canopy is reduced, at least temporarily, and in that the browse is made more available and palatable to livestock and wildlife.

The resistance of any woody species to burning may be related to species (322) and to the age and size of the tree (123) in addition to the role of the regeneration system. Species differences are more closely related to morphological features (in turn related to external factors such as insulation) than to differences on the cellular level such as innate physiological tolerance of heating (123). Regardless of species, fire resistance increases with the age of woody plants as lignification (the process by which cells of trees assume their woody character), trunk diameter, bark thickness, and elevation of the canopy increase.

Damage to velvet mesquite by fire is inversely related to its basal stem diameter. One researcher has reported that velvet mesquite of less than 0.5 inch basal diameter was severely damaged whereas little damage was incurred by plants 2 to 6 inches in diameter (48). Obviously, intensity of the heat and the duration of exposure to it are critical, and the longer the exposure to high temperatures, the larger the basal diameter which can be expected to suffer irreparable damage from fire. With species such as honey mesquite, and under typical Texas conditions, only the smaller plants are usually controlled by burning, and only then if they are burned with adequate fuel. Since honey mesquite is a vigorous crown sprouter, periodic fires will suppress its growth but kill relatively few of the plants.

The state of health of trees is important in determining their response to fire. Old trees which are infested with insects and diseases may be more susceptible to fire injury than their younger, healthy counterparts. Honey mesquite trees which have suffered borer attacks burn more readily than do undamaged trees (334). The borer damage apparently allows the wood to dry and opens it to oxygen for combustion.

Living cells of woody plants are equipped with a natural insulator from heat—bark (123). The efficiency of bark as an insulator varies with its thickness; composition; freedom from cracks, fissures, and defects; structure; moisture content; and percentage of cork or outer bark. These factors, collectively, determine the thermal conductivity of bark—its ability to transmit heat. Generally the bark forms a shell of low conductivity around the central core of the stem. The bark serves to protect the cambium and associated conductive tissues. Since the outer bark is the only protection for the cambial tissues, thin-barked hardwood seedlings are less resistant to thermal injury than are older trees with a thick outer covering. Moisture in the bark may serve as a heat conductor as does moisture in the soil (123). Moisture content increases the specific heat—the ability to absorb heat—of bark. Thus, the cambium may suffer greater damage from heat when the bark is thin and contains relatively high amounts of moisture than when the bark is thick and dry. Differential bark moisture content may partially explain the resistance of some tree species to fire damage in the fall and winter, times of low bark moisture content, compared to the spring and early summer, when moisture content is high. Cable (47) reported more damage to woody plants burned in the summer than from fire at any other season.

Elevation of the canopy determines the position of the foliage, buds, and stems in relation to the flames of the fire front. Short plants positioned directly in the flame will obviously incur more damage than a large tree with the canopy elevated well above the fire. Although heating by convection will damage, at least partially, the canopies of large trees, the intensity of the heat may not be adequate to kill the aerial growth points. This principle can be used effectively in the maintenance of savannah, in which the large, scattered trees are of value for livestock shade.

I have taken advantage of differential tree size to reclaim brushy live oak savannah with fire. Large live oak trees, usually in widely spaced mottes of several individuals, typify this vegetation type. In the absence of fire, running live oak and other woody shrubs of relatively small stature (less than 6 feet tall) dominate the spaces between the mottes. Winter burnings effectively open the spaces, converting them to herbaceous species desirable for grazing and only minimally damaging the large live oaks in the mottes, since their canopies are well above the fire front. Only under high wind conditions do the fires sweep into the crowns of the large live oaks.

Plant phenology. Phenology refers to the stage of plant growth, the state of the periodic biological phenomena such as flowering and seeding, as studied in relation to the influence of factors such as climate. The response of woody plants to the season of burning is closely related to their phenological and physiological state of development (123). Deciduous woody plants are usually damaged most from burning in the spring when food reserves are depleted. Among evergreen species this trend may not hold, since some accumulation of food reserves may occur in the winter because of active fall and early winter growth, especially in regions with long growing seasons.

The importance of timing fires in relation to carbohydrate storage patterns was noted more than forty years ago by Aldous (2). He timed burns for buckbrush control to coincide with the low point in carbohydrate storage. However, the low point of carbohydrate storage for sumac was in June, a period when the vegetation would not carry a fire. Consequently, Aldous controlled buckbrush by burning but did not control sumac.

The time of optimum response of woody plants to fire must be matched with the times of least detrimental effect on the desirable herbaceous species. Fire exerts two major influences on grasses—heat and top removal, which interplay to regulate resultant damage (315, 336). Greatest damage usually occurs at full leaf development, when the energy reserves have been transported out of the roots. The later a burning occurs following a rainy season needed to promote plant growth, the higher the expected damage due to prolonged stress on the plant's energy reserve system without replenishment. However, plant phenology is geared so tightly to season that one cannot be discussed in detail without consideration of the other.

Season of burning. Season is a critical consideration in planning a burning since it is related to both plant phenology and expected weather conditions. On a range in the Texas High Plains where annual average precipitation is about 21 inches, fall, spring, and summer burning may reduce overall herbage production for two subsequent growing seasons (306). Blue grama apparently benefits from fire, while less desirable grasses such as red threeawn may be damaged.

In South Texas where about 30 inches of rainfall is received annually, burning in the fall or in the winter, or a combination of the two seasons, may result in higher herbage production than on adjacent unburned ranges (40). Ranges burned in the fall produced the most herbage in one study (40). The forb population was reduced, but grass production was increased. Burning for two successive years, once in the fall and once in the winter, increased total herbage production and resulted in the same proportions of grasses and forbs on both the burned and unburned areas. In another study, apparently under less rainfall, burning of South Texas range in the fall did not change grass production at the end of the first year. Filly panic, buffalograss, and meadow dropseed were more abundant on burned than on unburned areas, whereas plains bristlegrass decreased in abundance following burning (39). Burning reduced production of forbs primarily by decreasing western ragweed and Texas broomweed.

Response of herbaceous range plants to burning depends to a great extent on moisture conditions following the fire. In an area with average annual precipitation of 24 to 28 inches, herbage yields following burning in the spring were increased by 41 percent during a year when 23 inches of rainfall occurred but were increased by only 13 percent in a year when only 6.5 inches were received (333). During the wetter year burning increased yields of little bluestem but did not affect production of sideoats grama or tall grama. During the dry year, production of all three species was lower on the burned area. These grasses occupy upland sites, and reduced production during the dry year was attributed to removal of the mulch and blackening of the surface, resulting in a hotter, drier environment than existed on similar unburned areas. Vine mesquite and meadow dropseed occupy lowland sites and responded positively to burning during both rainfall conditions. Although production for the site was unchanged during the wet year, these species did spread into areas opened by the fire (331). During the dry year, grasses of the lowlands sites received runoff water from occasional intense storms, and production was maintained at a high level. In another area having a moderate fuel load (about two thousand pounds per acre), burning increased total production and the grazing use of tobosa, did not affect buffalograss, and decreased the density of common broomweed, western ragweed, and horsetail conyza (130).

During a study of burning on several major grass species of West Texas, winter-spring precipitation varied from average to 40 percent above normal (333). Texas wintergrass, a cool-season species, and the rhizomatous form of sideoats grama were harmed by fire. The rhizomatous form of sideoats grama tolerates fire during exceptionally wet years, but apparently it never benefits from burning (333). Buffalograss, blue grama, and sand dropseed tolerate burning but usually do not benefit from it and actually may be harmed if burning occurs during dry years. Vine mesquite, Arizona cottontop, little bluestem, plains bristlegrass, and Texas cupgrass increased for one to two years after burning (333).

Density and vigor of Lehmann lovegrass were not affected by a winter burning which was adequate to kill 90 percent of the live oak sprouts infesting a site in south central Texas (334). Since Lehmann lovegrass is relatively coarse and unpalatable when mature, burning may be used as a management tool to improve stands for grazing.

Burning may increase the abundance of some species, particularly native legumes, which are beneficial to livestock and wildlife. Periodic burning is used in the southeastern part of Texas to perpetuate "fire followers" such as wild partiridge pea and to improve range forage value (129).

Response of Range Animals to Burning

Range burning results in a supply of highly palatable, nutritious feed, aids in promoting grazing distribution if entire pastures are burned (spot burning results in spot grazing), and may be used to attain certain botanical compositions of forage by timing of the burn. For example, in one Florida study, burning on one-fourth of the range in November and an additional one-fourth in January increased the weaned calf crop from 56 percent to 75 percent and increased calf weights by 192 pounds to 234 pounds over those from unburned range (165). The most common vegetation on the Florida range was pineland threeawn, a species that is not palatable when mature. However, after the burning it was sparse, palatable, and nutritious (112, 113); protein content of its forage increased, and fiber content decreased (165). Similar improvement in forage quality occurs after burning Texas species. Late spring burning of little bluestem decreases crude fiber, cell wall constituents, cellulose, and lignin and increases crude protein, ether extract, nitrogen-free extract, and ash (3).

Burning is an effective practice for increasing use of species with inherently low palatability, such as Gulf cordgrass (219) and tobosa (332), resulting in improved carrying capacity and higher animal performance. Increased protein and phosphorus content of the forage and increased consumption of top growth by livestock, especially during the winter on the Coastal Prairie, are generally reflected in improved animal production efficiency (219).

Burning also promotes efficiency of livestock management by improving distribution of grazing animals. For example, cattle may concentrate along the roads and around feeders during the winter in sections of Coastal Prairie infested by Macartney rose (108). Following burning, the cattle use the pastures more primarily because of the early supply of green forage.

Combining Fire with Other Techniques

Burning may be used to control some brush species which are not controlled by other brush management techniques. For example, most juniper species are not controlled by foliage treatments with most herbicides but are susceptible to burning. The best use of burning, however, is as a maintenance tool following other brush management methods.

Fire has proven to be a highly effective tool for accelerating range improvement following aerial spraying or mechanical management techniques, especially in the wetter parts of the state. Aerial spraying opens the woody plant canopy, allowing fine fuel to develop in adequate quantity and continuity to allow effective burning. Also, a certain amount of drying of the standing woody plants apparently occurs following herbicide application. This drying aids in the combustion of species such as Macartney rose (248). If the burning is delayed following spraying until those plants which were only top-killed by the sprays begin to develop basal sprouts, the fire may be used effectively to suppress the woody plant regrowth.

Fire is also an excellent "cleanup" method following practices such as chaining of light stands for which raking and stacking are not merited. Honey mesquite stems on the ground following chaining may be removed by burning with 2,000 pounds (moderate load) of fine fuel per acre in northwestern Texas (130). However, few live honey mesquite trees are killed, and only a few of the standing dead stems are burned down.

8

Biological Brush Management

BIOLOGICAL control methods use natural enemies (plant-feeding and disease-causing organisms) to reduce or eliminate the economic impact of an undesirable plant species (5, 150). Eradication is never the objective of biological plant control (149, 217). Biological control may be achieved by the direct action of the control agent (the direct damage it causes by boring into or consuming plant parts), or by its indirect action to reduce the vigor and/or reproductive capability of the plants or promote conditions for secondary infections (5, 151). An effective biological control agent may need only to reduce the competitive advantage of the target species. Some view the use of grazing animals more as a cultural approach to plant control, but selective grazing may be logically included with biological methods (315). Vertebrates have been employed to a much lesser extent in biological control than have insects (104).

Action of Biological Agents

The action of biological agents may be categorized, generally, as pathogenic in nature, as any attack which depletes the food reserves of the plant, or as any action which is detrimental to normal reproduction (217). Pathogens damage the host plant by producing toxins, by degrading the physiological and/or structural balance of the plant at the cellular level, and by other mechanisms. Hormone systems may be imbalanced, the function of the vascular system altered, or enzyme systems degraded. Such action of a biological agent may kill

This chapter was developed in collaboration with Dr. D. N. Ueckert, Texas Agricultural Experiment Station, San Angelo.

the target plant or at least reduce its competitive advantage and/or prevent its successful reproduction.

Food reserves may be reduced by the defoliating activity of insects or by damage to the storage system, as by root boring activity. The boring activity of insects may also create areas for infection by primary or secondary plant pathogens.

In general, the success of the biological control agent depends on the degree and extent of other environmental stresses that are exerted on the target species. An efficient competitor growing in a favorable environment obviously will not succumb to an attack by the biological agent as readily as a species already under environmental stress. In an example from Australia, the lacebug (*Teleonemia scrupulosa*) in Queensland more effectively controls drought-stressed lantana than those plants growing under more favorable conditions (217). Management, as it affects the target species, may expedite the action of the biological agent by intensifying competitive stress.

Range animals may be employed to selectively graze or browse plants to reduce or eliminate their impact in the ecosystem. This reduction or elimination should be reflected by a corresponding increase in the density, production, and vigor of associated species of higher ultimate value to the land manager. Selective grazing takes advantage of the different preferences of livestock for the target species of forage plants. In row crops, for example, this approach has used geese to selectively remove grass seedlings from cotton fields. Because of the diversity in species of rangeland vegetation, foraging preference may not be so clear-cut, but the same approach can be employed. For example, deer and goats tend to use relatively large amounts of browse, whereas cattle are considered to use primarily grasses. However, cattle may also use certain portions of woody plants such as the twigs and young leaves of winged elm (60) and Macartney rose during certain times of the year. Also, cattle use relatively high amounts of forbs during certain growth stages and during stress periods such as drought.

Biological brush management, with its connotation of being a "natural" approach, is appealing to most of the general public. It has been highly effective in some instances; however, the success rate of research efforts to develop biological methods of plant control is relatively low. The successes widely applauded include the effective control of pricklypear in Australia by the moth *Cactoblastis cactorum* and the reduction of the introduced Klamathweed by leaf beetles of the genus *Chrysolina* in the northwestern United States. Biological weed control, especially by insects or pathogens, is viewed conservatively because (1) there is fear that the risks associated with the parasite organism may outweigh the potential for effective control—that the parasite organism may change its feeding habits once the target organism is limited and turn to economically important crops—and (2) there are conflicts of opinion about the undesirability of the target species; for example, although pricklypear is generally considered a range management problem, it is of value as a feed source for cattle in times of drought (151, 217). The first of these reasons is losing its force because of accumulating evidence of the success of biological pest management, greater assurance against disproportionate risk, recent advances in host specificity studies, and recent developments in the criteria for selecting effective biological control agents.

Harris (125) reviewed the criteria that have been used for selecting biological weed control agents. He felt that a major reason that many biological control attempts have failed is because the selection of "safe" biological control agents has preempted attention from the selection of those that will be effective in controlling the target plant. He developed a scoring system that incorporates twelve criteria for recognizing effective agents, or at least for eliminating the most ineffective. The twelve criteria are the following:

1. *Host specificity.* Oligophagous species score higher than more specialized feeders.
2. *Direct damage inflicted.* Insects that destroy vascular or supporting tissue score higher than those that mine leaves, form galls, defoliate, suck plant juices, or damage seedlings; insects that prevent seed production of annuals or biennials score higher than those that prevent seed production of long-lived perennials or short-lived plants not dependent on seeds.
3. *Indirect damage inflicted.* Insects that transmit diseases or that create conditions favorable for secondary infections score higher than those that do not.
4. *Phenology of attack.* Insects that attack during a limited period, thus increasing plant susceptibility to frost, drought, or interspecific competition, and those that attack the target plant throughout its growing season or reproductive season score higher than those

that attack for shorter periods of time or at times that are not particularly detrimental to the weed.

5. *Numbers of generations.* Insects with four or more generations per year score higher than those with fewer generations.

6. *Number of progeny per generation.* Those with over one thousand progeny score higher than those with fewer.

7. *Extrinsic mortality factors.* Insects that are subject to extensive mortality from specialized enemies, including diseases, and that are relatively immune to nonspecific enemies score higher than those that are controlled naturally by nonspecific enemies or ecological factors and that are subject to extensive mortality from other competitors for the host.

8. *Feeding behavior.* Gregarious or colonial feeders score high than solitary feeders.

9. *Compatibility with other control agents.* Those insects that are compatible score higher than those with poor compatibility which might restrict possibilities for introducing additional agents.

10. *Distribution.* Species that cover the full geographical range of the target weed score higher than those with more restricted range.

11. *Evidence of effectiveness as a control agent.* Species that have proven effective for control of the target weed in other biological control attempts score higher than those that have not proven effective.

12. *Size of agent.* Species which have a dry body weight of over 50 milligrams score higher than smaller species.

This scoring system provides a quantitative method for evaluating biological weed control agents. Zwölfer and Harris (340) have outlined the procedure for introducing a new phytophagous insect for biological weed control. They have discussed host-determined adaptations of phytophagous insects, laboratory tests to determine potential host range of an insect and the plants attacked by related insects, analysis of host-plant specificity, and starvation and negative-oviposition tests on economic plants.

The approaches to biological plant management include (1) augmentation of existing natural enemies of native or alien weeds by means of periodic releases of mass-reared insects or pathogens, (2) conservation of existing natural enemies or the manipulation of their environment to enhance their effectiveness as weed control agents,

(3) importing natural enemies from abroad for the control of alien weeds, and (4) using an insect pest of a closely related species of plant that occurs where the target plant does not occur, perhaps near the center of origin of the target species (105). After release and colonization, the ideal biological control agent then provides continuous and adequate suppression of its host over most of its geographical range.

However, in over one-half of the attempts for biological weed control the results have been less than ideal. Frick (96) has outlined possibilities for augmentation of unsuccessful or partially successful suppressants in order to increase their effectiveness, which should increase the number of successful biological weed control programs and generally broaden the scope of biological control. Methods of augmentation of biological suppressants discussed by Frick include (1) modification of habitat to reduce or eliminate mature growth of target species, for example, by felling mature trees or by controlled burning, (2) management of livestock grazing to increase the competitive advantage of desirable plants, (3) reduction in the abundance of the target weed by mechanical or chemical means, (4) increase in the host suitability or nutritional value of the target species by fertilization or with sublethal doses of herbicide such as 2,4-D, and (5) increase in the population density of the suppressant by distributing suppressants from areas of surplus, by releasing suppressants reared on host-plant cultures or artificial diets in insectaries, or by reducing natural enemies of the suppressants. The importation of natural enemies from abroad for the control of alien weeds will probably remain the basic approach during the next few decades (105). However, in many areas, such as the rangelands of Texas and much of the other western states, the major noxious plants are natives rather than aliens. There is hope and strong possibility that importation of foreign insects can be equally successful against native weeds (132).

Recent work has shown (1) that insects available for control of a weed are not limited to those attacking it in its native habitat but include species that attack closely allied or other plants in other areas, (2) that where native plants are serious weeds, their abundance may sometimes be reducible by the introduction of alien insects which attack the same or related plant species or races, (3) that while past successes have all been obtained against perennial weeds, annuals may also be controlled biologically, (4) that while some phytophagous insects may lack host specificity, as shown by starvation tests, and so may involve risks for economic plants, the risk has generally been overestimated, (5) that for many weeds safe insects are available, and (6) that in some instances plant diseases may prove feasible for weed control (330).

Plant pathogens and phytophagous mites are receiving considerable attention as biological weed control agents. There is a wide variety of pathogens among bacteria, fungi, viruses, nematodes, mycoplasms, and possibly *Rickettsiae* from which to select candidates for biological weed control (54). A rust fungus (*Puccinia chondrillian*) was introduced into Australia from Italy in 1971 as a biological control agent for skeleton weed, which it is showing promise of success in controlling (320). Secondary infections in pricklypear in Australia by soft rot bacteria and by the fungal parasites *Gloeosporium lunatum*, *Phyllosticta concava*, and *Montignella opuntiarum* were found to be effective in controlling the cactus once the initial damage had been inflicted by larvae of the moth *Cactoblastis cactorum* (69). Common persimmon can be effectively controlled by application of spores of the persimmon wilt (*Cephalosporium diospyri*) to freshly cut stumps or to wounds made in the live wood of standing trees (58, 114, 115, 328). The host-specific eriophyid mite (*Aceria boycei*) has been exported from California to the Soviet Union for ragweed control, and another species of *Aceria* has been transferred from Central Asia to the Soviet Union for biological control of Russian knapweed (105).

Biological control is not without its limitations. This approach will probably never be the solution to all weed and brush problems on rangelands. Weed species or situations least suited to biological control are (1) those weeds that are valued in certain situations into which the control agent may spread, (2) brush and weed problems (such as occur in the mixed brush of the South Texas Plains and Edwards Plateau resource areas of Texas) where many weed species occur together, (3) those weeds that are closely related to plants of economic importance, (4) weeds that require instantaneous control, (5) weeds whose eradication is required or which can be tolerated only at very low population densities, and (6) weeds that are highly

geographically localized unless these have been recently introduced
and threaten to become widespread (126).

Insects and Pathogens for Brush Management

Probably the most widespread concept of biological weed control
is the use of insects or pathogens. The use of insects by man for plant
management is an attempt to shift parasite-host relationships in favor
of the parasite—a delicate biological balance which is often difficult to
manipulate effectively.

Control of pricklypear in Australia by insects is the classic example of success with biological control methods. A few years after
the introduction of pricklypear as an ornamental hedge and forage
plant to Australia, nearly 30 million acres of rangeland had become
useless for grazing due to infestations of the cactus (217). An additional 30 million acres were seriously infested with pricklypear. Most
control measures available at the time of infestation required an investment which exceeded the value of the land. Consequently, several insect species were introduced to attempt biological control, with greatest success achieved with the moth borer *Cactoblastis cactorum*.
Larvae of the moth burrow inside above-ground parts of pricklypear
and consume the tissues. Damaged tissues are further attacked by secondary organisms such as bacteria and fungi. As a result, pricklypear
(mostly *Opuntia stricta*) was effectively controlled (but not eradi-
cated) in Australia by the tunneling moth in only a few years.

In the past five years considerable research in Texas has been
focused on control of honey mesquite, the most widespread brush
problem. Although honey mesquite is a persistent perennial with ability to perpetuate itself vegetatively, its only means of spread is by
seed. If its reproductive capacity is reduced, the possibilities of honey
mesquite containment by other methods can be improved.

A survey in West Texas has resulted in the identification of more
than fifty insect species representing thirty-one families and six orders
in honey mesquite flowers and pods (287). Evidently two species of
insects, conchuela (*Chlorochroa ligata*) and a seed beetle (*Algarobius
prosopis*), were most damaging to the production of viable honey
mesquite seeds. Conchuela reduced honey mesquite seed production

by at least 70 percent, at the population densities evaluated, by sucking the juices from the seeds. The seed beetle during its larval stage consumes the seed cotyledons. Net effect of seed beetle activity was a reduction of about 22 percent in the production of viable seeds. Native insect populations reduced the number of pods produced per honey mesquite tree, the number of seeds per pod, and the percentage of viable seeds.

Unfortunately, conchuela is a pest of cotton, which precludes its use in most areas where honey mesquite is a management problem. The seed beetle is evidently host specific to honey mesquite and may warrant additional study as a potential biological management method. Since the seed beetle winters in grassland mulch, there is an obvious compatibility between good range management and perpetuation of the seed beetle population (287).

Leaf-footed bugs (*Mozena obtusa*) feed by sucking the juices from immature pods of honey mesquite. Feeding of leaf-footed bugs increases the abortion of immature honey mesquite pods, decreases the dry weights of pods and seeds, and reduces the percentage of germination of seeds. In one study it was found that a density of four leaf-footed bugs per honey mesquite pod caused 89 percent abortion of the immature pods; seed germination was reduced to about 4 percent. As the density of leaf-footed bugs per pod was increased, the dry weight of surviving seeds was decreased. In the absence of leaf-footed bugs, seed germination was about 65 percent. Seedlings that developed from pods infested with leaf-footed bugs were less vigorous, based on sprout weight, than those from insect-free pods. With development of adequate population densities, leaf-footed bugs have potential for seriously reducing the spread of honey mesquite, for these insects are apparently host specific—they are not known to damage economically important plants (310).

The net effect of insects on reproduction of honey mesquite was demonstrated by comparing reproduction potential of trees protected from insect damage by insecticide spray with that of unprotected trees (287). Trees sprayed in the spring produced about eighty-nine pods per tree, with the pods containing more than twelve seeds, each with over 50 percent viability. In comparison, unsprayed trees produced about sixty-five pods per tree, with each pod containing ten seeds, of which about 25 percent were viable.

Several species of insects significantly reduce the canopy area of honey mesquite, occasionally to the extent that adequate foliage may not be left for the effective activity of foliar-active herbicides. Theoretically, prolonged extensive canopy reduction would eventually kill the trees or perhaps weaken the plants for increased effectiveness of subsequent management techniques such as burning or mechanical methods. However, any method which damages the canopy is not compatible with use of foliar-applied herbicides.

Twig girdlers (*Oncideres rhodosticta*) damage parts of honey mesquite canopies, the extent of damage varying from year to year. The twig girdler is a long-horned beetle (Fig. 8.1), the larvae of which are called round-headed borers (230, 313). The female girdler chews a ring into the live wood of honey mesquite stems about 0.3 to 0.4 inch in diameter and deposits about eight eggs beneath the bark (230). After the eggs hatch (ten to fourteen days), the larvae feed upon the dying wood up the stem from the girdle. During years of high twig girdler activity, total canopy area of honey mesquite is significantly reduced (Fig. 8.2). Such attacks, especially when the plant is weak-

8.1. The mesquite twig girdler is a long-horned beetle which may cause severe reduction in honey mesquite canopies. (*Courtesy D. N. Ueckert*)

8.2. Branches killed by twig girdlers on honey mesquite (*above*) were removed to illustrate the impact of the insect on total canopy area of individual trees (*below*) in years of high girdler activity. (*Courtesy D. N. Ueckert*)

ened by environmental stresses, will reduce food reserves as a result of reduced photosynthetic area and consequently hold promise for biological control (230, 313).

Although each female twig girdler damages only one branch, 98 percent of the eggs hatch to produce larvae which feed on the sapwood of the plants (230). Each larva consumes about 0.1 cubic inch of honey mesquite wood. However, over 30 percent of the girdled branches are broken off by winds or livestock before the adults emerge, parasites and predators kill 15 to 22 percent of the larvae, and a high percentage of the twig girdlers die of undetermined causes. Therefore, before the twig girdler reaches full potential, procedures will have to be developed to improve its survivability.

Another species which attacks the canopy of honey mesquite is the cutworm *Melipotis indomita*. During 1972 a honey mesquite stand near Paint Rock, Texas, had the canopy reduced by an average of 58 percent from infestations of cutworms (309). However, the cutworm populations were restricted to bottomland and heavy clay range sites where honey mesquite had been damaged by a late spring freeze. In some areas the cutworms reduced the honey mesquite foliage by 95 percent.

Insect activity may augment the effectiveness of other brush management practices. For example, wood boring activity by certain insects is common in honey mesquite trees killed by fire or drought (312). Boring activity of insects enables standing dead trunks to burn more completely by improving aeration in them (334). However, the extent of borer activity apparently varies depending on previous treatment of honey mesquite (312). In one comparison, boring activity was highest in trees basally sprayed with diesel oil plus 2,4,5-T, was intermediate in trees top-killed by basal treatment with diesel oil and by burning, and was insignificant in trees which had received aerial broadcast sprays of 2,4,5-T. Therefore, ranchers planning to use prescribed burning to remove standing dead honey mesquite could expect best results where basal treatments and burning were used as the initial practices (312).

The blue cactus borer (*Melitara dentata*) consumes the pulpy material within pricklypear cladophylls. Mortality of pricklypear attribute to this insect was 29, 59, and 68 percent respectively in 1972, 1973, and 1974 (308). Although the potential impact of this insect in cactus management appears obvious, considerable disagreement may exist about a high degree of cactus control in South Texas, where pricklypear furnishes reserve cattle feed during drought, is the preferred food of javelina, and is relished by other wildlife species.

Other insects which occur on pricklypear are cactus bugs (*Chelinidea* spp.) and cochineal insects (*Dactylopius* spp.) (308). These species suck the juices from pricklypear pads, and although they rarely inflict high degrees of direct damage, they serve to open the succulent pads to secondary infection by pathogens.

Large acreages of creosotebush are periodically defoliated by walkingstick (*Diapheromera covilleae*), sometimes two years in succession. It has been estimated that the defoliation of creosotebush by walkingstick insects increased production of black grama and blue grama by 203 pounds per acre (103 percent) and production of annual forbs by 31 pounds per acre (122 percent) (311).

Hewitt and his coworkers (132) have reviewed the literature on insects affecting several noxious brush species of the western United States, including sagebrush, rabbitbrush, mesquite, creosotebush, cactus, and others. Stevens, Giunta, and Plummer (297) have discussed possibilities for biological control of juniper and pinyon pine in Utah. Peterson (230) has reported that a leaf blight (*Cercospora sequoiae* Ell. and Ev. var. *juniperi*) infesting eastern red cedar in the midwest has killed fifteen- to twenty-year-old trees. Although looked upon as a problem which damages windbreaks in Nebraska, the leaf blight might have promise for reducing the juniper problem in Texas.

Many have discouraged attempts at biological control of noxious rangeland plants in Texas because most of the serious and widespread noxious plants are native species. However, several species of native plants have been controlled by the planned or accidental introduction of alien insects or diseases. Two native species of pricklypear (*Opuntia littoralis* and *O. oricola*) were successfully controlled on Santa Cruz Island off the coast of southern California by the introduction of a cochineal insect (*Dactylopius* sp.) from Hawaii in 1951 (106, 107). The removal of native chestnut trees from the forests of the eastern United States by the accidentally introduced fungus *Endothia parasitica* also shows that native plants (including native noxious weeds) may be more readily controlled than alien species (151). Huffaker (151) cited two other examples, including the pathogenicity of the alien white-pine blister rust, *Cronartium ribicola*, for native white pines in North America and the essential annihilation of Bermuda cedars on some islands of Bermuda by the accidentally introduced scale insects *Carulaspis visci* and *Lepidosaphes newsteadi*.

Native weeds often have close relatives of similar habits, phenology, and chemical and physical characteristics in other countries. It is essential that exploration be conducted for insects and other natural enemies of those closely related weeds which, if introduced into this country, might effectively control the native weeds (151). DeLoach (68) has recently discussed the advantages and limitations of various methods of biological control of native weeds, factors that influence the chances of success in finding effective biotic suppressants, factors to be considered in ranking target weeds in order of priority for research and control, conflicts between the beneficial and the harmful effects of weeds, and possible adverse ecological effects that could result from biological control of native weeds on southwestern rangeland.

Brush Management with Goats

"Goating" of woody plants has been used extensively in Texas and other areas of the Southwest for range improvement (65, 199, 200). Goats consume large amounts of browse, primarily from low-growing, shrubby forms of plants such as oaks, sumacs, and hackberries (Fig. 8.3). Very careful grazing management is essential to prevent goats from damaging desirable species. When the availability of preferred host species becomes limited, goats often turn to alternate food resources.

It has been recommended that on a year-long basis one goat is needed for every 2 to 3 acres of rangeland to give effective brush control (315). For short-term grazing—for example, a thirty-day period —five to eight goats per acre are required for effective brush control. Stocking rate and length of grazing period, to a point, depend directly upon the intensity of the brush problem. The short-term approach, grazing with high stocking rates, has been much more effective than grazing on a year-long basis with only a few goats per acre. Usually goats must be used for two to three successive years before the brush cover is reduced enough that the number of animals can be reduced.

8.3. Goats, which like large amounts of browse in their diet, are excellent biological agents for brush control. (*Courtesy L. B. Merrill*)

After the initial heavy browsing period to cut down woody-plant forage production, a reduced number of goats may be used for maintenance control of brush sprouts. Spanish and Angora goats have been used for brush control in Texas. When used properly, these goats can serve a dual purpose in the ranching operation; Spanish goats are marketed primarily for their meat, and Angora goats are the source of mohair as well as meat.

When the range manager considers range improvement with goating, as with other methods he must take into account the economics of the brush management procedure. Improvement in the range condition plus the goat products marketed should pay for (1) the original purchase cost of the goats, (2) extra shelter and fencing that are required to keep the goats in the treatment area, and (3) predator control practices required for maintenance of the goat herd (315).

. Goats select from a much wider variety of plants than do other livestock species (200). They may shift their diet from herbaceous . broad-leaved plants and preferred shrubs, especially under grazing pressure, to less desirable woody plants such as oaks and persimmon.

On the Sonora Research Station in the Edwards Plateau, Angora goats have grazed at a heavy stocking rate for twenty-three years, have browsed the less desirable trees and shrubs to a height of 7 feet, and have reduced the overall brush cover by 83 percent. During this time, condition of the range increased from fair to high fair.

Spanish goats are apparently more effective browsers than Angora goats. In a study near Sonora, Texas, Spanish goats consumed new growth of shin oak, hackberry and lime prickly ash but did not use Texas wintergrass, Texas cupgrass, and sideoats grama (65). Angora goats used these three grasses to a height of 1.5 inches and allowed shin oak shoots to reach a height of 6 inches. Following chaining, Spanish goats stocked at 85 percent of the stocking rate (cattle, sheep, and goats at 45 animal units per section) have effectively controlled brush regrowth (199).

Following bulldozing and cabling of brush in the Grand Prairie of Texas, Angora goats readily consume the sprouts of oaks and other woody species (193). In the mid-1950's many ranchmen of the area used goats after applying mechanical brush management. Goats did not replace cattle, but rather were added to consume the browse. The practice usually was to concentrate goats on rangeland immediately after mechanical brush control and to stock lightly with cattle. Results of an economic evaluation of the practice showed that in five years the goat enterprise had paid for the goats purchased; the cost of maintaining, housing, and caring for the goats; and all the year-to-year costs (193). Earnings from the goats, meat and mohair, covered the cost of clearing nearly 520 acres of rangeland at 1957 costs.

As long as adequate browse is available, there is little competition between cattle and goats for available forage (199). Consequently, the goats can be stocked in addition to the stocking capacity of the cattle, especially when goating is applied as a short-term practice. However, as the browse is controlled, stocking rates of the goats must be adjusted downward in proportion to avoid competition between goats and cattle (193). During these later stages of goating, managerial effectiveness is critical.

No other domestic animals are as valuable for brush managements as goats. Cattle eat a variety of woody species, but to only limited extent. Browsing by cattle is usually restricted to new growth and to certain seasons. For example, cattle may browse winged elm intensively from late spring (May 1) to midsummer (July 1), but to only a minor extent during other seasons (60). The degree of consumption of twigs of winged elm by cattle is apparently directly related to the crude protein and moisture content of the twigs. Generally only the new growth is of the quality that is preferred by cattle. Preference by cattle and deer for a number of woody species was increased following mechanical top removal, which promotes succulent regrowth (38). However, even under optimum conditions the preference by cattle for most woody plants is so low that effective control rarely occurs.

Grazing with mature cattle during the winter has controlled small soapweed on grassland in the Nebraska Sandhills (315). Gary reported 51 to 63 percent use of sprouts of salt cedar by cattle during summer grazing in Arizona (99). Sheep grazing in late fall effectively controls big sagebrush in Utah if the practice is initiated before the sagebrush becomes too dense and if sheep grazing is repeated periodically (98).

Economics of Biological Control

The economic benefit of biological control of Klamathweed to California, accrued to 1973, has been estimated at $51 million (105). Wilson (329) has estimated that £35 million per year are spent worldwide on pesticide research and some £6,000 million per year on the purchase of pesticides versus only £2 million per year (almost entirely by various governments) for the biological control of both insect pests and weeds. The cost of controlling weeds with herbicides and biologically is almost the reverse of the amount spent on them (127). The biological control of a weed costs between $0.5 million and $1 million (127), while the cost of developing a new pesticide is in the order of $8 million (49). There is also the annual cost of the chemicals required to maintain control (127). The return on investment in biological control research appears to be many times that invested in pesticides. Hence, from a financial standpoint, biological control may justify a larger investment than it is receiving.

According to Andres (6), the total research program for biological control of a weed species by the introduction of foreign suppressants averages one to two million dollars at current prices. He reported benefit-cost ratios up to 200:1 and even to 1000:1 for recent successful projects on biological control of weeds. Biological control is less expensive because the biological suppressants spread naturally from a few release sites, become permanently established, and exert a constant pressure on the weed, whereas chemical or mechanical controls must be applied periodically to part or all of the infested area.

9

Brush Management for Wildlife Habitat

THE term *range improvement* generally connotes an increase in the grazing capacity of rangeland (19), and increased grazing capacity generally infers the capability of the rangeland to support larger numbers of domestic livestock. Unfortunately, game animals historically have been largely omitted from consideration in rangeland improvement and development programs (103). However, they have become of adequate economic importance that they now must be considered to be an integral part of efficient systems of rangeland resource use.

During the past decade the desire of the urbanite to spend an increasing amount of his leisure time hunting, fishing, hiking, camping, and undertaking other forms of outdoor recreation has added a new dimension to range management by lending a dollar value to wildlife and to the range resource for nonconsumptive uses. With an adequate harvest, the net return per animal unit of white-tailed deer (six to seven mature deer, roughly the equivalent of a 1,000-pound cow with calf) can exceed that of livestock (233). The public demand on rangeland is bound to increase. Fortunately, the potential value of leasing rangeland for hunting rights may be added to traditional values for livestock production with the proper range management programs.

As the economic value of wildlife has increased, range managers have realized that the impact of brush management on wildlife habitat is a critical consideration in their development of improvement schemes. Highly sought-after game species such as white-tailed deer, wild turkeys, javelinas, feral hogs, squirrels, various species of upland game birds, and introduced species of exotic ungulates must have their habitat requirements met if the landowner is to capitalize on the opportunity to augment his income (176, 319).

The effect of brush control on wildlife results from the interactions of the specific control technique with environmental conditions (36) and wildlife species. Many of the cause-effect relationships surrounding these interactions are not clearly understood. Resource managers have seen both detrimental and beneficial effects and thus may have mixed feelings about the role of brush management in game habitat management.

The relative quality of game habitat is related to the particular mixture of plant species, including woody as well as herbaceous plants, remaining after the brush control operation. Woody plants provide many of the specific habitat needs—food, cover, and roosting and nesting sites—of wildlife. These requirements must be considered for each game species as brush management plans are developed. Obviously, specific habitat requirements of wild animals vary somewhat among species, so a positive response of one species to a given brush manipulation technique may be accompanied by a negative response from another species. We may presume that any alteration of the vegetative cover serves to either accelerate or retard plant succession and, subsequently, may have a varying influence on different species. As Box (36) has so aptly stated, ". . . the game manager may actually manipulate the relative amounts of various plants by using different [brush] control techniques. The field is no longer one of brush control but one of habitat manipulation by brush management."

In general, brush management practices change the character of wildlife habitat by altering plants' relative proportions (botanical composition), height, density, canopy cover, and relative availability for use by animals. Broad differences in the impact of brush management methods on the vegetation may be emphasized by contrasting broadcast chemical treatments with mechanical methods. The effects of hormone herbicides on woody plant communities are fairly subtle, at least initially, compared to those of mechanical approaches such as chaining or root plowing. Spraying is generally completed much more rapidly and causes less physical disturbance of the habitat, and vegetation change is less abrupt than with mechanical brush control techniques (19). Spraying reduces competition by at least partial, and often complete, removal of the brush canopy, but woody trunks and branches left standing serve as screen or cover. Although most mechanical methods are applied much more slowly than aerial spraying, they result in drastic, immediate physical alteration of the habitat. Mechanical methods severely reduce the screen, but those which disturb the soil usually increase the abundance and diversity of forbs. Severe soil disturbance, as by root plowing, may increase seasonal production of forbs, improving food availability for some species, although it may reduce the cover of woody plants below the habitat requirements of other species. Conversely, sprays usually reduce forbs for at least one year after treatment. Yet both aerial spraying and root plowing can be employed without degradation of wildlife habitat and with substantial improvement of livestock production.

Although technology affords the bases for proper application of brush management, common sense must be exercised when it is applied to the management of wildlife habitat. One would logically anticipate that overkill of brush would be the most common tendency among range managers steeped in the traditions associated with livestock production. Conversely, the fear of removing too much brush might cause the landowner to leave too much. In 1947, Blakey recognized that there was an upper limit to requirements for brush cover for quality wildlife habitat (21). He emphasized that "Encroachment of brush jungle upon formerly open forest and prairie range is insidious in that it has both good and bad effects upon certain wildlife species, and in some areas has the constant potential for near total exclusion of all valuable forms." Since economical and ethical game management is directed at production as well as harvest (302), and production is dependent on the development and maintenance of quality habitat, it is imperative that brush management procedures be chosen in view of the specific habitat (food and cover) requirements of game animals.

Requirements of White-tailed Deer

Probably more discussion about proper brush management schemes has centered on white-tailed deer habitat, especially in South Texas, than on any other game species–habitat complex. The increase in density and stature of woody plants has stimulated extensive brush clearing efforts to improve carrying capacity for livestock, particularly cattle. These brush clearing efforts have disturbed those who recognize the need for some brush as quality habitat for the continued production of trophy-sized deer.

Both the structure and composition of woody-plant communities are important to white-tailed deer, although relative importance among communities varies with season. Recent study in South Texas has shown that the "mesquite drainage, guajillo scrub and hackberry drainage" are the most preferred brush types in the fall, winter, and spring (158). On an annual basis, the honey mesquite drainage is most used, with the guajillo scrub and the hackberry drainage used about equally by deer. Mesquite drainages generally are dominated by thick stands of honey mesquite 4 to 10 feet tall and typically are classified as tight sandy loam range sites. The guajillo scrub is dominated by a moderate density of guajillo 2 to 4 feet tall and usually occurs on shallow sandy loam range sites. Hackberry drainages are dominated by thick stands of netleaf hackberry on the same soil and range sites as the honey mesquite drainages. However, some species may be substituted from site to site without reducing use by deer.

The affinity of white-tailed deer for several brush types results because many brush species of similar growth form provide adequate food, cover, and shelter (74, 158, 192). Providing cover, especially during activities such a mating, may well be the most important role of brush for deer. Although many, if not most, woody plants will be browsed, and almost any moderately thick stand of brush will provide some food, only a few brush species are especially relished by white-tailed deer.

White-tailed deer require a given amount of screen, and their limited use of root-plowed areas or areas where the brush has been knocked down by other methods is apparently the result of the absence of sufficient screening cover over a relatively large area. Avoidance of such areas is apparently a relative occurrence, however, since white-tailed deer may be observed periodically in savannahs, tame pastures, and cleared areas. Inglis and McMahan (158) succinctly summarized the requirement of brush by deer as follows: "Brush to deer is simply brush; the animals do not distinguish between composition types of brush, or between any of the structural attributes of brush, such as height, pattern, or density. But lack of brush over extensive areas causes much reduced use by deer. Deer are attracted to dense herbaceous vegetation; thus, the quality of typical brushlands as deer habitat is largely a function of the range site."

Range managers concerned with white-tailed deer habitat should consider leaving drainages intact and treating upland sandy loam range sites, at least in South Texas, to leave a pattern of brush types. This consideration is apparently not so much related to the preference of white-tailed deer for a particular brush type as to their preference for areas which produce herbaceous food. Any brush management practice, employed in moderation, that will foster the production of forbs on these sites likely will not be detrimental to deer.

In at least two studies (19, 158) the relation of range site to the production of preferred foods has been documented as a critical consideration for white-tailed deer habitat. In both cases the sites were sandy loam. Obviously the presence of such sites varies with location, and some management units may completely lack the preferred sites. However, if general food preferences are understood, the range manager can take steps to improve the available sites which are most preferred by deer.

Based on analyses of deer rumen contents in the spring of 1970 and 1971 in South Texas, forbs and browse, as general forage classes, contributed most to the diet (86). Deer had access to three major range sites, with some overlap of species that were available. Although several species were noted as important from year to year and among sites, ten species apparently contributed the bulk of the animals' diet. Important forbs were perennial lazy-daisy, ground-cherry, and winecup. Apparently perennials were more important in the diet than annuals. Preferred woody plants were spiny hackberry, lotebush, honey mesquite, guayacan, catclaw acacia, coma (bumelia), and pricklypear. Honey mesquite beans and Texas persimmon fruits were highly important. The importance of mast to game animals justifies leaving at least scattered mature woody plants. Although standing dead plants provide screen, their failure to produce seeds and fruits detracts from habitat quality.

Although ten species were most common in the diets of white-tailed deer (86), more than eighty-three plant taxa were encountered in the sampling, indicating the importance of botanical diversity in deer habitat. Although food habits certainly depend on the relative availability of plants, diet apparently also is influenced by preferences of individual deer. Preference apparently varies with age, sex, and season and among individuals of the same age and sex within a season. Therefore, an intermixture of vegetation types providing a reasonable level of diversity is an apparent requisite for quality deer habitat.

The importance of forbs is illustrated by the results of studies of the midsummer diet of white-tailed deer on two soil types in Coastal Prairie vegetation. These animals had access to highly diverse mixed-brush stands of sufficient stand thickness to easily meet cover and browse requirements. Even with the high availability of browse, forbs made up at least 50 percent of the diet. Relative preference of food items apparently varies with range site as it regulates the availability of plant species. On clay soils the diet was 70 percent forbs and 22 percent browse (including mast) (74). On sandy soils forbs made up 53 percent of the deer diets and browse (including mast) contributed 45 percent. Whitetail diets may shift within a site, as dictated by plant species availability and phenology, according to season and climate. During dry periods white-tailed deer consume the leaves, succulent branch tips, and mast of browse plants in South Texas (74). As the mast crop is reduced by feeding and the browse matures, the deer diet is composed primarily of forbs. Although only three or four plant species made up more than half the diet, fifty-eight species were identified in the diet (74). Again, *diversity of plants* is an important consideration for quality white-tailed deer habitat. Regardless of range site, the most important deer foods are usually perennials, and grasses are an insignificant part of their diets during the summer.

White-tailed deer are primarily grazers during the winter in South Texas. Their complex diet shifts with season as winter dormancy gives way to spring "greenup." According to Chamrad and Box (52), herbaceous plants make up about 90 percent of the diet, with forbs contributing almost 70 percent during the winter on the Coastal Prairie. During this winter period browse affords only about 5 percent of their diet. Since deciduous brush species are without foliage during the winter and evergreens do not develop significant vegetative growth, available green plant matter is afforded primarily by cool-season forbs.

Use of habitat types by white-tailed deer in the Rolling Plains of Texas follows much the same pattern as that noted for South Texas. Relatively undisturbed bottomland habitats with deep soils and dominated by brush species such as desert sumac, agarito, net-leaf hackberry, one-seeded juniper, and lotebush usually support the highest density of deer (61). Canopy cover of such sites is normally about 20 percent. The least preferred habitats in this region are uplands which support a shrub canopy cover of only 4 percent and are dominated by catclaw mimosa and agarito usually less than 3 feet tall. These upland sites are usually adjacent to upland savannah habitat, a smooth, nearly level upland with a shrub canopy cover of about 3 percent dominated by honey mesquite.

The sand shinnery oak habitat, common in the Rolling and High Plains of Texas, usually supports fewer white-tailed deer than does undisturbed bottomland habitat but is more preferred than upland habitat (61). Sand shinnery oak occurs on sites with deep, fine sand, usually with less than 10 percent canopy cover, and with shrubs most of which are less than 18 inches tall. Since the sand shinnery oak provides little concealment, attraction of the white-tailed deer is apparently related to availability of food. Sand shinnery oak browse and acorns are preferred by deer and may provide more than 10 percent of the total food items in the fall and winter (61). Also, the presence of sand shinnery oak mottes, scattered circular clumps of thick, relatively tall oak stems, apparently provides adequate cover for white-tailed deer, especially in conjunction with adjacent habitats dominated by honey mesquite.

Use of open areas by white-tailed deer is facilitated when adequate cover is available in adjacent habitats, but there is a threshold level of cover necessary for high deer densities. In the Coastal Prairie, I have observed large herds of white-tailed deer using open areas 1,000 to 2,000 feet wide between strips of Macartney rose. In other areas deer will routinely use tame pastures and may even become a nuisance on cropland. Invariably, however, with minor disturbance the deer will quickly disappear back into the woody plant cover. When cover requirements are met, the quality of herbaceous vegetation (in terms of the abundance and diversity of the forbs) apparently dictates the preference of white-tailed deer for certain habitats.

Based on the preceding discussion, the following conclusions are pertinent to designing brush management schemes for white-tailed deer:

1. Woody plants are important to white-tailed deer habitat by furnishing both food and cover. However, deer do not distinguish types of brush if minimal cover requirements are met; the affinity of whitetails for specific range sites is related to food.

2. On a year-round basis, white-tailed deer depend most heavily on forbs for the bulk of their diet. Undoubtedly browse is an important (perhaps even critical) component of their diet, but the importance obviously varies with season and type of growth.

3. Although a few key plant species usually contribute the majority of the diet within a given season and range site, white-tailed deer use a great number of species. Therefore, range improvement practices which promote species diversity as well as plant production should be considered for quality white-tailed deer habitat.

4. Although the same forage classes are preferred, white-tailed deer diets may vary among range sites within a season. Availability and growth stage of vegetation are important, but individual preference may be the regulating factors for diet at any given time.

5. Deer consume some grasses, although relatively few, and cattle utilize some forbs. However, the high preference of deer for forbs and of cattle for grass, unless one of the two forage classes becomes limiting, should preclude competition between the two species (86).

Herbicides and Wildlife Habitat

Unfortunately, relatively few studies have assessed the impact of commonly used herbicides on wildlife habitat. Consequently, only broad generalizations have been possible, and too often herbicide use has not been viewed objectively by game managers. Broadcast herbicide applications may have negative effects on wildlife habitat, but, applied properly, they may improve habitat.

Aerial sprays can be used to reduce the incidence of low-preference browse species, thus allowing preferred species to increase and to improve deer habitat (171). The influence of herbicides such as 2,4,5-T on the forb population is usually restricted to the year of application, since phenoxy herbicides have short-lived residual effects. The dead tops of woody plants and regrowth provide cover for deer following aerial spraying with 2,4,5-T. Therefore, use of the herbicide does not degrade white-tailed deer habitat unless treatments are repeated until the brush is completely removed (61). Since herbicides may vary significantly in species selectivity and residual effects, only general statements concerning their effects on game habitat are possible. For example, picloram controls a broader spectrum of broadleaved species, both woody and herbaceous, and has longer residual life in the grassland ecosystem than does 2,4,5-T at the same application rate.

Relative affinity of white-tailed deer for rangeland aerially treated with herbicides such as 2,4,5-T plus picloram is predominantly associated with food and is closely correlated with production and diversity of forbs (19). Posttreatment reductions in numbers of deer on large areas that are completely sprayed parallel the responses of forbs to hormone herbicides. When the effect of the sprays on forbs is eliminated (after about two and one-half years in one study [19]) and forb production returns to normal, numbers of deer are no different between treated and untreated areas. The response of deer to aerial sprays of 2,4,5-T plus picloram is less pronounced when only 80 percent or less of the rangeland is sprayed in alternate strips compared to complete spraying. Strip spraying is a logical compromise when both livestock and white-tailed deer share the habitat.

Game species such as nilgai antelope may not respond so profoundly to herbicide treatment as white-tailed deer since the antelopes' diet is much more variable than that of deer (19, 284). Nilgai antelope are evidently less dependent on forbs and browse and more dependent on grasses than are deer, or they have the capability to more effectively use grasses in their diet.

Feral hogs and javelina may leave areas treated with aerial sprays because of the reduced availability of fruiting parts of woody plants and because of the control of pricklypear. Fruiting parts of woody plants constitute approximately 50 percent of the summer, fall, and winter diet of feral hogs (295), and pricklypear is the singularly most important food item of javelina (160). In a study by Beasom and Scifres (19), numbers of feral hogs and javelina were significantly reduced in pastures which were completely sprayed with 2,4,5-T plus picloram. Leaving 20 percent of the habitat untreated was not adequate to preserve the javelina populations.

If roosting sites are protected, it is expected that spraying in strips will not seriously degrade wild turkey habitat. Wild turkeys use a broad range of food items which may enhance their adaptability to the manipulation of their habitat.

Aerial spraying has two primary advantages which allow integration of the objectives of brush management for livestock production with those for maintenance of wildlife habitat:

1. Aerial spraying can be completed relatively rapidly with a minimum of initial disturbance to wildlife, aside from aircraft noise and the presence of men during the time of treatment.

2. The effects of herbicides on the vegetation are relatively subtle. Defoliation may require several weeks, and trunks and branches remain standing, affording screen. Although the canopy cover is drastically reduced, not all woody plants are killed. Those species which resprout provide new succulent growth for browsing, and herbicides can be applied in strips to preserve adequate forbs for white-tailed deer habitat.

Mechanical Brush Management and Wildlife Habitat

Mechanical practices, such as chaining, quickly knock down the larger woody plants, exerting an almost immediate effect on wildlife habitat. In one study on the Rolling Plains, chaining of bottomland sites reduced the white-tailed deer population to eight or ten per one hundred acres compared to seventeen deer per one hundred acres on unchained bottomland habitat (61). Chained bottoms two miles wide supported three deer per one hundred acres, whereas those only one mile wide supported eleven deer per one hundred acres. This contrast suggests that chaining small areas, sparing logically placed strips and clumps of woody vegetation to provide travel lanes and escape cover for deer, is more desirable than complete brush removal (61).

Shredding stimulates the development of regrowth and may increase the preference for several browse species by white-tailed deer (232). However, this increased preference may be restricted to the season of treatment. By the second growing season after shredding, the woody sprouts increase in size, age, and "thorniness" and are not necessarily preferred by white-tailed deer over untreated plants. Shredding also increases the availability of browse by bringing it within easy reach of the animals.

Shredding may not increase preference by white-tailed deer for those species such as huisache which are normally highly preferred. However, the preference by deer for species such as spiny hackberry and lotebush, two of the less preferred species in the mature state, may be dramatically increased by shredding during the growing season or top removal (232).

Not only is regrowth preferred by deer over mature woody plants, but nutritional quality of the immature growth is also usually higher. Crude protein content of the regrowth of many species may be higher than that of its mature growth. Roller chopping may induce the same changes as shredding in browse quality and availability.

New growth is usually tall enough the year after shredding or roller chopping to provide cover for quail, for turkey nesting, and for fawning (38). In three to five years brush regrowth may be sufficiently high to provide cover for adult deer and javelina.

Root plowing, improperly applied, may drastically alter wildlife habitat. Root plowing may essentially eliminate browse and reduce cover but stimulate forb production. On deeper sites, root plowing may essentially eliminate the brush for ten to twenty years and, with adequate rainfall, provide high amounts of range forage for grazing animals. However, root plowing of broad expanses reduces quality habitat for white-tailed deer (67) and reduces numbers of deer on the treated area, at least for one or two years. Therefore, it is advisable to root plow only the deeper range sites, leaving adjacent sites with a brush cover for deer habitat, and to emphasize development of edge effect, the leaving of irregular rather than straight lines of standing brush to facilitate concealment of deer and make more avenues available for their escape to cover. (These irregular brush lines result in a larger proportion of brush to open areas than is possible with straight lines. The wildlife biologists also refer to "interspersion" of types of vegetation which offer diversity of habitat—the basis for the term *edge effect.*) Root plowing followed by seeding with species such as Kleingrass may be valuable in developing habitat for upland game birds such as bobwhite quail (122), although a portion of the brush (15 percent or so) apparently is still required to provide adequate cover for quail. By leaving some brush cover and using a species such as Kleingrass which produces relatively large, plump seeds, bobwhite quail habitat can be maintained and carrying capacity of the rangeland for livestock can be improved.

Prescribed Burning and Wildlife Habitat

Fire has great potential for manipulation of range wildlife habitat (334). Properly applied burnings may result in a plentiful supply of palatable herbaceous forage, reinstate diversity within the vegetation system, and reduce the effects of several types of parasites. Fire rarely harms wildlife directly and then only when all escape routes are closed during burning. Exclusion of natural fires and the lack of planned burning in Texas have resulted in the development in many areas of dense jungles which limit the carrying capacity of wildlife (21). In my opinion, brush stands can become overmature for best use by wildlife, and habitat quality can be improved by converting these decadent stands to a diversity and size which afford a more available supply of nutritious browse and a more open brush stand. Fire may well be the most logical tool for this sort of vegetation conversion.

Where repeated herbicide use greatly reduces the forb population, prescribed burning may restore broad-leaved plants to the range ecosystem (248). White-tailed deer make heavy use of burned areas on the Coastal Prairie, especially in early spring when succulent forb growth is available.

Since animals as well as vegetation of the grassland ecosystem have evolved under the influence of fire, burning may be a requirement for success of some game species. For example, the abundance of Attwater's prairie chicken parallels the incidence of fire on the Coastal Prairie (175), and prescribed burning may be used to attract the birds to areas not previously used by them (51). The prairie chickens engage in booming, roosting, loafing, and feeding on or immediately adjacent to the burned areas. Attwater's prairie chickens may locate their nests within four hundred yards of burned areas where booming occurs in the spring following the burning (51). Burning promotes growth of succulent vegetative parts and tends to increase seed production, both important components of the prairie chickens' diets.

Since wild turkeys eat seeds and fruiting parts of several plant species, mostly grasses (18, 102), prescribed burning may improve wild turkey habitat in much the same manner that it functions to augment Attwater's prairie chicken. Also, burning may increase the availability of browse and promote its use by both cattle and white-tailed deer.

In enumerating the benefits of prescribed burning for improvement of wildlife habitat in southeastern Texas, Blakey (21) emphasized:

Benefits derived for wildlife are evident in the physical recovery of range in usable condition, improvement in wildlife food resources and cover relationships, and response by various animals in their activities on the range. Deer congregate in the cut-over areas within a matter of hours or days. Turkeys are attracted by the burning and the increased crop of their preferred foods. Quail find a suitable year-around range where they could not exist before. Doves feed in the burned-over tracts. Jacksnipes and sandhill cranes prefer the burned sites and congregate there. Only a portion of the wintering population of song and insectivorous birds is temporarily readjusted to unburned tracts. Predators find less protection for their movements. All in all, we find this a very satisfactory, efficient, and economical means of habitat improvement. Managers of range land should give attention to the possibilities of its use wherever the principles and mechanics of cutting and burning may be properly applied.

In my experience, the simultaneous use of rangeland for quality wildlife habitat and livestock production has never been in conflict, *if common sense is exercised in the development of a sound resource management plan.* An effective management plan always includes an inventory of resources as the working basis. If the resources available are developed for their best use based on the resource inventory, an effective balance between wildlife habitat and grazing land for livestock is not only possible but also a desirable goal. The balance can only be maintained, however, if the response of the resources is continually monitored to allow necessary management adjustments to coincide with vegetation trend.

10

Brush Management Systems

To this point brush management practices have been treated primarily as singular approaches to range improvement, with little reference to the overall management system. This approach allows the principles for the successful application of each method to be described, but brush management is rarely planned without consideration of the overall needs of the management unit—usually the entire ranching enterprise. Knowledge of individual brush management techniques is only one step toward effective range improvement. The theory of the weakest link applies to the fullest in this case. Any brush management practice is only as successful as the associated managerial ability is sound. This point was aptly made by Dyksterhuis (75): "Though many practices besides management of grazing are applied on ranges (artificial seeding, rodent control, brush control, burning, mechanical treatment of soil, fertilization, etc.), the succession process in response to grazing treatment ultimately determines the success or failure of any of them. . . . Control of weedy plants can be highly effective and economical on rangelands *if* it is integrated with other practices to hasten secondary succession. If it is not, professional rangemen should try to avoid being party to the practice." The ultimate success of range improvement is measured by the land manager in terms of economic net returns to the ranching enterprise. Furthermore, success is usually a reflection of overall managerial ability in the ranching enterprise rather than an absolute measure of the effectiveness of a given brush management technique.

No brush management method, whether chemical, mechanical,

This chapter was developed in collaboration with Drs. R. E. Whitson and M. M. Kothmann, Department of Range Science, Texas Agricultural Experiment Station, Texas A&M University.

biological, or prescribed burning, is without its unique strong points and characteristic weaknesses. There are only a few cases in which single-treatment approaches have maximized long-term benefits to the ranching enterprise. Instead, several carefully selected treatments applied over a considerable period of time are usually required to optimize net returns to management.

The word *system* has more than fifteen definitions and a multitude of uses. Meanings which may apply directly to brush management systems include (1) a coordinated body of methods or a complex scheme or plan of procedure; (2) any formulated, regular, or special method or plan of procedure; and (3) due method or orderly manner of arrangement or procedure. A brush management system, then, may be considered a plan of procedure in which the application of the individual methods is coordinated by the manager in an orderly manner. Thus, the resource manager must become familiar with the applicability of all available methods and their specific place in a sequential arrangement for maximum results.

Proper sequencing and applicaton of two or more brush management practices in a well-designed improvement plan will yield maximum long-term benefits, but long-range planning is often difficult, since a degree of uncertainty is associated with each step. Consequently, in planning the brush management system, flexibility in the timing of the primary methods and applicable alternative methods must be considered. Since effective brush management on rangeland is not a "one-shot" affair but a perennial component of the overall plan for management of land resources, some important considerations in the planning stages should include:

1. *Natural resource potential.* Potential production of the rangeland must be projected based on precipitation (including average annual and seasonal distribution), soils, growing season, and related factors. To effectively formulate this projection, the manager must develop an accurate resource inventory relating the relative proportions of vegetation-soil complexes on the management units and determine the following:

   A. Available information about the production potential of that portion of the enterprise that is to be subjected to improvement practices, and additional information needs

   B. The percentage of land area, by management unit, that is amenable to improvement through brush management

C. The projected degree (intensity) of brush management needed to optimize usable vegetation

D. Applicable practices for the area, their sequencing, and the expected rate of change in production following their application

2. *Management objectives.* Overall organizational objectives may best be related as a series of goals to be attained within a specified time framework. These goals must be based on long-term objectives of the enterprise for use of natural resources and will require decisions pertaining to

A. The relative importance to be placed on potential income from livestock and wildlife resources

B. The projected roles of tame pasture and cultivated forage crops in relation to natural grazing resources

3. *Economics.* Although the brush management practice with potential for maximum net pay-back is usually considered to be the logical choice by management, the choice of method is tempered by

A. The estimated benefits, costs, and alternative uses of capital

B. The financial resources available for range improvement efforts

C. Requirements for contract work and the amount of work that can be accomplished with equipment, supplies, and labor controlled by the enterprise

D. A logical, economically feasible time frame for attaining maximum range improvement

Before a brush management system can be developed, some basic concepts of range management must be clearly understood by the resource manager. Those principles with direct practical utility in developing brush management systems include range condition and trend, the key species–key area concept, and the general principles of grazing management.

Range Condition and Trend

Different kinds of rangeland complexes of soil and climatic conditions, called range sites, have potential for supporting different kinds and amounts of vegetation. Many vegetation types may successively occupy the same range site in response to different grazing treatments (76). The ultimate vegetation of the range site, based on its natural potential, is referred to as climax vegetation. Climax vegetation is more productive for grazing than any other successional stage. *Range condition* refers to the kinds and amounts of vegetation a site supports in relation to its potential or climax. Range condition is more than a reflection that an area has a favorable growing season or simply has received good rains. It is the "state of health" of the range in terms of what it could or should be under normal climate and the best management that can be practiced (79). *Range condition trend* is the direction of vegetation change from its current condition—whether the health of the range is improving or deteriorating.

Range condition is usually a quantitative estimate of botanical composition (the relative proportions of plant species) based on weight or ground cover relative to what the coverage of the climax vegetation should be. It can be viewed as "the percentage of the present vegetation which is original vegetation for the site" (79). Based on these composition estimates, range condition may be classed as excellent, good, fair, or poor (Fig. 10.1). Range condition is excellent when 76 to 100 percent of climax vegetation is supported on a site, good when 51 to 75 percent of the climax vegetation is represented, fair when 26 to 50 percent is present, and poor when 25 percent or less of the resident vegetation occurs in climax.

Range plants are classified based on their response to overgrazing. *Decreasers* are highly preferred species, whether grasses, grasslike plants, forbs, or shrubs, which decline under overgrazing. As decreasers decline, another group of climax species called *increasers* tends to become more abundant. However, under continued overgrazing the increasers are also overused and begin to decline in abundance. There are, however, some increaser species which under continual overgrazing may tend to progressively increase— post oak in Post Oak Savannah climax is an example. Under good management a very low proportion of the vegetation is afforded by *invaders*, those opportunistic species, generally of low grazing value, which fill voids created by the removal of decreasers and increasers under overgrazing. Decreasers and increasers, then, are species of

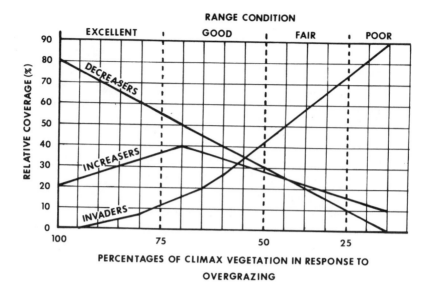

10.1. Relationships between major variables used to classify range condition.

undisturbed and relatively stable climax communities, whereas the invaders are not (79). As range condition declines, invaders, including brush, compose an increasingly higher percentage of the vegetation.

Overgrazed land therefore is land that supports unsatisfactory kinds and proportions of plants compared to what could grow on the site (76). Classification of range condition is useful, then, in relating to what degree the site has been overgrazed and the degree of improvement possible by grazing management. Excellent range condition indicates the ultimate balance between grazing use and site potential, while good, fair, and poor range conditions reflect grades of overuse. It follows then, that unless the management unit is under proper grazing management, range condition cannot be improved on a sustained basis by brush management. It is in this vein that most misunderstandings concerning the role of brush management arise.

The removal of brush changes, at least on the short term, the proportion of invaders to other species classes. Release of herbaceous plants from competition with woody plants usually increases their production, especially in wet years. This result may be viewed as an upward trend. However, under overgrazing, voids left by control of woody invaders will simply be filled by herbaceous opportunists and seedlings of woody plants. In fact, control of brush without grazing management may be significantly detrimental to the range. On badly deteriorated rangeland often the only desirable plants present are next to a thorny shrub which has protected them from grazing.

On ranges in poor to high fair condition because of the presence of brush, rest from grazing should be the first step to restoration in a brush management program. Rest from grazing allows the climax perennials to improve in vigor and produce seed and enables them to effectively compete with invaders for the voids remaining after the brush is removed.

Key Species–Key Area Concept

Range condition classification is a tool for determining the departure of vegetation from its potential and deciding whether the vegetation change is in the right direction. However, this tool does not present a workable method of determining proper grazing on a day-to-day basis. Pastures are usually composed of a number of range sites, each of which supports a relatively large number of plant species. Under grazing, the plant species will be used to varying degrees depending on their availability and the preferences of the grazing animals. Just as excessive cover of brush indicates overgrazing, the prosperity of desirable species indicates proper grazing. To consider the degree of use of all plant species in making the decision about proper use of a pasture is difficult and impractical. Therefore, one or more plant species (*key species*) may be used to indicate proper use. The key species should be well distributed and should be a major species on the management unit.

Some species, present in lesser numbers than the key species, may be more highly preferred by the grazing animals. Such species will be overused before proper use is made of the key species, and they eventually may be sacrificed. The manager must decide the advisability of overusing such preferred species. If they are representative of the climax, and potentially of high importance for grazing (that is, if they were allowed to increase on the range, their grazing capacity would be substantially increased), then use of the entire range should be reduced to allow them to fulfill their potential. Otherwise, the range manager is justified to sacrifice them for the sake of highest sustained forage yield.

As certain species are selected as indicators of proper use of a range, so a representative area, the *key area*, may be selected on which to base use of the management unit. Certain areas, especially those containing water, salt, or supplemental feed, will be necessarily sacrificed to heavy use by livestock. This cannot be avoided under continuous grazing. Also, it must be accepted that certain other areas, by virtue or their physical features or their distance from water, salt, or feeding grounds, will be used lightly. That area which normally supports most of the grazing is generally used as the key area. The key area may conceivably be composed of several range sites. When use of the key area is correct, use of the pasture is correct.

Grazing Management

Grazing management, broadly speaking, is the manipulation of livestock grazing to achieve desired results (170); it generally includes maintenance or improvement of range vegetation, efficient use of the forage resource, and production of animal products from livestock or wildlife. As Kothmann (169) has defined it, "Grazing management includes stocking rates (ratio of animals to land area) and grazing systems (schemes for alternately grazing and resting pastures)."

Since proper grazing management is the basic range improvement practice, brush management is only as successful as it is allowed to be by the grazing management system on which it is superimposed. In their discussion of the importance of grazing management and honey mesquite control, Hoffman and Merrill (201) emphasized that

Planned management of grazing will increase benefits from brush control and is essential to the continued success of a brush control program. Mesquite control is valuable for releasing growth of native forage plants and for improving conditions of all animal life. Forage plants need rest from grazing, and a systematic deferred-rotation grazing program is the most satisfactory method of attaining systematic rest periods. . . . A grazing rotation program can be initiated either entirely on native rangeland, in conjunction with tame pastures, or in conjunction with feedlots. A grazing management program combined with mesquite control should be outlined in step-by-step procedures for at least a 15-year period. Such planning will assure maximum benefits from mesquite control in the overall range program.

Although the practice of herding livestock is as old as the history of civilization, grazing management technology is still in the developmental stages. The application of grazing management can draw heavily on scientific principles, but it is still largely an art that is acquired through years of experience, with a sound scientific base and a keen sense of perception. Kothmann (170) prepared a list of definitions appropriate here to avoid confusion in discussion:

1. *Continuous grazing.* The grazing of a specific unit by livestock throughout a year or grazing season. The term is not necessarily synonymous with year-long grazing.
2. *Intermittent grazing.* Grazing rangeland or tame pastureland for indefinite periods at irregular intervals.
3. *Deferred grazing.* The use of deferment in the grazing management of a unit but not in a systematic rotation including other units.
4. *Grazing system.* A specialization of grazing management which defines systematically recurring periods of grazing and deferment for two or more pastures or management units.
5. *Rotational grazing.* A form of grazing management, generally used on tame pasture or cropland pasture, which embraces periods of heavy stocking followed by periods of rest for herbage recovery during the same season.

The essentials of grazing management required for optimum use of forage can be grouped into four categories: proper stocking, proper season of grazing, proper distribution of grazing, and proper kind and class of livestock and wildlife. Proper stocking is considered by many to be the single most important factor involved in grazing management. Grazing management increases production of livestock and wildlife by improving vegetation (168) and functions generally by increasing production per animal (hence increasing total production for the overall management unit) rather than depending necessarily on increased numbers of animals (Fig. 10.2).

Most range plants are well adapted to tolerate grazing, but only to a certain degree and only at certain times. Much research

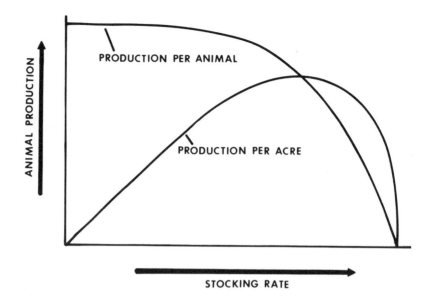

10.2. Relationship between stocking rate and animal production. Production per animal is highest at low stocking rates, while production per acre increases to a point and then declines (168).

has been done to determine the tolerance of different forage species to grazing, but much is still needed. The tolerance of plants to grazing is correlated to the levels of reserve food supplies in the plant at the time of grazing. Thus, the critical stages for top removal of forage plants are during the early growth stage and again during the period of rapid stem elongation before flowering. Forage plants retain adequate foliage to manufacture food for maintenance of the root system, for production of new foliage, and for reproduction, whether by seeds or vegetatively. Since almost all desirable range plants are perennials, their food reserves must be adequate at the beginning of the dormant period so they will be sustained during winter or during other periods of stress such as drought. Reserves are also necessary to support the initial growth required for foliar replacement following dormancy.

Proper stocking. The proper ratio must be maintained between animal numbers and grazeable forage so that the animals can meet their intake requirements and the plants can meet their requirements for growth and reproduction (168). At low stocking rates production per acre may be too low for economic feasibility (Fig. 10.2).

As stocking rate is increased, production per animal decreases, but production per acre increases to a point and then declines drastically. Under conditions of overstocking, neither production per animal nor production per unit area is optimum.

The amount of grazeable forage on the range is the primary consideration when the proper stocking rate is being determined. Usually 25,000 to 35,000 pounds of total forage are required to support an animal unit (1,000-pound cow with calf, or the equivalent; see Table 10.1) for a year. This quantity is considerably more than is actually consumed by an animal unit in a year (about 9,500 pounds). Not all plants produced on the range are consumed by grazing animals, since plant species vary in palatability. Some are very palatable and will be selected first, while others may never be used. Thus, to avoid destructive overuse of the most desirable species it is generally necessary to forego use of some secondary species, which will only be used after the most desirable species are seriously overgrazed.

Animals also prefer certain parts of plants. Leaves, which almost always have a higher nutrient content, are generally selected over stems. A stocking rate heavy enough to cause a high degree of use is usually reflected by the inclusion of more stems and other low-quality forage in the animals' diets. Significantly amounts of forage must be left ungrazed so that the plants can retain enough leaves to remain photosynthetically active and to maintain the nutrient content of the animals' diet at the highest level.

Forage is also lost or made unavailable for grazing through the action of insects, rodents, trampling, weathering, and other such causes. Also, some vegetation cover is necessary for soil stabilization and prevention of erosion. The amount of vegetation cover required varies with the soil type, rainfall intensity and distribution, slope, and other physical factors. However, two thousands pounds of mulch and standing live plant material per acre has generally been adequate for conditions in central Texas.

Grazing deferment. Some ranges are suitable for grazing during all seasons, while others are accessible only during certain seasons. Plants are more susceptible to damage from grazing during certain seasons than during others. Year-long grazing practiced over a period of years will almost always result in deterioration of the range vegetation, especially if stocking rate is not carefully adjusted to meet annual fluctuations in forage production. The seasonal suitability of a unit must be determined before the grazing plan can be developed.

A period of rest from grazing is necessary to maintain the vigor of range plants and improve the composition of the vegetation. These rest periods, called periods of deferment, should be scheduled to allow the plants an opportunity to regain vigor and reproduce and to allow new plants to become established. This deferment is achieved either through the use of deferred grazing or with a planned grazing system.

Grazing Distribution. Animals seldom graze vegetation uniformly, so proper grazing distribution is critical for the efficient use use of range forage. Patterns of use of range forage may be classified as *area-selective* and *species-selective* grazing.

Area-selective grazing—the grazing of certain areas in preference to others—may be attributed to the size and shape of pastures; the location of water, salt, and bedding grounds; topography; soil factors (fertility, texture, and so on); prevailing winds; and the kinds and classes of animals. The opportunity for area-selective grazing is greater in large than in small pastures. Acute angles at the junctions of fences may be used less by livestock than square corners. Sheep use slopes and ridge tops much more readily than do cattle, which prefer to graze on level bottomlands. Sheep and goats graze into the wind, while cattle and horses graze with the wind. Distribution of young stocker animals may differ from that of a mature cow with a calf in the same pasture.

The location of water and salt within the pasture has a strong influence on grazing distribution. Each animal will visit these locations at least once daily, resulting in increased localized use of the forage.

Species-selective grazing—the preferences exhibited by animals for certain plant species—may also result in poor grazing distribution. Most plant species are not uniformly distributed over the range but are associated with rather localized soil, topographic, and moisture differences. Within a given area, plants of a single species frequently occur in clumps or colonies. Where the preferred plant species are restricted in distribution, species-selective grazing may appear to be area-selective grazing. However, species-selective grazing can still occur where different plant species are intermingled rather uniformly over an entire pasture.

Management practices should be selected to achieve the most uniform possible use of all available forage. While uniform use of all plant species and areas is a goal, it is rarely, if ever, fully achieved. Therefore, only those areas of the pasture and those plant species which will be used must be considered in determining the grazing capacity and subsequent stocking rate.

Combinations of grazing animals. In most regions there is a choice available with respect to the kinds of animals—usually cattle, sheep, horses, and goats—that may be stocked. Wildlife, especially white-tailed deer, are also present in many areas. Each kind of animal has characteristic preferences and requirements with respect to diet, type of terrain, and other habitat characteristics. The kinds of animals best suited to the given management area should be carefully selected. If species of animals other than those considered best adapted to the area are used, the manager must recognize the limitations of the vegetation in meeting the animals' requirements.

Because different kinds of animals prefer different plant species and different types of terrain, a combination of species can frequently use an area more efficiently than can a single species. It is often possible to graze more animals without damage to the resource by using combinations of species than by using any single species. If the proper stocking rate is used, the degree of competition between kinds of animals is negligible. As stocking rates are increased to the point that the availability of preferred forages is limited, the degree of competition between kinds of animals is increased.

The calculation of stocking rates using different kinds of animals is facilitated by use of animal-unit conversion factors. These factors relate the different kinds of animals to a common base—their forage consumption. An animal unit is the number of animals which consume twenty-six pounds of forage per day. The animal-unit conversion factor is a *general guide* for determining the numbers of

TABLE 10.1.
Animal-Unit Conversion Factors.

Animal-unit Equivalent	Kind and Class of Animal
1	Cow (1,000 pounds) with calf
1.25	Mature bull
0.6	Stocker (500 to 600 pounds)
0.75	Yearling heifer
0.143–0.167	Doe goat (with or without kid)
0.143–0.167	Doe white-tailed deer (with or without fawn)
0.2	Ewe with lamb
0.25	Mature ram
1.25–1.5	Horse

animals of different species which exert equivalent grazing pressure on the range (Table 10.1).

Structural improvements. The resource manager can make better use of the range by implementing structural improvements, such as the arrangement of watering locations to improve grazing distribution, fence construction, the building of walkways in low marsh ranges, and salting, which contribute to better efficiency in the use of forage. Frequently these improvements must be made before deferred grazing or a grazing system can be used successfully.

Forage located more than a mile from any water source will generally receive little use, since travel time limits the amount of time animals will spend grazing. Salt should not be placed near water but should be located in areas which need to be used more. Fences should be constructed as nearly along the boundaries of range sites as possible. This last improvement method promotes uniform use of the range by creating pastures with more homogeneous vegetation and topography. Not only is grazing distribution improved, but application of other management procedures to each type of vegetation is also facilitated. Generally, square pastures with water centrally located are most efficient. The following questions should be considered while planning and selecting fence routes:
1. How will the proposed fences likely affect cattle movement, natural drift, and patterns of use? A poorly located fence can isolate portions of the range or create pockets and "cow traps."

2. Do the fences fit in properly with the long-range plan of management?
3. Will the carrying capacity of pasture units created by fencing be equal, or nearly so? If pasture units are seriously unbalanced, rotation may be impossible or at least ineffective because the normal beneficial effects of rest or deferment will be nullified by extreme overstocking in the light-capacity pastures.

Grazing systems. Ranges that are in poor condition or vigor should be deferred from grazing for the entire growing season of the desirable species. Where reproduction of desirable species is desired, the range should not be heavily grazed until after seed is set. Limited grazing after plant maturity is generally not detrimental and may even assist in range improvement. It is wise to defer grazing during the spring following seed dissemination to allow young plants to become established. Brush management practices and range seeding should always be accomplished by deferment of grazing during the season of installation of the practice and sometimes the following growing season. The proper use of a carefully selected grazing system allows the resource manager to meet all these needs to improve his range. These systems are based on planned deferments of grazing.

Planning deferments for several management units within an operation can be difficult, and not all units may receive the needed deferment unless a formal, systematic grazing plan is used. Therefore, grazing systems have been designed which use several pastures and are based on rotation of the livestock among pastures on a predetermined schedule (Fig. 10.3). Each of the pastures should regularly be deferred during different seasons of the year.

A deferred-rotation grazing system that works well with many brush management practices is the "two-pastures, one-herd" system (269). Only one pasture is treated in a given year, and practices such as herbicide application may be timed for the spring or the fall as dictated by the susceptibility of the brush (Table 10.2). With this particular system, rest periods which include the spring growing season can maximize the benefits of the brush management techniques. With careful thought the ranch manager can developed combinations of brush management practices for use with other grazing systems which will take advantage of scheduled rest periods.

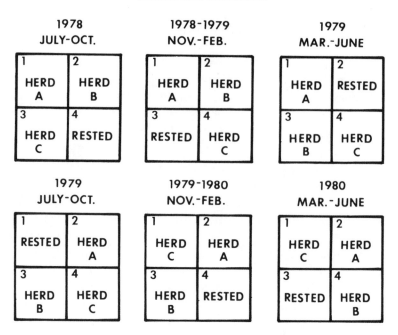

10.3. Schedule for grazing and rest under the Merrill grazing system. Each pasture is grazed for twelve months and rested for four months. The four pastures should have approximately the same carrying capacities (168).

Economic Considerations

Too often brush management is viewed only as a one-time investment. Initial cost of brush management practices is only a part of the total cost, and the investment should not be based only on initial treatment cost and simple projections of the stocking rate for domestic livestock. Unfortunately, brush management is often "sold" on potential increases in stocking rate without full consideration of all economic implications. For example, if the present carrying capacity for domestic livestock is thirty animal units (A.U.) per section (one A.U. per twenty-one acres), and it is anticipated that the stocking rate can be increased to forty-three A.U. per section (one A.U. per fifteen acres), then the additional pounds of beef obtained from the added thirteen A.U. and any improvement in percentage of calf crop, weaning weight changes, or reduced opera-

TABLE 10.2.
Incorporating Herbicide Application for Maximum Range
Improvement in a Two-Pastures, One-Herd Grazing System (269).

Time period	Pasture 1	Pasture 2	Spring (May 1– June 10)	Fall (Sept. 15– Oct. 15)
Oct. 1–Feb. 1	Graze	Rest	—	Pasture 1
Feb. 1–June 1	Rest	Graze	—	—
June 1–Oct. 1	Graze	Rest	Pasture 2	—
Oct. 1–Feb. 1	Rest	Graze	—	Pasture 2
Feb. 1–June 1	Graze	Rest	—	—
June 1–Oct. 1	Rest	Graze	Pasture 1	—

* Application refers to foliar broadcast treatment, and dates in parentheses are generalized to aid in understanding.

tional costs associated with the original thirty A.U. must pay for:[4]

1. Cost of the initial practice and any secondary practices such as fencing or water development in addition to those used when the rangeland was carrying thirty A.U. per section
2. Cost of purchasing the additional thirteen A.U.
3. Any decreased sources of revenue (for example, if game production or quality and associated revenues are altered by the practices)
4. All additional variable costs (veterinary cost, supplemental feeding, additional breeding males, livestock handling and care, fertilizer, marketing, and so on)
5. The opportunity cost associated with the investment and added breeding stock (For example, if the total investment in brush management was $19,200 per section, the rancher could invest the $19,200 in a savings account paying, for example, 5 percent. Thus, the brush management practice would have to pay $6,529 per year in simple interest in addition to capital recovery, added variable costs, and reduced revenues before the practice would break even.)

[4] Changes in value of the land were not considered, since disposition of the land would be necessary to realize an effect on land value by the brush management practice. One must realize also that changes in land value affect factors such as tax base and the "borrowing power" of the landowner.

The burden of cost often is assigned to the total carrying capacity after treatment, and the costs (fixed and variable) associated with each added animal unit and alternative investments are not properly considered. Also, the effect of initiating the management practice on cash flow within the ranch unit must be considered in relation to payback periods imposed by lending institutions. The binding of capital over extended periods often complicates the management strategy in that improvement capital must be repaid quicker than increased productivity will allow.

Since the land resource manager analyzing the feasibility of brush management is invariably faced with decisions for which the exact final outcome cannot be anticipated, a certain amount of risk and investment uncertainty is expected. However, there are some relatively simple procedures which can aid the resource manager in the decision-making process.

Long-term investments may be defined as capital expenditures which require longer than one year to recover. The decision maker must preselect criteria on which to base acceptance or rejection of alternative long-term investments following economic evaluation. Some of the more common criteria that are used by resource managers are urgency or need, payback period, simple rate of return, and discounting or present-value analysis.[5]

Urgency or need. If a stock pond is washed out and is the only source of water for a large pasture, it must be replaced. Exterior fencing that has been destroyed is another example of a necessary investment. Such repairs must be made if the range resource is to be used; the only real decision involves the selection of the method of least cost to replace the fence or rebuild the pond. This type of investment is common and does not require detailed economic analysis. Unfortunately, many investments with high potential profitability are postponed or not considered when this approach is adopted for all decisions. The result is that many opportunities to increase profits from the ranching operation are lost.

Payback period. Payback period is the amount of time required

---

[5] In the following discussion, material contained in R. D. Aplin and G. L. Caslen, *Capital Investment Analysis: Using Discounted Cash Flows* (Grid, Inc., 1973), was used as a guideline for the discussion of long-term investments and adapted to economic situations faced in range management.

for the initial investment to be recovered from its expected earnings. For example, assume that the establishment of an improved pasture costs five thousand dollars and that annual earnings are expected to increase fifteen hundred dollars each year from the improvement. The length of time for the investment to be recovered is less than four years (5,000 ÷ 1,500 = 3.33). Normally the resource manager establishes a maximum payback period, ranks several investment alternatives, and rejects any that exceed that period, requiring longer to recover the original investment than is desirable.

There are sound arguments for using the payback period as the criterion for selecting investments. If the manager has to borrow the investment money which must be repaid within a given time period, this method allows selection of only those investments which "pay their own way." In this case the criterion becomes more a measure of liquidity than of profitability.

The payback period method is limited, however, in that the entire life of the investments is not considered. Profitability of a given investment may be ignored, violating the basic premise for adopting economic evaluation. For example, assume that two projects have potential for use on the management unit. Based on the payback period, the investment in one project may be recovered in three years while the other is expected to require eight years. However, the first project might have only a three-year life and return 4 percent on the original investment compared to the second project, which might have a fifteen-year life and return 20 percent. Obviously, the second investment opportunity has greater potential for returning profits to the enterprise. The payback period method ignores returns over the total life of the project and the timing of returns during the life of the treatment. Consequently, investments with returns early in the life of the investment would be favored over those which might afford greater profit later in the life of the investment.

Simple rate of return. This investment criterion uses average annual net returns, the total size of the investment, and annual depreciation to determine the annual rate of return on an investment. For example, assume that average annual net returns are five thousand dollars, depreciation is two thousand dollars per year, and the initial cost of the improvement is twenty-five thousand dollars. Simple rate of return is calculated as: $r = (E - D) \div C$, where r = rate of return,

E = average annual net return not including depreciation, D = average annual depreciation, and C = amount of capital required by the investment. Thus, $r = (5,000 - 2,000) \div 25,000 = 12$ percent.

Although this criterion considers the entire life of the project, the rate of return does not correspond with interest rates quoted by financial and investment firms. Thus, the simple rate of return cannot be directly compared to the cost of borrowing money or to the returns from a certificate of deposit, bond, or savings account but offers a means to eliminate some investments based on the magnitude of the return.

Both these criteria—simple rate of return and payback period—ignore the timing of cash flows over the length of the investment. Timing is important in economic evaluation of investment practices such as brush management, because a dollar which is available today has more value than one which is received ten years hence. For example, $1.00 received today, if allowed to accrue interest in a savings account at 6 percent, would total $1.79 at the end of year ten. Another way to view this principle is to ask the question, "What would have to be invested today at 6 percent interest in order to have a dollar at the end of year ten?" The answer is $0.56. Both approaches illustrate that time has value and that returns derived from an investment early have more value than those produced later.

Discounting or net present value. This criterion properly accounts for the timing of funds.[6] It requires the resource manager to establish a rate of return on a proposed investment before carrying out the project. The chosen rate of return may be based on the return from secure investments such as savings accounts, certificates of deposit, government bonds, or other similar investments plus a return for ac-

---

[6] A related criterion is referred to as an internal rate of return or yield. The determination of the yield of an investment is carried out in a manner similar to conducting a net-present-value analysis. The principal difference is that the rate of return is found which will result in a net present value of zero rather than the discount rate being predetermined. The net-present-value method and the yield method generally result in the same decision. However, the net present value has less restrictive assumptions concerning reinvestment of net cash inflows and is generally easier to use than the yield method. The yield method has some advantages over the net-present-value method in capital rationing problems and in comparing different investment magnitudes.

cepting the increased level of risk and uncertainty inherent in adopting the brush management practice. In general, the greater the amount of risk and uncertainty, the greater the percentage of return required to attract investors. The amount of return for risk and uncertainty would depend on the resource manager's perception of the brush management practice and his personal risk-return preference.

Present value analysis is considered superior to the first two criteria discussed because it considers the timing of cash flows arising from the investment over the entire life of the treatment. Timing is critical to determining the economic feasibility of a brush management practice, because such range improvement practices are generally not short-term decisions, and time translates into cost when alternative investments exist.

The timing of investments, annual net cash returns, and salvage values have to be estimated over the projected life of the investment or selected planning period to conduct a net-present-value analysis. The net cash flow is determined by summing the investment costs and annual net cash returns and/or cost savings for each year of the planning horizon. These annual cash flows are discounted to a net present value and summed over the planning period. Tables are commonly used to simplify the math required in carrying out a net-present-value analysis and are typically presented over a range of discount rates and time periods (148). The values in Table 10.3 for alternative interest rates are used to multiply the respective cash flows occurring in a given time period. For example, a $1,000 cash flow occurring in year five using a 10 percent discount rate would result in a present value of $620; that is, $620 invested today at 10 percent would be equivalent to $1,000 if allowed to compound in a certificate of deposit paying 10 percent until the end of year five.

The total net present value must be zero or greater for an investment alternative to be judged economically feasible. For example, if the net present value of a project is $2,300, this implies that the investment has been recovered, opportunity costs have been paid on the investment, all increased operational costs have been paid, and the investment has produced surplus cash flow. A positive net present value indicates that the practice is profitable and that $2,300 has been gained over the next best alternative. In other words, the resource

TABLE 10.3.

Present Value of One Dollar Due at the End of N Years
for Use in Present-Value Analysis (5).*

Year	Interest Rate (%)						
N	6	7	8	9	10	12	14
0	1.	1.	1.	1.	1.	1.	1.
1	.945	.934	.925	.917	.909	.892	.877
2	.890	.873	.857	.841	.826	.797	.769
3	.841	.793	.793	.772	.751	.711	.674
4	.792	.762	.735	.708	.683	.635	.592
5	.749	.712	.680	.649	.620	.567	.519
6	.705	.666	.630	.596	.564	.506	.455
7	.666	.622	.583	.547	.513	.452	.399
8	.627	.582	.540	.501	.466	.403	.350
9	.593	.543	.500	.460	.424	.360	.307
10	.558	.508	.463	.422	.385	.321	.269
11	.528	.475	.428	.387	.350	.287	.236
12	.497	.444	.397	.355	.318	.256	.207

* Present value of one dollar is defined as $(1 + r)^{-n}$ where r = percentage rate and n = time period (length of investment). This relationship may be used to calculate present values at interest rates or time periods not included in the table.

manager could have spent an additional $2,300 on the brush management project (at the time of its establishment) and would have been as well off economically if he had invested in his next best alternative.

Present-value analysis is not a simple task. The decision maker must make realistic projections concerning production responses, costs, prices, and risks associated with carrying out a given practice. The more accurate a manager's information and projections, the more effective will be his decisions. The value of an improved decision may ultimately mean the difference in economic survival for the ranching enterprise.

A present-value analysis for brush management requires the following information:

1. Identification of brush management alternatives and an estimate of production changes over time following implementation of the practice

2. Identification of costs which change as a result of adopting the brush management practice

3. Cost of production and projections concerning product prices for the planning period
4. A discount rate selected as a decision criterion
5. Net present value of the selected practice
6. Acceptance or rejection of the alternative investment(s)

The following example is presented only for illustrative purposes, since each land management problem is economically unique. However, the approach may be suitable for evaluating similar brush management and other range improvement alternatives.

Consider a ranching unit of which 4,700 acres of rangeland in poor condition support a heavy cover of mixed brush under a rainfall regime of more than 30 inches annually. Soils are adequate to produce considerably more forage, as evidenced by adjacent similar sites in good range condition, planted to row crops, or used as tame pastures. In its present condition the area supports one animal unit per 25 acres.

Management experience and available technical information indicates a potential for increasing the carrying capacity of the range to one animal unit per 15 acres by brush management using aerial application of herbicides. Since some brush cover is desirable for white-tailed deer habitat, an important commodity to the ranch, it is decided to treat 75 percent of the area in alternating strips rather than treating the entire 4,700 acres (323).

Under sound management practices it has been demonstrated that the spraying treatment has a life expectancy of ten years; in at least five of those years production is at its maximum under average rainfall. Range production is usually at its maximum within two years following initiation of treatment unless it is limited by drought or mismanagement. Production will diminish, unless additional treatment is applied, during the final three years until the area returns to its original state of productivity. Major additional benefits (in addition to increased carrying capacity) indicated from experience and available technology are that calving percentage may increase from the present 70 to 85 percent, calf weights (heifers and steers averaged) may be increased from 415 to 440 pounds at sale time, and labor costs for handling and caring for the herd will be decreased by at least $0.65 per acre (323). The low bid for application of the herbicide is $12.50 per acre.

Thirty cows will be added the year of treatment, forty cows at the end of the first year, and fifty-five cows at the end of the second year.[7] The additional calves will be sold the year after they are added. The calf crop and weaning weight changes are expected to begin the third year and be effective through year eight, when herbicide effectiveness is expected to diminish. Labor savings begin in year one and are assumed to occur through year eight. At the end of year eight, calves as well as thirty producing cows will be sold. The thirty cows will be sold because of limitations in forage production and are assumed to be in addition to normal cull cows being sold. Forty additional cows will be be sold in year nine, and fifty-five additional cows in year ten. Calf crop and weaning weight changes shift to their original values in years nine and ten. These production changes are summarized in Table 10.4.

Added costs and returns must be identified over the ten-year planning period by developing a partial budget for each year of the project. The partial budget identifies only the costs and revenues which change as a result of adopting the brush management practice. The added revenues are compared to added costs (expressed in present-value terms) to determine profitability of a given practice in a present-value analysis. An enterprise may be losing money, from a total-budget standpoint, before and after adoption of a practice. However, the economic merit of the brush management practice is judged only on the changes which occur as a result of its adoption. Of course the enterprise would be losing less money, from a total-budget standpoint, if the brush management practice was judged economically feasible and was adopted.

Use of a partial budget to obtain estimates of the changes in cash flow which occur each year of the ten-year planning period is illustrated in Table 10.5. To improve understanding of how the values in Table 10.5 were derived, detailed calculations are provided in Table 10.6. Table 10.7 illustrates the procedure to itemize annual changes which are expected to occur as a result of adding cows.

---

[7] Under actual conditions the treated management unit should be deferred for part of the year of treatment and no additional animals should be considered until the growing season of the year after treatment. However, the example was developed for ease of presentation and simplicity, so deferment costs were not considered.

TABLE 10.4.
Projected Annual Livestock Changes of the Hypothetical
Project Described in the Text.

Year	Cows Added	Cows Sold	Calf Crop (percent)	Weaning Weights (pounds)	Labor Savings (dollars per acre
0	30	—	70	—	—
1	40	—	70	415	.65
2	55	—	75	415	.65
3	—	—	85	440	.65
4	—	—	85	440	.65
5	—	—	85	440	.65
6	—	—	85	440	.65
7	—	—	85	440	.65
8	—	30	80	440	.65
9	—	40	75	415	0
10	—	55	70	415	0

Cattle prices are projected at $40 per hundredweight for weaned calves over the life of the treatment. Cows are assumed to be added the last day of the year before they produce a calf for sale. Thus, bred heifers are assumed to be purchased at $250 each, and bulls are assumed to cost $750 with a 1:25 ratio of bulls to cows.

Treatment of 75 percent of the area will allow maintenance of a stable deer herd; that is, revenues from hunting will not fluctuate and will exceed added livestock revenues which could potentially be obtained from the untreated 25 percent. Maintenance of the deer herd by spraying in strips has been economically verified (323).

Results of the economic analysis of the hypothetical brush management problem are displayed in Table 10.8. The total net present value for the alternative is $39,890 or $8.99 per acre. This value represents the net increase in profits over the entire ten-year planning period. It pertains only to the increase (or decrease) in profits compared to production of the 4,700 acres if left untreated. The hypothetical rancher originally could have spent an additional $8.99 per acre and would have been as well off as if he put the same amount of dollars into an alternative investment which would pay 7 percent.

Given the present value criterion of 7 percent, this example in-

TABLE 10.5.
Projected Annual Net Cash Flow Estimates for Hypothetical
Project Described in the Text.

Partial Budget	Year						
	0	1	2	3–7	8	9	10
Increased revenues (dollars)							
Added calves	—	3,486	8,715	18,700	18,700	11,827	6,391
Increased weaning weights (original cows)	—	—	1,588	1,263	1,263	—	—
Increased calf crop (original cows)	—	—	—	4,765	3,168	1,434	—
Cow sales*	—	—	—	—	6,500	8,500	11,000
Reduced costs (dollars)							
Labor savings	—	3,055	3,055	3,055	3,055	—	—
Total benefits	—	6,541	13,358	27,783	32,686	21,761	18,391
Increased costs (dollars)							
Variable cows costs†	—	1,821	4,249	7,588	7,588	5,766	3,339
Cow purchase†	8,250	10,750	15,250	—	—	—	—
Treatment costs‡	44,062	—	—	—	—	—	—
Reduced revenues (dollars) (none for this problem)							
Total costs	52,313	12,571	19,499	7,588	7,588	—	—
Net Annual Benefit or Loss (dollars)	−52,313	− 6,030	+ 6,141	+20,195	+25,098	+15,995	+15,052

* Cows are assumed to be sold for $200 per head and bulls for $500 per head. These cows represent a reduction in herd size and are not cull cows. Cull cows are assumed to sell for enough in all other years to purchase a replacement heifer, thus maintaining herd size.

† Cows were assumed to cost $250 per head and bulls to cost $700 per head (one bull per twenty-five cows). Cull cows are assumed to sell for enough to purchase a replacement heifer in order to maintain the herd.

‡ 4,700 acres × $12.50 per acre × 0.75 of the area treated by the strip method.

TABLE 10.6.
Partial Budget Procedure for Years Three through Seven of the
Hypothetical Project Described in the Text.

Added revenues
  Added calves (125 cows × 0.85 × 440 lb. × $0.40) $18,700
  Increased weaning weights on original cows
  ((4,700 acres ÷ 25 × 0.96)* ×25 lb. × 0.70 × $0.40   1,263
  Increased calf crop from original cows
  ((4,700 acres ÷ 25 × 0.96)* × 0.15 increase × 440 lb. × $0.40   1,263
                                                               $24,728
Reduced costs
  4,700 acres × $0.65   3,055
                                          Total benefits $27,783
Increased costs (see Table 10.7)
  Increased cow cost ($60.70 × 125 cows)   7,587
Reduced revenues   0
                                          Total costs ....$ 7,587
Net benefit $20,195

---

* Since 4 percent of the herd was bulls, adjustment by 0.96 is necessary
to accurately calculate overall increase in weaning weights.

vestment alternative would be judged economically feasible. If the net
present value had been negative, it would have been rejected.

Financial feasibility must also be considered by the decision
maker. Financial feasibility questions concern the ability of a resource
manager to balance high needs for funds early in the brush management program against the relatively slow payback of those funds. Note
from Table 10.8 that the project did not break even until the seventh
year (somewhat earlier if added equity is considered from the added
cows). Thus, financing of brush management is a common problem.
Typically, payback periods for borrowed funds are not long enough
for the investment to meet debt repayment schedules. Thus, resource
managers must (1) be large enough to finance their own improvement
practices (or at least a large portion of them) or (2) have an outside
source of income to pay for the improvement practice. Many times
ranch managers have to reject a superior investment opportunity because of financial feasibility problems.

Obviously, results of this analysis could be altered significantly
by choice of a different discount rate or by changes in projected live-

TABLE 10.7.

Projected Annual Fixed and Variable Costs for Current and Added Cow Producing Units in the Hypothetical Project Described in the Text.

Item	Current Cost per cow	Increased Cost per Added Cow
Variable costs		
Feed	$ 11.75	$ 11.75
Salt and minerals	1.70	1.70
Veterinary care	2.00	2.00
Repairs and maintenance	2.80	2.80
Marketing	4.00	4.00
Bulls	6.00	6.00
Replacement heifer	6.00	6.00
Transportation	4.75	2.75
Miscellaneous	1.50	1.50
Interest on operating expenses	1.80	1.70
Total variable costs	$ 42.30	$ 40.20
Fixed costs		
Land charge	$ 35.00	$ —
Depreciation	11.50	2.50
Taxes	18.00	2.00
Insurance	1.00	—
Fixed labor and management	30.00	—
Interest on investment	22.50	16.00
Total fixed cost	$118.00	$ 20.50
Total cost	$160.30	$ 60.70

stock production estimates, projected cattle prices, anticipated degree of range improvement, life expectancy of the practice, and costs and salvage values for the additional animal units. However, the concept and procedure are sound if applied properly to a specific management situation.

This analysis was finite in that the project was undertaken with the anticipation that the results of brush management would expire after the life expectancy of the treatment. Under proper management, investment in follow-up brush management would be planned for maintenance of range improvement. In our example such a decision would be required before year six of the project. Of course, subsequent analysis would be adjusted for additional costs and changes in stocking rates.

TABLE 10.8.

Present Value of Projected Net Income from Investment in the
Hypothetical Project Described in the Text Based on a 7-percent
Discount Rate and Cattle Prices Averaging $0.40 per Pound

Year	Total Cows in Herd	Projected Change in Net Cash Flow*	Present Value of $1.00†	Present Value of Projected Income	Cumulative Present Value of Projected Income
0	180	−52,313	1.000	−52,313	−52,313
1	210	− 6,030	0.934	− 5,632	−57,945
2	250	− 6,141	0.873	− 5,361	−63,306
3	305	20,195	0.816	16,479	−46,827
4	305	20,195	0.762	15,388	−31,438
5	305	20,195	0.712	14,379	−17,059
6	305	20,195	0.666	13,450	− 3,609
7	305	20,195	0.622	12,561	8,952
8	305	25,098	0.582	14,607	23,558
9	275	15,995	0.543	8,685	32,244
10	235	15,052	0.508	7,646	39,890
11	180	0	—	—	—

*Estimates of cash flow changes are derived from development of a partial budget for each year of the planning period. Estimates are presented in Table 10.5.

†Present-value factors are obtained from Table 10.3.

The analysis, for the sake of simplicity, did not include consideration of game leasing. Although it was assumed that the white-tailed deer population would remain stable after brush treatment, the impact of brush management on wildlife must be considered for accurate analysis. Also, no cost of deferment was considered, although good range management dictates deferment following treatment to promote the effects of the brush management practice. Any deferment should be included at a cost equivalent to local grazing lease prices for the anticipated deferment period.

Finally, there is no quantitative expression of additional benefits which result from brush management. Such benefits may include
1. Reductions in losses due to parasites.
2. More docile and easier-to-handle livestock.
3. Reduction in requirements for supplemental feeding during stress periods.

4. Reduction in the number of breeding males. The economic analysis of the hypothetical brush management project included an additional bull for each twenty-five head of cows.
5. Improved livestock distribution.
6. Improved efficiency of water use.
7. Improved habitat for upland game birds.

System Development

Once the resource manager understands the basic range management techniques, especially grazing management, and can apply economic analysis to his projections concerning the application of brush management, he can begin to develop the brush management system. Usually the system is developed for a given management unit within an enterprise. Because of the interdependency of units, change in the production status of one affects all the others, and all decisions ultimately relate to the entire enterprise.

The fundamental consideration, perhaps better termed "commitment," of the manager is development of objectives. The resource management staff must set production goals in an atmosphere of realism and with a certain degree of flexibility. Production goals may include desired levels of livestock production, needs to maintain or improve wildlife habitat, contribution of row crops to potential use of the management unit subject to improvement, and so forth. This determination of the desired degree of improvement is usually more easily ascertained than is the proper, perhaps acceptable, rate of change of production that can be achieved by the natural resource.

Rate of range improvement is a prime consideration from the standpoints of both cost spreading and ranch management. Completing all brush management in a single year will not give full return on the investment on most ranches, since livestock would not be available to fully use the improved productivity. Even progressive improvement over a period of years will require good management to adjust grazing periods and numbers of livestock to properly use the treated pastures.

Needs for attaining production potential of the management unit may be isolated when current level of productivity (actually the history of production) is evaluated in consideration of the critical limiting factors such as excessive brush cover. Past grazing management, responses to improvement efforts, and the need for structural improvements must be analyzed. The intensity, extent, and composition of the brush infestation must be ascertained. Theoretically, the range manager, before considering treatment methods, should take steps to make sure that brush is the primary factor that keeps the current level of productivity from equaling the potential level.

Once the range manager has set his objectives for potential change in production of the management unit, he must select the brush management treatment. At this point all treatment alternatives, including no treatment, must be carefully studied. In some cases the number of possible treatment methods will be reduced by the nature of the brush infestation, but more usually it will be limited by cost factors. Some of the more effective treatments, in terms of percentage of brush killed, may be quickly eliminated because they are economically unfeasible. At this point the alternatives should be evaluated with some economic method such as present-value analysis. Also, a sequence of treatments, rather than just the initial treatment, should be selected. Since the initial treatment may affect the choice of subsequent ones, a brush management program, not just a series of treatments, will begin to emerge.

Once the applicable treatments have been selected, the brush management system may be designed. This step, one of the most critical, includes projected treatment sequencing. At this point treatments are no longer viewed simply as "what will work" but as those procedures that can be fitted together over time to result in the desired degree of change at the desired rate.

The remainder of this discussion is developed on the basis that the range improvement approach will be properly integrated with the grazing management system. Systems selected for discussion are combinations of herbicide and a mechanical method, herbicide and prescribed burning, and a mechanical method with both herbicide and prescribed burning. These systems serve only as examples since the number of possible approaches is limited only by the ingenuity of the resource manager.

Herbicide and mechanical method. One of the most successful control procedures for honey mesquite is aerial spraying followed by chaining. To complete the program, a second spraying must usually follow the chaining to control any plants which survive the initial treatment sequence. When the surviving population density is relatively low, power grubbing or individual-plant treatments may suffice to maintain the treated area.

The initial treatment is usually an aerial application of 0.5 pound of 2,4,5-T, 2,4,5-T plus picloram, or 2,4,5-T plus dicamba per acre in areas where honey mesquite is the dominant problem. These herbicides may be easily incorporated into a grazing system. After maximum control has been accomplished from the herbicide, usually within two to three years, the chaining will be most effective. The spray will control a high percentage of the small plants which cannot be controlled by chaining, and the chaining will uproot most of the large surviving mesquite plants, especially those not killed by the spray. The choice of the third and any subsequent treatments depends on the density of surviving plants. Potential subsequent treatments might include prescribed burning, grubbing, or basal spraying. Completion of such a program may require seven to ten years, but by such long-range planning high levels of range improvement may be attained for as long as twenty years with little additional brush management effort.

This combination of treatments has been successfully applied to honey mesquite infestations in northern and western Texas as well as heavy mixed-brush stands of South Texas. After herbicidal control is achieved, the speed of the chaining operation facilitates working and handling of livestock and may improve grazing distribution where heavy debris results.

Although they are highly effective, range improvement systems such as that just described are expensive in the early stages of improvement. One such system installed in 1973 in South Texas cost $24.00 per acre before maintenance costs were considered. However, the treatment life has been projected at fifteen years before additional brush management efforts will be required. Under average rainfall and growing conditions for that area, carrying capacity has been increased from one animal unit per 18 acres to one animal unit per 10 acres, so each animal unit, on a simple consideration of the investment, must repay about $16.00 per year to the enterprise for range improvement.

Combination methods. With rising costs the selection of treatments for brush management systems becomes more critical. Prescribed burning is a low-cost practice and has been installed for less than two dollars per acre in southeastern Texas with little or no loss in grazing under a two-pasture, one-herd rotation system. After the initial burn is installed, the costs of subsequent burns are reduced to slightly less than fifty cents per acre in some cases.

One example of incorporating mechanical methods, herbicides, and fire is a recently developed system used to improve rangeland in the Texas Coastal Prairie infested by Macartney rose (248). The concepts underlying this system may be applied to rangeland in other resource regions with proper modification according to the brush problem, rainfall, soils, and the necessary management factors.

Past efforts at management of Macartney rose have been only partially effective. Shredding spreads cane segments over the soil surface, and those segments, when pressed into moist soils, take root and increase stand densities. In many cases multiple applications of 2,4-D (in one case seven successive annual applications) have suppressed Macartney rose but have resulted in only a low level of control. Repeated herbicide applications virtually eliminate desirable forbs, essential for high-quality wildlife habitat, from the grassland community. Range forage produced between the Macartney rose plants is avoided by cattle, resulting in poor distribution of the grazing animals and inefficient use of the rangeland.

The range improvement system should be initiated by the mechanical reduction of undisturbed, dense stands of large Macartney rose without spreading the plants. Such spreading can be controlled by raking and stacking or by chaining and burning the debris. The initial mechanical practice reduces the Macartney rose top growth to a manageable level and releases herbaceous species necessary to provide adequate amounts of fuel for subsequent prescribed burnings.

Within eighteen to twenty-four months after the mechanical operation, a herbicide may be effectively used to control the Macartney rose. Herbicides containing picloram (2,4,5-T plus picloram was selected in this case) more effectively control the brush than phenoxy herbicides, but 2,4-D alone can be used. The herbicide is applied in the fall (September–October) to minimize the hazard of damaging adjacent, sensitive crops and at a time when the pasture is deferred from grazing.

Selection of the method of herbicide application depends directly on the effectiveness of the mechanical operation. Under proper conditions both raking and chaining will control at least a limited number of plants. For large areas of dense regrowth, aerial application of herbicide is most feasible, although drift to adjacent crops is always a consideration in Macartney rose–infested areas. At 1 pound per acre, 2,4,5-T plus picloram has been found to completely reduce the top growth and kill over 60 percent of the Macartney rose population. Herbicide treatment and grazing deferment further release range forage plants to spread and increase in vigor.

On small areas of light to moderate regrowth, ground broadcast applications of 1 pound of 2,4,5-T plus picloram per acre in at least 10 gallons of carrier per acre may be used as the second step in the improvement system. If the regrowth occurs in small areas of scattered stands, individual plant treatment with 2,4,5-T plus picloram at 2 to 4 pounds per 100 gallons of carrier has been used successfully. The top growth was completely controlled, and more than 80 percent of the plants may be killed.

Although the herbicide treatments provide good control, the dry Macartney rose stems and canes may remain standing for considerable lengths of time. The dry standing material restricts the release of forage, presents difficulties in working and handling livestock, and restricts optimum use of the range. This standing debris may be removed by prescribed burning.

Within eighteen to twenty-four months after application of the herbicide, ample time to maximize effects of the chemical, the prescribed burning may be effectively installed. Under research and actual ranch conditions, properly applied prescribed burnings removed over 95 percent of the debris and controlled the Macartney rose regrowth. The prescribed burnings restored the forb component of the community, improving the diversity of vegetation required for quality wildlife habitat. Preliminary indications are that at least two years, perhaps three, may elapse following the burning before a maintenance treatment is required. If regrowth is limited, burning may be used to maintain range improvement. Otherwise, herbicides may be used to control remaining plants.

Scientific Names of Selected Plants and Animals

Herbaceous Plants

Common Name	Scientific Name
Alkali sacaton	*Sporobolus airoides*
American snoutbean	*Rhynchosia americana*
Annual lazy-daisy (Kidder doze-daisy)	*Aphanostephus kidderi*
Arizona cottontop	*Digitaria californica*
Bahiagrass	*Paspalum notatum* var. *notatum*
Bearded swallowwort	*Cynanchum barbigerum*
Bermudagrass	*Cynodon dactylon*
Big bluestem	*Andropogon gerardii*
Big sandbur	*Cenchrus myosuroides*
Black grama	*Bouteloua eriopoda*
Bladderpod	*Lesquerella* spp.
Blue grama	*Bouteloua gracilis*
Brownseed paspalum	*Paspalum plicatulum*
Buffalograss	*Buchloë dactyloides*
Buffelgrass	*Cenchrus ciliaris*
Bundle flower	*Desmanthus* spp.
Burrograss	*Scleropogon brevifolius*
Bush muhly	*Muhlenbergia porteri*
Christmas bush	*Eupatorium odoratum*
Colonial bentgrass	*Agrostis hyemalis* var. *tenuis*
Common broomweed	*Xanthocephalum dracunculoides*
Common curlymesquite	*Hilaria belangeri*
Cotton	*Gossypium* spp.
Creeping bentgrass	*Agrostis stolonifera* var. *palustris*
Creeping red fescue	*Festuca rubra*
Cucumber	*Cucumis sativa*
Dallisgrass	*Paspalum dilatatum*
Dropseeds	*Sporobolus* spp.
Erect dayflower	*Commelina erecta*

False mallow .... *Malvastrum* spp.
False ragweed .... *Parthenium hysterophorus*
Field bean .... *Phaseolus vulgaris*
Field bindweed .... *Convolvulus arvensis*
Filly panic .... *Panicum hallii* var. *filipes*
Flax .... *Linum* spp.
Golden dalea .... *Dalea aurea*
Goldenrod .... *Solidago* spp.
Grain sorghum .... *Sorghum vulgare*
Grama .... *Bouteloua* spp.
Green sprangletop .... *Leptochloa dubia*
Ground-cherry .... *Physalis* spp.
Gulf cordgrass .... *Spartina spartinae*
Hairy grama .... *Bouteloua hirsuta*
Hall's panicum .... *Panicum hallii*
Heath aster .... *Aster ericoides*
Hibiscus .... *Hibiscus* spp.
Hooded windmillgrass .... *Chloris cucullata*
Horsetail conyza .... *Conyza canadensis*
Italian ryegrass .... *Lolium perenne*
Japanese brome .... *Bromus japonicus*
Klamathweed (St. Johns–wort) .... *Hypericum perforatum*
Kleingrass .... *Panicum coloratum*
Lehmann lovegrass .... *Eragrostis lehmanniana*
Longspike silver blustem .... *Bothriochloa saccharoides*
                                       var. *longipaniculata*
Machaeranthera .... *Machaeranthera* spp.
Meadow dropseed .... *Sporobolus asper* var. *drummondii*
Needle-and-thread .... *Stipa comata*
Needlegrasses .... *Stipa* spp.
Nightshade .... *Solanum* spp.
Perennial lazy-daisy .... *Aphanostephus skirrhobasis*
Pineland threeawn .... *Aristida stricta*
Plains bristlegrass .... *Setaria leucopila*
Prairie gaillardia .... *Gaillardia fastigiata*
Red threeawn .... *Aristida longiseta*
Rice .... *Oryza sativa*
Russian knapweed .... *Centaurea repens*
Salt-marsh aster .... *Aster subulatus* var. *australis*
Sand bluestem .... *Andropogon gerardii* var. *paucipilus*
Sand dropseed .... *Sporobolus cryptandrus*
Seacoast bluestem .... *Schizachyrium scoparium* var. *littoralis*
Seashore saltgrass .... *Distichlis spicata*
Showy sundrops .... *Oenothera speciosa*

Sideoats grama . . . . *Bouteloua curtipendula*
Silver beardgrass . . . . *Andropogon ternarius*
Skeletonweed . . . . *Lygodesmia juncea*
Smooth bromegrass . . . . *Bromus inermis*
Soybeans . . . . *Glycine max*
Squirreltail . . . . *Elymus longifolius*
Sunflower . . . . *Helianthus annuus*
Switchgrass . . . . *Panicum virgatum*
Tall dropseed . . . . *Sporobolus asper* var. *asper*
Tall fescue . . . . *Festuca arundinacea*
Tall grama . . . . *Bouteloua pectinata*
Tanglehead . . . . *Heteropogon contortus*
Texas broomweed . . . . *Xanthocephalum texanum*
Texas cupgrass . . . . *Eriochloa sericea*
Texas wintergrass . . . . *Stipa leucotricha*
Tobosa . . . . *Hilaria mutica*
Tomato . . . . *Lycopersicon esculentum*
Vine mesquite . . . . *Panicum obtusum*
Weeping lovegrass . . . . *Eragrostis curvula*
Western ironweed . . . . *Vernonia baldwinii*
Western ragweed . . . . *Ambrosia psilostachya*
Western wheatgrass . . . . *Agropyron smithii*
Western whorled milkweed . . . . *Asclepias subverticillata*
Wheat . . . . *Triticum aestivum*
White-margin euphorbia . . . . *Euphorbia bicolor*
Wild honeysuckle . . . . *Lonicera* spp.
Wild partridge pea . . . . *Cassia fasiculata*
Willows . . . . *Salix* spp.
Winecup . . . . *Callirhoë involucrata* var. *lineariloba*
Wright's threeawn . . . . *Aristida wrightii*
Yellow Indiangrass . . . . *Sorghastrum nutans*

Woody Plants, Vines, and Cacti
Not Described in Chapter 3

Big sagebrush . . . . *Artemisia tridentata*
Bermuda cedar . . . . *Juniperus bermudiana*
Buckbrush . . . . *Symphoricarpos orbiculatus*
Coma . . . . *Bumelia celastrina*
Dog cactus . . . . *Opuntia schottii*
Downy hawthorne . . . . *Crataegus mollis*
Grapes . . . . *Vitis* spp.
Lantana . . . . *Lantana* spp.
Little walnut . . . . *Juglans microcarpa*
Narrow-leaf forestiera . . . . *Forestiera angustifolia*

Net-leaf hackberry .... *Celtis reticulata*
One-seeded juniper .... *Juniperus monosperma*
Pinyon pine .... *Pinus edulis*
Poison oak .... *Rhus toxicodendron* var. *toxicodendron*
Rabbitbrush .... *Chrysothamnus* spp.
Sagebrush .... *Artemisia* spp.
Southern dewberry .... *Rubus trivialis*
Sycamore .... *Platanus occidentalis*
Velvet mesquite .... *Prosopis glandulosa* var. *velutina*
Western snowberry .... *Symphoricarpos occidentalis*
White pine .... *Pinus monticola*

Wildlife

Dove (mourning dove) .... *Zenaida macroura*
Feral hog .... *Sus scrofa*
Jacksnipe .... *Capella gallinago*
Javelina (collared peccary) .... *Dicotyles tajacu*
Nilgai antelope .... *Boselaphus tragocamelus*
Quail (bobwhite quail) .... *Colinus virginiana*
Sandhill cranes .... *Grus canadensis*
White-tailed deer .... *Odocoileus virginianus*
Wild turkey .... *Meleagris gallopavo*

Metric-English System Unit Equivalents

Metric Unit	*Equivalent English Unit*
Centigrade	Equivalent to Fahrenheit − 32° times 0.5555
Centimeter (one hundredth meter)	0.394 inch
Gram (one thousandth gram)	0.0352 ounce; 0.0022 pound
Hectare	2.471 acres
Kilogram	2.205 pounds
Kilometer	0.621 statute mile
Liter	0.264 gallon (roughly 1 quart)
Meter	3.28 feet; 0.9144 yard
Micron (one millionth meter; one thousandth millimeter	0.0000394 inch
Milligram (one thousandth gram)	0.0000352 ounce
Milliliter (one thousandth liter)	0.0338 fluid ounce
Millimeter (one thousandth meter)	0.0394 inch

Glossary

ABAXIAL. In reference to leaf surfaces, on the side away from the axis.

ABIOTIC. Nonliving components of the ecosystem.

ABSCISSION. The dropping of plant parts such as leaves usually following the formation of a separation layer.

ABSORPTION (of herbicides). The movement of herbicides across the surface barriers to the inner leaf tissues.

ACHENE. A small, dry fruit, hard, one-seeded, and indehiscent such as the seed of thistles and others of the *Compositae*.

ACID EQUIVALENT. The theoretical yield of parent acid from the active ingredient content of a formulation.

ACID SOIL. A soil giving an acid reaction, below pH 7.

ACTINOMYCETE. Any of several rod-shaped or filamentous aerobic or anaerobic bacteria of the family *Actinomycetaceae*.

ACTIVE INGREDIENT. The chemical compound in a formulated product that is responsible for herbicidal activity.

ACUMINATE. Tapering at the end, such as with a leaf, to a gradual point.

ACUTE. Terminating in a sharp or well-defined angle.

ADAXIAL. Facing the primary axis.

ADSORPTION. The concentration of material at the contact zone of two substances.

ADVENTITIOUS. In reference to buds and roots, arising in an irregular or unusual position.

ALKALI SOIL. A soil that has either so high a degree of alkalinity (pH 8.5 or higher) or so high a percentage of exchangeable sodium (15 percent or higher) or both that the growth of most crop plants is reduced.

ALKALOIDS. Any of a large class of organic, nitrogen-containing ring compounds of vegetable origin and sometimes synthesized, some of which are liquid but most of which are solid, that have a bitter taste, that are usually water soluble and alcohol soluble, that combine with acids without the loss of a water molecule to form water-soluble hydrochlorides, hydrobromides, or the like, and that usually exhibit pharmacological action, as nicotine, morphine, or quinine.

ALLERGENIC. Causing allergic sensitization.

ALLUVIAL SOILS. An azonal group of soils developed from material transported and relatively recently deposited by streams.

ALTERNATE. Not opposite each other on the stem but occurring at regular intervals at different levels, as leaf arrangement on some plants.

ANIMAL UNIT (A.U.). Considered to be one mature cow and its calf or equivalent. Conversion factors have been developed to equate other animal types to the standard animal unit.

ANIMAL-UNIT MONTH (A.U.M.). The amount of feed or forage required by an animal unit for one month.

ANNUAL PLANT. A plant that completes its life cycle and dies in one year or less.

APICAL DOMINANCE. Influence exerted by a terminal bud in suppressing the growth of lateral buds. The regulation of growth of buds or other plant parts below the uppermost, or apical, meristem (bud).

AUXIN. An organic compound, active at low concentrations, which promotes growth by cell enlargement.

AXIL. The angle formed beween any two organs such as leaf and stem (the leaf axil) or bud and stem.

AXILLARY. Situated in the axil of a leaf, stem or similar organ.

BACKFIRE. Fire intentionally ignited to remove combustible materials in the path of advancing flames; burns into (not with) the wind.

BARK. All tissues outside the cambium.

BERRY. A fleshy or pulpy fruit such as a grape.

BICOMPOUND. Doubly compound.

BIENNIAL. A plant which normally requires two growing seasons to complete its life cycle.

BIOMASS. The sum total of living plants and animals above and below ground in an area at a given time.

BIOTIC. Living components of an ecosystem.

BIPINNATE. Leaves doubly pinnate; pinnate with the divisions pinnate.

BRANCH. A division or subdivision of the stem or trunk (main axis) of a tree. A limb or offshoot of a main stem.

BROWSE. 1. (n) That part of current leaf and twig growth of woody plants available for animal consumption.

2. (v) Act of consuming browse.

BRUSH. A growth of shrubs or small trees usually of a type undesirable to livestock or timber management, but which are sometimes useful or can be managed for wildlife.

BRUSH CONTROL. Any practice employed to reduce the influence of brush in the management or use of the land.

BRUSHLAND. Land on which the dominant vegetation is woody plants of no commercial value.

BRUSH MANAGEMENT. Management and manipulation of stands of brush to achieve specific management objectives.

BUD. A small protuberance of plant tissue at the tip of a stem (terminal bud) or in the axil where a branch and stem or leaf and stem join (axillary bud) or on the surface of a stem or root which contains rudimentary leaves, inflorescences or both.

BUD OPENING. Bud burst, the result of seasonal stimulation of bud growth; the buds, due to the onset of growth, swell and open, exposing a rosette of closely compacted rudimentary leaves or inflorescences.

BUD ZONE. An accumulation of buds on the base (crown) of honey mesquite and plants of similar growth habit. Botanically, a compressed section of radially enlarged stem at the extreme lower end of tree trunks which supports many buds responsible for stem regrowth when the top growth is disturbed (see also CROWN).

BUNCH GRASS. Grass with characteristic growth habit of forming a bunch or tuft.

CALCAREOUS. Containing or like calcium carbonate; chalky.

CALF CROP. The number of calves weaned from a given number of cows bred, usually expressed as a percentage.

CALIBRATE. To determine, check, or rectify the delivery per unit area of herbicides, fertilizers, seeds, or such from machinery used for their application.

CALICHE. A layer in the soil horizon more or less cemented by secondary carbonates of calcium or magnesium precipitated from the soil solution. May occur as soft, thin horizon or hard, thick horizon.

CAMBIUM. The layer of delicate tissue, responsible for all radial trunk growth, between the inner bark (phloem) and the wood (xylem) of stems and branches of woody plants.

CANOPY. Collectively, the foliage and stems, excluding the main trunk, of trees. Canopy cover is the ground area covered by the canopy.

CAPSULE. A dry fruit with more than one seed-bearing compartment; splits open to release seeds when dry (mature).

CARCINOGEN. A substance or agent which produces or incites cancerous growth.

CARRIER. Any material, liquid or solid, used to dilute and facilitate the dispensing of herbicides.

CARRYING CAPACITY. The maximum stocking rate possible without inducing damage to vegetation or related resources.

CATKIN. A dry, scaly infloresence (flowering head) typical or oaks, willows, and birches.

CELLULOSE. An inert carbohydrate, the chief constituent of the cell walls of plants.

CHAPARRAL. 1. A shrub community composed of sclerophyllous species. 2. A dense thicket of stiff or thorny shrubs or dwarf trees.

CHLOROPHYLLS. Green pigments necessary to the process of photosynthesis.

CHLOROSIS. Yellowing of normally green plant tissues; loss of chlorophyll.

CLADOPHYLL. A branch modified in the form of and functioning as a leaf, such as the pads of cacti.

CLASS OF ANIMAL. Age and/or sex group of a kind of animal.

CLASS OF LIVESTOCK. Age and/or sex group of a kind of livestock.

CLAYPAN. A dense and heavy soil horizon underlying the upper portion of soil, presumably formed in part by the accumulation of clay brought in from the horizons above by percolating water.

CLIMATE. The average weather conditions of a place over a period of years.

CLIMAX. See POTENTIAL VEGETATION.

COLLOID (soil). Inorganic and organic matter having very small particle size and a correspondingly high surface area per unit of mass.

COMPETITION. The struggle for existence within a trophic level in which the living organisms compete for a limited supply of the necessities of life.

COMPOSITION (species composition). The proportions by cover, weight, density, and the like of a species in the total population of a given area.

COMPOUND. Two or more parts united as one whole; for example, a compound leaf which is divided into two leaflets.

COMPOUND LEAF. A leaf divided into two or more parts or leaflets.

CONTACT HERBICIDE. A herbicide that kills only the plant tissue with which it comes in contact, as contrasted to translocated herbicides.

CONTINUOUS GRAZING. The grazing of a specific unit by livestock throughout the year or for that part of the year during which grazing is feasible.

CORDATE. Heart-shaped.

CORK. An outer tissue of bark, exterior to the phellogen (secondary meristem external to the true cambium).

COROLLA. The internal envelope of floral leaves of a flower.

COTYLEDONS. Embryonic foliage, the first leaves (usually one in grasses and two in most broad-leaved species) to emerge upon germination; "seedling leaves."

CRENATE. Scalloped, or with broad rounded teeth.

CROWN. The enlarged base of a woody stem, mostly under the surface of the soil immediately above the roots, supporting many buds which replace the top growth of the woody plant following disturbance.

CUTICLE. The relatively thin wax-like covering of the epidermis of plants, usually in reference to leaves.

DECIDUOUS. Seasonally shedding leaves; not evergreen.

DECREASER. Plant species of the original or climax vegetation that will decrease in relative amount with continued overuse.

DECUMBENT. Stems or branches lying or trailing on the ground with the extremity tending to ascend.

DEFERMENT. Delay or discontinuance of livestock grazing on an area for an adequate period of time to provide for plant reproduction, establishment of new plants, or restoration of vigor of existing plants.

DEFERRED GRAZING. Discontinuance of grazing by livestock on an area for a specified period of time during the growing season to promote plant reproduction, establishment of new plants, or restoration of vigor by old plants.

DEFERRED-ROTATION GRAZING. Discontinuance of grazing on various parts of a range in succeeding years, allowing each part to rest successively during the growing season in order to permit seed production, establishment of seedlings, or restoration of plant vigor. Two, but usually three or more, separate units are required. Control is usually insured by unit fencing but may be obtained by camp herding.

DEGREE OF USE. The proportion of the current year's forage production that is consumed and/or destroyed by grazing animals.

DEHISCENCE. The opening of an anther, fruit, or other structure, permitting the escape of reproductive bodies contained within.

DENSITY. The number of individuals in relation to the space in which they occur. The number of individuals per unit area.

DILUENT. Any material, liquid or solid, used to dilute active ingredients in the formulation or in the fiield application of herbicides.

DIOECIOUS. Plants unisexual, with male and female flowers on separate plants.

DISCLIMAX. A stable vegetation that due to disturbance is held at a successional stage below the potential indicated by climate and soils.

DIVERSITY. An attribute of vegetation composed of many species of plants as contrasted to stands of single species.

DOMINANT. Plant species or species groups, which by means of their number, coverage, or size have considerable if not the major influence or control upon the conditions of existence of associated species.

DORMANCY. A temporary inactivity of tissues, especially buds and seeds, due primarily to influence of season, physiological limitations, or excesses or morphological features which prevent active growth.

DRIFT. 1. The movement from the point of origin or displacement of materials, especially the lateral displacement of herbicide sprays, causing movement away from the target area.

2. The natural movement of animals; also, the movement of materials by wind or water.

DROP (DROPLET). A small amount of liquid produced more or less in a spherical mass; collectively, drops form the spray sheet.

DROP SPECTRUM. The array of drop characteristics, usually in reference to size, in a spray; the proportions of sizes of drops in the spray.

DRUPE. A fleshy or pulpy fruit with inside hard and stony.

DRUPELET. A diminutive drupe such as a blackberry.

ECESIS. The establishment of an individual after migration to a new community or area.

ECOLOGY. The study of the interrelationships of organisms with their environment.

ECOSYSTEM. Organisms together with their abiotic environment, forming an interacting system and inhabiting an indentifiable space.

EFFECTIVE PRECIPITATION. That portion of the total precipitation that becomes available for plant growth.

ELLIPTICAL. Like an ellipse, broadest at the middle, tapering broadly and evenly toward each end.

EMULSIFIER. Any material which facilitates formation of emulsions.

EMULSION. The suspension of one liquid in another, such as oil in water, forming a liquid preparation with the color and consistency of milk. (An invert emulsion is the reverse situation of the standard emulsion, the suspension of water in oil, forming a preparation with the consistency of mayonnaise).

ENCLOSURE. An area fenced to confine animals.

ENTIRE. In reference to leaves, margins without teeth or divisions.

ENVIRONMENT. Sum total of all external influences, substances, or conditions that affect resident organisms.

EPICOTYL. That part of the embryonic or seeding stem above the cotyledons.

EPINASTY. The curving and bending of plant parts due to increased growth on the upper surface of the plant part. Typical reaction of susceptible plants to hormone-type herbicides.

FASCICLED. In a close cluster.

FAUNA. The animals of a given region or period considered as a whole.

FERAL. Escaped from cultivation or domestication and existing in the wild.

FIRE GUARD (FIREBREAK). A natural or man-made barrier used to prevent or retard the spread of fire and in existence before the fire occurs.

FLAGGING. The result of incomplete defoliation of trees or partial foliage replacement following spraying, with a small percentage of individual branches retaining a proportion of their foliage.

FOLIAGE. Collectively, the leaves of plants, usually those green or live; mass of leaves, leafage.

FOLIATE. Having leaves.

FORAGE PRODUCTION. The weight of forage that is produced within a designated period of time on a given area.

FORB. Any herbaceous plant other than grasses, sedges, or rushes.

FORMULATION. 1. A herbicidal preparation supplied by a manufacturer for practical use.
2. The process, carried out by manufacturers, of preparing herbicides for practical use.

FREQUENCY OF OCCURRENCE. An expression of the presence or absence of individuals of a species in a series of samples or across a given area.

FRUIT. Part of the plant which bears the seeds.

FULL USE. The maximum use during a grazing season that can be made of range forage under a given grazing program without inducing a downward trend in range condition.

FUNGI. Mushrooms, molds, mildews, rusts, smuts, and so on, a group of organisms characterized chiefly by absence of chlorophyll and by their substistence upon dead or live organic matter; any of numerous thallophytes of the division fungi.

GAME. 1. Wild birds, fish and other animals hunted for sport or for use as food.
2. Wildlife species so designated by law, the harvest of which is regulated by law.

GAME RANGE. Range that is predominantly grazed by wildlife seasonally or year around.

GENUS. A group of closely related species clearly distinguishable from other groups.

GLABRATE. Becoming glabrous.

GLABROUS. Smooth, not pubescent or hairy.

GLAUCESCENT. Becoming glaucous (covered with a whitish waxlike coating).

GLOBOSE. Globelike, globe-shaped.

GLOBULAR. Globe-shaped, spherical.

GRANULAR. A formulation of herbicide in dry discrete particles of generally less than 10 cubic millimeters.

GRASSLAND. Land on which grasses are the dominant plant cover.

GRAZING MANAGEMENT. The manipulation of livestock grazing to accomplish a desired result.

GRAZING PERIOD. The length of time that livestock are grazed on a specific area.

GRAZING PRESSURE. The actual animal-to-forage ratio at a specific time; for example, three animal units per ton of standing forage.

GRAZING SYSTEM. A specialization of grazing management which defines systematically recurring periods of grazing and deferment for two or more pastures or management units.

GROWTH REGULATOR. Chemicals which alter the rate and/or extent of growth used primarily for control of unwanted vegetation, although extremely low concentrations of these compounds, especially auxin-like chemicals, may promote growth.

GRUBBING. The physical act of removing almost entire plants by excavation and uprooting.

HABITAT. The natural abode of a plant or animal, including all biotic, climatic, and soil conditions or other environmental influences affecting life.

HALF-LIFE. The time required for one-half of an unstable material, such as a degradable herbicide, to undergo chemical change.

HARDPAN. A hardened or cemented soil horizon.

HEARTWOOD. The hard central wood of the trunk of a tree.

HERBACEOUS PLANT. A vascular plant that does not develop persistent woody issue above ground.

HERBAGE. Herbs taken collectively. Usually used in the same sense as forage, except that it may include material not available to animals and excludes browse.

HERBICIDE. Any chemical which is toxic to plants (phytotoxic); a specific group of pesticides.

HIRSUTE. With stiff hairs.

HUMUS. The well-decomposed, more or less stable part of the organic matter of the soil.

HYPOCOTYL. The part of the stem beneath the cotyledons in an embyonic or seedling plant.

INCREASER. Plant species of the original vegetation that increase in relative amount, at least for a time, with overuse.

INDEHISCENT. Fruit which does not open to release seeds.

INFILTRATION. The process by which water enters the soil through the surface.

INFLORESCENCE. The flowering part of plants; the structure supporting the flowers.

INVADER. Plant species that were absent or present in only very small amounts in undisturbed portions of the original vegetation of a specific range site and will invade following disturbance or continued overuse.

INVASION. The migration of organisms from one area to another and their establishment in the latter.

INVERT EMULSION. The suspension of water droplets in a continuous oil phase.

INVOLUCRE. A collection or rosette of bracts subtending a flower cluster.

KEY MANAGEMENT SPECIES. Forage species on which management of grazing of a specific unit is based.

LANCEOLATE. Usually referring to shape of leaf; elongate; shaped like the head of a lance.

LEACHING. The removal of materials in solution; in the case of herbicides, resulting in downward movement through the profile.

LEGUME. 1. Any plant of the family *Leguminosae,* including forage species such as alfalfa and the clovers and undesirable species such as honey mesquite.
2. The pod or seed vessel of plants in the family *Leguminosae.*

LIGNIN. An organic substance that, with cellulose, forms the chief part of woody tissue.

LINEAR. Long and narrow; leaves with parallel margins.

LIVESTOCK MANAGEMENT. Application of business methods and technical principles to livestock production.

LOBED. Margin cut rather deeply into curved or angular segments.

MANAGEMENT PLAN. A program of action designed to reach a given set of objectives.

MAST. The fruit of trees used as forage by animals.

MERISTEM. Localized tissue composed of cells which do not mature but remain capable of further growth and division.

MESIC. An environment having a balanced supply of moisture.

MIXED BRUSH. A brush community composed of two or more species of woody plants which often differ significantly in growth habit and/or form.

MONOECIOUS. Both sexes on the same plant but in separate parts.

MOTTE. A distinct clump, usually circular, of woody plants in open grassland or shrubland.

MUCRONATE. Having a short and small, abrupt tip.

MULCH. A layer of dead plant material on the soil surface.

MULTIPLE USE. Harmonious use of range for more than one purpose.

NECROSIS. Localized death of living tissue.

NEMATODE. Any unsegmented worm of the phylum or class *Nematoda* having an elongated, cylindrical body; a roundworm.

NUT. A hard, indehiscent, one-seeded fruit.

NUTLET. A diminutive nut.

OBLONG. Longer than broad, with nearly parallel sides.

OBOVATE. Inverted ovate; egg-shaped outline with the broader end not directly attached to the stem.

OBTUSE. Blunt or rounded at the end.

OILING. The practice of applying diesel oil, kerosene, motor oil, or similar hydrocarbons to the base of trees.

OLIGOPHAGOUS. Feeding on a limited variety of foods.

OPPOSITE. Leaves or buds occurring in pairs at a node.

ORGANIC SOILS. Soils containing organic matter in sufficient quantities to dominate soil characteristics.

OVATE. Egg-shaped outline with broader end attached to stem.

OVERGRAZED. Unsatisfactory kinds and proportions of plants related to what could grow on a given site.

OVERSTORY. The uppermost layer of plants, usually trees, shrubs, and/or vines.

OVERUSE. Use of an excessive amount of the current year's growth which, if it continues, will result in overgrazing and range deterioration.

PALATABILITY. The relish with which a particular species or plant part is consumed by an animal.

PALMATE. Lobed or divided so that the sinuses point to or reach the apex of the petiole without respect to the number of lobes.

PANICLE. A compound racemose infloresence.

PAPILIONACEOUS. Having an irregular corolla shaped somewhat like a butterfly, such as the pea and other leguminous plants.

PAPPUS. A crown or ring of hairlike structures forming a parachutelike appendage on achenes.

PATHOGEN. Any disease-producing organism.

PEDICELS. Supports for single floral structures.

PEDUNCLE. A flower stalk, supporting either a cluster or a solitary flower.

PELLET. A dry formulation of herbicide and other components in particles usually larger than 10 cubic millimeters.

PERCENT USE. Grazing use of current growth, usually expressed as a percentage of the weight removed.

PERENNATING STRUCTURE. Vegetative reproductive structures such as buds which give perennial character to plants.

PERENNIAL. A woody or herbaceous plant living from year to year, not dying after once flowering.

pH. Negative logarithm of the hydrogen ion concentration. A notation to designate or indicate degree of acidity or alkalinity. Indicates soil reaction.

PHENOLOGY. The study of periodic biological phenomena such as flowering, seeding, and the like, especially as related to climate.

PHLOEM. The food-conducting system of plants; transports substances manufactured in the leaves to the stems and roots.

PHOTOPERIOD. Length of diurnal period that a plant is exposed to light.

PHOTOSYNTHESIS. The production of carbohydrates from carbon dioxide and water in the presence of chlorophyll, using light energy and releasing oxygen.

PHREATOPHYTE. A deep-rooted species that absorbs its water from the water table or the soil above it.

PHYTOPHAGOUS. Herbivorous, feeding solely on plants.

PHYTOTOXIC. Injurious or toxic to plants.

PINNA. A primary division (leaflet) of a pinnate leaf.

PINNAE. One of the primary divisions of pinnate or compoundly pinnate leaves.

PINNATELY COMPOUND. A compound leaf with the leaflets arranged along the sides of a common axis.

PISTILLATE. Having pistils; without stamens.

PITH. The central cylinder of tissue in the stems of broad-leaved plants.

PLANT CONTROL. The reduction, sometimes complete, of the influence of undesirable plants on any given area or habitat.

PLANT KILL. An index, usually expressed as a percentage, of the population of plants dead as the result of any control effort.

PLUMOSE. Feathery or plumelike.

POD. Two-valved seed vessel; legume; fruit of members of *Leguminosae*.

POTENTIAL VEGETATION. The kind of plant community capable of perpetuation under the prevailing climatic and edaphic conditions. Climax vegetation.

PRAIRIE. An extensive tract of level or rolling land that was originally treeless, or essentially so, and grass-covered.

PRESCRIBED BURNING. The use of fire as a management tool under specified conditions for burning a predetermined area.

PROPAGULE. Any reproductive structure by which plants reproduce.

PROPER STOCKING. Placing a number of animals on a given area that will result in proper use at the end of a planned grazing period.

PROPER USE. A degree and time of use of a current year's growth which, if it continues, will either maintain or improve the range condition consistent with conservation of other natural resources.

PUBERULENT. Minutely pubescent.

RACEME. A simple inflorescence with flowers pedicelled upon a common axis.

RANGE. Rangelands and also many forest lands which support an understory of periodic cover of herbaceous or shrubby vegetation amenable to certain range management principles or practices.

RANGE CONDITION. The state and health of the range based on what the range is naturally capable of producing.

RANGE CONDITION TREND. The direction of change in range condition.

RANGE IMPROVEMENT. 1. Any structure or excavation to facilitate management of range or livestock.

2. Any practice designed to improve range condition or facilitate more efficient utilization of the range.

3. An increase in the grazing capacity of range; that is, improvement in range condition.

RANGELAND. Land that is used as range.

RANGE MANAGEMENT. A distinct discipline founded on ecological principles and dealing with the husbandry of rangelands and range resources.

RANGE SCIENCE. The organized body of knowledge upon which the practice of range management is based.

RANGE SITE. An area of land having a combination of soil, climate, and natural life that is significantly different from that of adjacent areas.

RATE. The amount of herbicide equivalent, usually expressed as pounds per acre, applied per unit area.

REGROWTH. Plant growth originating from original stems, branches, and/or roots after the original plant growth has been physically removed or killed and left in place.

REVEGETATION. The reestablishment or improvement of vegetation through either natural or mechanical means; that is, natural revegetation or artificial revegetation.

REVOLUTE. Rolled backward from margins or tip.

RACHIS. The axis of an infloresence when somewhat elongated, as in a raceme.

RESIDUE (herbicide). Detectable herbicide residing some time after the application process.

RHIZOME. A horizontal underground stem, usually sending out roots and above-ground shoots from the nodes.

RUMEN. The first stomach of ruminating animals.

SALINE SOIL. A non-alkali soil containing sufficient soluble salts to impair its productivity.

SAMARA. An indehiscent, usually one-seeded, winged fruit, as of the elm or maple.

SAPWOOD. The softer part of the wood between the inner bark and the heartwood.

SAVANNAH. A grassland with scattered trees, whether as individuals or clumps.

SCABROUS. Rough to touch.

SCARIFICATION. To make scratches or superficial incisions on the surface of an object, especially to scratch, nick, or otherwise disturb the hard coat of seeds such as those of honey mesquite.

SECONDARY SUCCESSION. Plant succession occurring where original vegetation was removed or destroyed but on fully developed soil.

SERRATE. Having sharp teeth pointing forward.

SERRULATE. Finely serrate.

SESSILE. Without a stalk.

SHINNERY. Short, thick growth of oaks, usually of sand shinnery oak, vasey oak, or running live oak.

SHRUB. A plant that has persistent, woody stems and a relatively low growth habit and that generally produces several basal shoots instead of a single bole.

SIMPLE (leaf). Undivided as opposed to compound.

SITE. The place or seat of any specified thing.

SOD. Vegetation which grows to form a mat of soil and vegetation.

SOD GRASSES. Stoloniferous or rhizomatous grasses which form a sod or turf.

SOIL APPLICATION. Applied primarily to the soil surface rather than to vegetation.

SOIL TEXTURE. The coarseness or fineness of soil.

SOIL TYPE. A group of soils having genetic horizons similar in differentiating characteristics, including texture and arrangement in the soil profile, and developed from a paricular type of parent material.

SPATULATE. Oblong, the basal end tapered like a spatula.

SPECIES COMPOSITION. The proportions of various plant species in relation to the total on a given area. May be expressed in terms of cover, density, weight, and so on.

SPECIFIC GRAVITY. The ratio of the density of any substance to the density of some other substance, especially the ratio of density of material such as wood to a standard such as water.

SPIKE. Simple inflorescence, the flowers sessile upon a common axis.

SPINE. A sharp, rigid outgrowth from the stem; thorn.

SPINESCENT. Becoming spinelike; ending in a spine.

SPRAY DRIFT. Movement of airborne spray from the intended area of application.

SPRAY PATTERN. The density, distribution of sizes, and general outline of contact of a spray on any environmental surface.

STAMEN. The pollen-bearing organ of a flower, consisting of the filament and the anther.

STAMINATE. Having a stamen or stamens.

STAND. An effective number of one or more specific plant species of the same life form.

STIPULAR. Pertaining to a stipules, a small appendage at the base of a petiole or leaf.

STOCKING RATE. The area of land which the operator has alloted to each animal unit for the entire grazeable period of the year.

STOLON. A horizontal stem which grows along the surface of the soil and roots at the nodes.

STOMA (pl. STOMATA). Small openings or pores on the surfaces of leaves which function primarily in gas exchange.

SUCCESSION. The process of vegetational development whereby an area becomes successively occupied by different plant communities of higher ecological order.

SURFACTANT. Surface active agents; materials which facilitate spreading and wetting of sprayed surfaces and which may also aid in emulsifying or dispensing herbicides.

SUSCEPTIBILITY. Lack of tolerance for treatment, as with herbicides.

SUSPENSION. Finely divided solid particles dispersed in a solid, liquid, or gas.

SWATH. The width of area treated in one pass, as when brush is aerially sprayed.

SYNERGISM. Complementary effects of two or more different chemicals resulting in an effect that would be greater than that expected from the sum of the effects of the chemicals applied independently.

TAME PASTURE. Grazing lands, planted primarily with introduced or domesticated native forage species, that receive periodic renovation and/or cultural treatments.

TENDRIL. A slender, clasping, winding stem or foliar growth.

THREE-FOLIATE. Having three leaflets, as in a compound leaf.

TRANSLOCATION. The movement of materials from one place to another, especially the movement of herbicides within plant systems.

TRIFOLIATE. Three-leaved.

TRUNCATE. Ending abruptly, as cut off at the tip.

TWIG. The growth made by the shoot of a woody plant during the previous season.

UNDERSTORY. Plants growing beneath the canopy of another plant. Usually refers to grasses, forbs, and low shrubs under a tree or brush canopy.

UNDULATE. Having a wavy surface or margin.

UNGULATE. Belonging or pertaining to the *Ungulata,* a group comprising all hoofed mammals.

VEGETATION. Plants in general, or the sum total of plant life above and below ground in an area.

VEGETATION TYPE. A plant community with distinguishable characteristics.

VEGETATIVE REPRODUCTION. Production of new plants or plant parts by asexual methods such as from buds on roots and stems.

VEIN. A vascular bundle forming a part of the framework of the conducting and supporting tissues of a leaf or other expanding organ.

VENATION. The arrangement of the vascular bundles, or veins, of a leaf.

VOLATILITY. The ability of a liquid to change to a gas, such as the vaporization of herbicides under high temperatures.

WATERSHED. A total area of land, above a given point on a waterway, that contributes runoff water to the flow at that point.

WETTABLE POWDER. A finely divided dry herbicide formulation that can be suspended readily in water.

WILDLIFE. Undomesticated vertebrate animals considered collectively, with the exception of fishes.

WOLF PLANT. A plant that, though of a species generally considered palatable, is not grazed by livestock.

XEROPHYTE. A plant adapted to survival under conditions of a limited supply of water in the habitat.

XYLEM. The plant cells which transport water and minerals in plants and collectively form the woody tissues of plants.

Literature Cited

1. Adams, D. F., C. M. Jackson, and W. L. Babesberger. 1964. Quantitative studies of 2,4-D esters in air. *Weeds* 12:280–283.
2. Aldous, A. E. 1934. *Effects of Burning on Kansas Bluestem Pastures*. Kan. Agr. Exp. Sta. Tech. Bull. No. 38. 65 pp.
3. Allen, L. J., L. H. Harbers, R. R. Schalles, C. E. Owensby, and E. F. Smith. 1976. Range burning and fertilizing related to nutritive value of bluestem grass. *J. Range Manage.* 29:306–308.
4. Allison, D. V., and C. A. Rechenthin. 1956. Root plowing proved best method of brush control in South Texas. *J. Range Manage.* 9:130–134.
5. Anderson, W. P. 1977. *Weed Science*. St. Paul, Minn.: West Publ. Co. 598 pp.
6. Andres, L. A. The economics of biological control of weeds. *Aquatic Bot.*, in press.
7. Anonymous. 1968. *Twenty-two Plants Poisonous to Livestock in the Western States*. U.S. Dept. Agr. Inf. Bull. 327. 64 pp.
8. Arnold, K., L. T. Burcham, R. L. Fenner, and R. F. Gray. 1951. Use of fire in land clearing. I. Controlled burns by planned application. *California Agr.* 5: 9–11.
9. Arnold, W. R., and P. W. Santelmann. 1966. Response of native grasses and forbs to picloram. *Weeds* 14:174–176.
10. Ashton, R. M., and A. S. Crafts. 1973. *Mode of Action of Herbicides*. New York: John Wiley and Sons. 504 pp.
11. Bailey, G. W., A. D. Thruston, Jr., J. D. Pope, Jr., and D. R. Cochrane. 1970. The degradation kinetics of an ester of silvex and the persistence of silvex in water and sediment. *Weed Sci.* 18:413–419.
12. Baldwin, B. C. 1963. Translocation of diquat in plants. *Nature* 198(4883):872–873.
13. Barnett, A. P., E. W. Hauser, A. W. White, and J. H. Holladay. 1967. Loss of 2,4-D in washoff from cultivated fallow land. *Weeds* 15:133–137.
14. Baur, J. R., and P. W. Morgan. 1969. Effects of picloram and ethylene on leaf movement of huisache and mesquite seedlings. *Plant Physiol.* 44:831–838.

15. ———, and R. W. Bovey. 1969. Distribution of root-absorbed picloram. *Weed Sci.* 17:524–527.

16. ———, ———, R. D. Baker, and I. Riley. 1971. Absorption and penetration of picloram and 2,4,5-T into detached live oak leaves. *Weed Sci.* 19:138–141.

17. Beadel, H. L. 1962. Fire impressions. *Proc. Tall Timbers Fire Ecology Conf.* 1:1–6.

18. Beasom, S. L. 1975. Range management trends and wild turkey food habits. In *Rangeland Resources Research, 1971–74*. Texas Agr. Exp. Sta. PR-3341.

19. ———, and C. J. Scifres. 1977. Population reactions of selected game species to aerial herbicide applications. *J. Range Manage.* 30:138–142.

20. Benson, L., and R. A. Darrow. 1954. *The Trees and Shrubs of the Southwestern Deserts*. Tucson: Univ. Arizona Press. 437 pp.

21. Blakey, H. L. 1947. The role of brush control in habitat improvement on the Aransas National Wildlife Refuge. *Trans. North Amer. Wildl. Conf.* 12:179–185.

22. Boehring, N. N., P. W. Santelmann, and H. M. Elwell. 1971. Reponses of eastern red cedar to control procedures. *J. Range Manage.* 24:378–382.

23. Bovey, R. W. 1971. Hormone-like herbicides in weed control. *Econ. Bot.* 24:385–400.

24. ———, and C. J. Scifres. 1971. *Residual Characteristics of Picloram in Grassland Ecosystems*. Texas Agr. Exp. Sta. Bull. 1111. 34 pp.

25. ———, and F. S. Davis. 1967. Factors affecting the photoxicity of paraquat. *Weed Res.* 7:281–289.

26. ———, ———, and H. L. Morton. 1968. Herbicide combinations for woody plant control. *Weed Sci.* 16:332–335.

27. ———, ———, and M. G. Merkle. 1967. Distribution of picloram in huisache after foliar and soil application. *Weed Sci.* 15:245–249.

28. ———, H. L. Morton, and J. R. Baur. 1969. Control of live oak by herbicides applied at various rates and dates. *Weed Sci.* 17:373–375.

29. ———, ———, ———, J. D. Diaz-Colon, C. C. Dowler, and S. K. Lehman. 1969. Granular herbicides for woody plant control. *Weed Sci.* 17:538–541.

30. ———, ———, R. E. Meyer, T. O. Flynt, and T. E. Riley. 1972. Control of yaupon and associated species. *Weed Sci.* 20:246–248.

31. ———, J. R. Baur, and H. L. Morton. 1970. Control of huisache and associated woody species in South Texas. *J. Range Manage.* 23:47–50.

32. ———, R. E. Meyer, F. S. Davis, M. G. Merkle, and H. L. Mor-

ton. 1967. Control of woody and herbaceous vegetation with soil sterilants. *Weeds* 15:327–330.

33. ———, R. H. Haas, and R. E. Meyer. 1972. Daily and seasonal response of huisache and Macartney rose to herbicides. *Weed Sci.* 20:577–580.

34. ———, S. K. Lehman, H. L. Morton, and J. R. Baur. 1969. Control of live oak in South Texas. *J. Range Manage.* 22:315–317.

35. Box, T. W. 1967. Brush, fire and West Texas rangeland. *Proc. Tall Timbers Fire Ecology Conf.* 6:7–19.

36. ———. 1964. Changes in wildlife habitat composition following brush control practices in South Texas. *Trans. North Amer. Wildl. Conf.* 29:432–438.

37. ———, and A. D. Chamrad. 1966. *Plant Communities of the Welder Wildlife Refuge.* Welder Wildlife Found. Cont. 5, Series B. 28 pp.

38. ———, and J. Powell. 1965. Brush management techniques for improved forage values in South Texas. *Trans. North Amer. Wildl. and Nat. Resour. Conf.* 38:285–294.

39. ———, ———, and D. L. Drawe. 1967. Influence of fire on South Texas chaparral communities. *Ecology* 48:955–961.

40. ———, and R. S. White. 1969. Fall and winter burning of South Texas brush ranges. *J. Range Manage.* 22:373–376.

41. Brady. H. A. 1971. Spray date effects on behavior of herbicides on brush. *Weed Sci.* 19:200–204.

42. Britton, C. M., and H. A. Wright. 1971. Correlation of weather and fuel variables to mesquite damage by fire. *J. Range Manage.* 24: 136–141.

43. Buckley, R. W. 1971. Influence of herbicides on rangeland vegetation of the Rio Grande Plain. Ph.D. diss., Texas A&M Univ., College Station. 93 pp.

44. Buechner, H. L. 1944. The range vegetation of Kerr County, Texas, in relation to livestock and white-tailed deer. *Amer. Midl. Nat.* 131:697–743.

45. Burnside, O. C., and T. L. Lavy. 1966. Dissipation of dicamba. *Weeds* 14:211–214.

46. Busby, F. E., Jr., and J. L. Schuster. 1971. Woody phreatophyte infestation of the middle Brazos River flood plain. *J. Range Manage.* 24:285–287.

47. Cable, D. R. 1972. Fire effects in southwestern semi-desert grass-shrub communities. *Proc. Tall Timbers Fire Ecology Conf.* 10:109–127.

48. ———. 1965. Damage to mesquite, Lehmann lovegrass and black grama by a hot June fire. *J. Range Manage.* 18:326.

49. Canadian Agricultural Chemicals Association. 1971. *Pesticides and the Environment.* Montreal. 16 pp.

50. Cantlon, J. E., and M. F. Buell. 1952. Controlled burning—its broader ecological aspects. *Bartonia* 26:48–52.

51. Chamrad, A. D., and J. D. Dodd. 1972. Prescribed burning and grazing for prairie chicken habitat manipulation in the Texas Coastal Prairie. *Proc. Tall Timbers Fire Ecol. Conf.* 10:257–276.

52. ⸻, and T. W. Box. 1968. Food habits of white-tailed deer in South Texas. *J. Range Manage.* 21:158–164.

53. Chang, In-Kook, and Chester Foy. 1971. Effect of picloram on germination and seedling development of four species. *Weed Sci.* 19:58–63.

54. Charudattan, R. 1975. Weed control with plant pathogens. *Agrichem. Age* 18(1):9–12.

55. Cooper, R. W. 1963. Knowing when to burn. *Proc. Tall Timbers Fire Ecology Conf.* 2:31–35.

56. Corbin, T. T., and R. P. Upchurch. 1967. Influence of pH on detoxification of herbicides in soil. *Weeds* 15:370–376.

57. Cords, H. P., and A. A. Badiei. 1964. Root reserves and susceptibility to systemic herbicides in two phreatophytes. *Weeds* 12:299–301.

58. Crandall, B. S., and W. L. Baker. 1950. The wilt disease of American persimmon, caused by *Cephalosporium diospyri*. *Phytopath.* 40(4):307–325.

59. Dahl, B. D., R. B. Wadley, M. R. George, and J. L. Talbot. 1971. Influence of site on mesquite mortality from 2,4,5-T. *J. Range Manage.* 24:210–215.

60. Dalrymple, R. L., D. D. Dwyer, and J. E. Webster. 1965. Cattle utilization and chemical content of winged elm browse. *J. Range Manage.* 18:126–128.

61. Darr, J. W., and D. A. Kelebenow. 1975. Deer, brush control, and livestock on the Texas Rolling Plains. *J. Range Manage.* 28:115–119.

62. Daubenmire, R. F. 1968. Ecology of fire in grasslands. In *Adv. Ecol. Res.* No. 5. New York: Academic Press.

63. Davis, F. S., M.G. Merkle, and R. W. Bovey. 1968. Effect of moisture stress on the absorption and transport of herbicides in woody plants. *Bot. Gaz.* 129(3):183–189.

64. ⸻, R. W. Bovey, and M. G. Merkle. 1968. Effect of paraquat and 2,4,5-T on uptake and transport of picloram in woody plants. *Weed Sci.* 16:336–339.

65. Davis, G. G., L. E. Bartel, and C. W. Cook. 1975. Control of gambel oak sprouts by goats. *J. Range Manage.* 28:216–218.

66. Davis, L. S., and R. E. Martin. 1960. Time-temperature relationships of test headfire and backfire. *Southeast Forest Exp. Sta. Note* No. 148. 2 pp.

67. Davis, R. B., and R. L. Spicer. 1965. Status of the practice of brush control in the Rio Grande Plain. *Texas Parks and Wildlife Dep. Cont. Fed. Aid Proj.* W-84-R. 41 pp.

68. De Loach, C. J. 1976. Considerations in introducing foreign biotic agents to control native weeds on rangeland. *Proc. IV Int. Symp. on Biol. Control of Weeds,* in press.

69. Dodd, A. P. 1940. *The Biological Campaign against Pricklypear.* Brisbane: Commonwealth Prickly Pear Board. 177 pp.

70. Dodd, J. D. 1968. Grassland associations of North America. In F. W. Gould, *Grass Systematics.* New York: McGraw-Hill. 382 pp.

71. ———. 1968. Mechanical control of pricklypear and other woody species in the Rio Grande Plains. *J. Range Manage.* 21:366–370.

72. ———, and S. T. Holtz. 1972. Integration of burning with mechanical manipulation of South Texas grassland. *J. Range Manage.* 25:130–135.

73. Donaldson, T. W., and C. L. Foy. 1965. The phytotoxicity and persistence in soils of benzoic acid herbicides. *Weeds* 13:195–292.

74. Drawe, D. L. 1968. Mid-summer diet of deer on the Welder Wildlife Refuge. *J. Range Manage.* 21:164–166.

75. Dyksterhuis, E. J. 1972. Past and present range management. *Proc. Silver Anniv., Dep. Range Sci., Texas A&M Univ.* pp. 7–11.

76. ———. 1958. Range conservation as based on sites and condition classes. *J. Soil and Water Cons.* 13:151–155.

77. ———. 1957. The savannah concept and its use. *Ecology* 38:435–422.

78. ———. 1952. Determining the condition and trend of ranges (natural pastures). *Proc. VI Int. Grassland Cong.,* vol. II, pp. 1322–1327.

79. ———. 1949. Condition and management of rangeland based on quantitative ecology. *J. Range Manage.* 2:104–115.

80. Eaton, B. J., H. M. Elwell, and P. W. Santelmann. 1970. Factors influencing commercial aerial applications of 2,4,5-T. *Weed Sci.* 18:37–41.

81. Ellis D., and J. L. Schuster. 1968. Juniper age and distribution on an isolated butte in Garza county. *Southw. Nat.* 13:343–348.

82. Elwell, H. M. 1968. Winged elm control with picloram and 2,4,5-T with and without additives. *Weed Sci.* 16:131–133.

83. ———, and W. E. McMurphy. 1973. *Weed Control with Phenoxy herbicides on Native Grasslands.* Okla. Agr. Exp. Sta. B-706. 23 pp.

84. Erne, K. 1966. *Studies on the Analytical Chemistry and Toxicology of Phenoxy Herbicides.* Stockholm: Nat'l Vet. Inst.

85. Evans, R. A., and R. D. Eckert, Jr. 1965. Paraquat-surfactant combination for control of downy brome. *Weeds* 13:150–151.

86. Everitt, J. H., and D. L. Drawe. 1974. Spring food habits of white-tailed deer in the South Texas Plains. *J. Range Manage.* 27:15–19.

87. Fisher, C. E. 1975. Personal communication.

88. ———, C. H. Meadors, and R. Behrens. 1956. Some factors that influence the effectiveness of 2,4,5-T trichlorophenoxyacetic acid in killing mesquite. *Weed Sci.* 4:139–147.

89. ———, ———, ———, E. D. Robison, P. T. Marion, and H. L. Morton. 1959. *Control of Mesquite on Grazing Lands.* Texas Agr. Exp. Sta. Bull. 935. 24 pp.

90. ———, H. T. Wiedemann, C. H. Meadors, and J. H. Brock. 1973. Mechanical control of mesquite. In *Mesquite Growth and Development, Management, Economics, Control, Uses,* ed. C. J. Scifres. Texas Agr. Exp. Sta. Mon. 1.

91. ———, ———, J. R. Walter, C. H. Meadors, J. H. Brock, and B. T. Cross. 1972. *Brush Control Research on Rangeland.* Texas Agr. Exp. Sta. MP-1043. 18 pp.

92. ———, J. L. Fultz and H. Hopp. 1946. Factors affecting action of oils and water soluble chemicals in mesquite eradication. *Ecol. Mon.* 16:109–126.

93. Fosberg, M. A., and R. W. Gurman. 1973. Fire climates in the southwest. *Agr. Met.* 12:27–34.

94. Frandsen, W. H. 1973. *Effective Heating of Fuel Ahead of Spreading Fire.* U.S. Dep. Agr. Forest Ser. Res. Paper INT-140. 16 pp.

95. Frey, W. K. 1951. Effects of herbicidal applications on common persimmon, *Diospyros virginiana.* M.S. thesis, Texas A&M Univ., College Station. 53 pp.

96. Frick, K. E. 1974. Augmenting the weed control effectiveness of phytophagous insects. Paper presented at Biological Control of Weeds Symposium, Entomol. Soc. Amer., Minneapolis, Minn., Dec.

97. Friesen, H. A. 1965. The movement and persistence of dicamba in the soil. *Weeds* 13:30–33.

98. Frischknecht, N. C., and L. E. Harris. 1973. Sheep can control sagebrush on seeded range if. . . . *Utah Sci.* 34(1):27–30.

99. Gary, H. L. 1960. *Utilization of Five-Stamen Tamarisk by Cattle.* Rocky Mtn. Forest and Range Exp. Sta. Res. Note 51. 4 pp.

100. Genter, W. A. 1964. Herbicidal activity of vapors of 4-amino-3,5,6-trichloropicolinic acid. *Weeds* 12:239–240.

101. Getzendaner, M. E., J. L. Herman, and B. VanGiessen. 1969. Residues of 4-amino-3,5,6-trichloropicolinic acid from application of Tordon herbicides. *J. Ag. Food and Chem.* 17(6):1251–2156.

102. Glazener, W. C. 1967. Management of the Rio Grande Turkey. In *The Wild Turkey and Its Management.* Washington, D. C.: The Wildl. Soc.

103. ———. 1958. *Wildlife Management as a Part of Range Management in Texas.* Welder Wildl. Cont. 19. Series B. 10 pp.

104. Goeden, R. D. 1975. How biological weed control is working. *Weeds Today* 6(4):4–9.

105. ———. 1973. Prospects for the biological control of weeds with insects. *Calif Weed Conf. Proc.* 25:116–125.

106. ———, C. A. Fleschner, and D. W. Ricker. 1968. Insects control pricklypear. *Calif. Agr.* 22(10):8–10.

107. ———, ———, and ———. 1967. Biological control of pricklypear cacti on Santa Cruz Island, California. *Hilgardia* 38(16):579–606.

108. Gordon, R. A., and C. J. Scifres. 1977. *Prescribed Burning for Improvement of Macartney Rose Infested Coastal Prairie.* Texas Agr. Exp. Sta. Bull. 1183. 15 pp.

109. Gould, F. W. 1975. *Texas Plants: a Checklist and Ecological Summary.* Texas Agr. Exp. Sta. MP 585(Rev.). 121 pp.

110. Gowing, D. P. 1960. Comments on herbicide mixtures. *Weeds* 8:379–391.

111. Green, M. B. 1973. Are herbicides too expensive? *Weeds Today* 4 (4):14–16.

112. Grelen, H. E., and E. A. Epps, Jr. 1967. Herbage responses to fire and litter removal on southern bluestem range. *J. Range Manage.* 20:403–404.

113. ———, and ———. 1967. Season of burning affects herbage quality and yield on pine-bluestem range. *J. Range Manage.* 20:31–33.

114. Griffith, C. A. 1970. The use of persimmon wilt (*Cephalosporium diospyri*) for control of common persimmon (*Diospyros virginiana*). *South. Weed Sci. Soc. Proc.* 23:254–257.

115. ———. 1967. *Persimmon control with the fungus persimmon wilt* Cephalosporium diospyri. Sturm Farm Field Rep., 1965–66. Ardmore, Okla.: Samuel Roberts Noble Found. 7 pp.

116. Haas, R. H., C. J. Scifres, M. G. Merkle, R. R. Hahn, and G. O. Hoffman. 1971. Occurrence and persistence of picloram in grassland water sources. *Weed Res.* 11:54–62.

117. ———, S. K. Lehman, and H. L. Morton. 1970. Influence of mowing and spraying dates on herbicidal control of Macartney rose. *Weed Sci.* 18:33–36.

118. Hahn, R. R., O. C. Burnside, and T. L. Lavy. 1969. Dissipation and phytotoxicity of dicamba. *Weed Sci.* 17:3–8.

119. Hall, R. C., C. S. Giam, and M. G. Merkle. 1968. The photolytic degradation of picloram. *Weed Res.* 3:292–297.

120. Hamaker, J. W., H. Johnston, R. T. Martin, and C. T. Redemann. 1963. A picolinic acid derivative: A plant growth regulator. *Science* 141:363.

121. Hamner, C. L., and H. B. Tukey. 1944. Herbicidal action of 2,4-

dichlorophenoxyacetic acid and trichlorophenoxyacetic acid on bindweed. *Science* 100:154–156.

122. Haney, R. L. 1976. The scientists tell me . . . rangeland improvement need not damage quail coveys. Texas Agr. Exp. Sta. News Release 88, June 16.

123. Hare, R. C. 1961. *Heat Effects on Living Plants.* U.S. Dep. Agr. Paper 183. 32 pp.

124. Harris, C. I. 1964. Movement of dicamba and diphenamid in soils. *Weeds* 12:112–115.

125. Harris, P. 1973. The selection of effective agents for the biological control of weeds. *Can. Entomol.* 105:1495–1503.

126. ———. 1971. Biological control of weeds. *Environ. Letters* 2(2): 75–88.

127. ———. 1971. Current approaches to biological control of weeds. In *Biological Control Programmes against Insect and Weeds in Canada, 1959–1968.* Tech. Commun. Commonw. Inst. Biol. Control 4. 266 pp.

128. Harris, V. M. 1958. Ecology, control and management of shin oak on the Edwards Plateau. Ph.D. diss., Texas A&M Univ., College Station. 114 pp.

129. Harshbarger, R. J., C. J. Perkins, and R. E. Martin. 1975. Legume response unrelated to fuel moisture at time of burning. *J. Range Manage.* 28:70–71.

130. Heirman, A. L., and H. A. Wright. 1973. Fire in medium fuels of west Texas. *J. Range Manage.* 26:331–335.

131. Herbel, C. H., G. H. Abernathy, C. C. Yarbrough, and D. K. Gardner. 1973. Root plowing and seeding arid rangelands in the southwest. *J. Range Manage.* 26:193–197.

132. Hewitt, G. B., E. W. Huddleston, R. J. Lavigne, D. N. Ueckert, and J. G. Watts. 1974. *Rangeland Entomology.* Soc. Range Manage. Range Sci. Ser. No. 2. 127 pp.

133. Hilton, J. L. (chm.). 1974. *Herbicide Handbook of the Weed Science Society of America.* Champaign, Ill.: Sci. Soc. Amer. 430 pp.

134. Hoffman, G. O. Personal communication.

135. ———. Undated. *Control of Baccharis.* Texas Agr. Ext. Ser. L-753. 2 pp.

136. ———. 1972. Texas persimmon—a pesky range problem. *Texas Agr. Prog.* 18(1):8–9.

137. ———. 1967. Controlling pricklypear in Texas. *Down to Earth* 23(1):9–12.

138. ———. 1966. Chemical control of Macartney rose and unpalatable weeds pays. *Down to Earth* 22(3):8–11.

139. ——. 1965. Watch out! Poison ivy can be anywhere. *Texas Agr. Prog.* 11(2):22–23.

140. ——, and B. J. Ragsdale. Undated. *Brush Control with AMS.* Texas Agr. Ext. Ser. L-423. 1 p.

141. ——, and ——. Undated. *Brush Control with 2,4,5-T.* Texas Agr. Ext. Ser. L-414. 1 p.

142. ——, and ——. Undated. *Chemical Brush Control Broadcast Aerial Application.* Texas Agr. Ext. Ser. L-415. 1 p.

143. ——, and ——. Undated. *Mesquite Control.* Texas Agr. Ext. Ser. MP-386. 6 pp.

144. ——, H. G. Hoermann, and J. V. Allen. 1969. Putting the heat on mesquite. *Texas Agr. Prog.* 15(1):15–17.

145. ——, and J. D. Dodd. 1867. How to whip pricklypear. *Texas Agr. Prog.* 13(3):16–18.

146. ——, and R. A. Darrow. Undated. *Pricklypear—good or bad?* Texas Agr. Ext. Ser. B-806. 7 pp.

147. ——, R. H. Haas, and B. E. Jeter. Undated. *Macartney Rose Control in Texas.* Texas Agr. Ext. Ser. MP-745. 12 pp.

148. Hopkin, J. A., P. J. Barry, and C. B. Baker. 1973. *Financial Management in Agriculture.* Danville, Ill.: Interstate Printers & Publishers. 459 pp.

149. Huffaker, C. B. 1964. Fundamentals of biological weed control. In *Biological Control of Insect Pests and Weeds,* ed. P. DeBach. New York: Reinhold Pub. Corp.

150. ——. 1963. Some concepts on the ecological basis of biological control of weeds. *Can. Entomol.* 94(5):507–514.

151. ——. 1957. Fundamentals of biological control of weeds. *Hilgardia* 27(3):101–157.

152. Hughes, E. E. 1967. Influence of environment on shoot growth and total carbohydrate reserves of saltcedar. *Weeds* 15:46–49.

153. ——. 1966. *Effects of Root Plowing and Aerial Spraying on Microclimate, Soil Conditions and Vegetation of a Mesquite Area.* Texas Agr. Exp. Sta. MP-812. 10 pp.

154. ——. 1966. Single and combination mowing and spraying treatments for control of saltcedar (*Tamarix pentandra* Pall.) *Weeds* 14:276–278.

155. ——. 1965. Basal and stump sprays for control of saltcedar. *Weeds* 13:338–340.

156. Humphrey, R. R. 1958. The desert grassland: A history of vegetational change and an analysis of the causes. *Bot. Rev.* 24:193–252.

157. Huss, D. L. 1954. Factors influencing plant succession following fire in ashe juniper woodland types in Real County, Texas. M.S. thesis, Texas A&M Univ., College Station. 80 pp.

158. Inglis, J. M. and C. A. McMahan. 1974. Use of Rio Grande Plain brush types by white-tailed deer. *J. Range Manage.* 27:369–374.

159. Janson, L. E., W. A. Gentner, and W. C. Shaw. 1961. Effects of surfactants on the herbicidal activity of herbicides in aqueous spray systems. *Weeds* 9:381–405.

160. Jennings, W. S., and J. T. Harris. 1953. *The Collared Peccary in Texas.* Austin: Texas Game and Fish Comm. 31 pp.

161. Johnston, M. C. 1962. Past and present grasslands of southern Texas and northern Mexico. *Ecology* 44:456–466.

162. Jones, F. B. 1975. *Flora of the Texas Coastal Bend.* Welder Wildlife Found. Cont. B-6. 262 pp.

163. ———, C. M. Rowell, Jr., and M. C. Johnston. 1961. *Flowering Plants and Ferns of the Texas Coastal Bend Counties.* Welder Wildlife Found. Series B-1. 146 pp.

164. Kirby, B., and P. W. Santlemann. 1964. Germination and emergence of winged elm seeds. *Weeds* 12:277–279.

165. Kirk, W. G., E. M. Hodges, F. M. Peacock, L. L. Yarlett, and F. G. Martin. 1976. Production of cow-calf herds: Effect of burning native and supplemental feeding. *J. Range Manage.* 27:136–139.

166. Klingman, D. L., C. H. Gordon, G. Yip, and H. P. Burchfield. 1966. Residues in the forage and in milk from cows grazing forage treated with esters of 2,4-D. *Weeds* 14:164–167.

167. ———, and W. C. Shaw. 1961. *Using Phenoxy Herbicides Effectively.* U.S. Dep. Agr. Farmers Bull. 2183. 24 pp.

168. Kothmann, M. M. 1977. Personal communication.

169. ———. 1975. Grazing management systems. *Texas Agr. Prog.* 21(2):22–23.

170. ———. 1974. Grazing management terminology. *J. Range Manage.* 27:326–327.

171. Krefting, L. S., and H. L. Hansen. 1969. Increasing browse for deer by aerial applications of 2,4-D. *J. Wildl. Manage.* 33:784–790.

172. Lee, W. O. 1970. Effect of picloram on production and quality of seed in several grasses. *Weed Sci.* 18:171–173.

173. Lehman, S. K., R. H. Haas, and B. E. Jeter. 1966. The effectiveness of picloram for control of Macartney rose. *Proc. So. Weed Conf.* 19:281–297.

174. ———, ———, and ———. 1965. *Control of Macartney Rose (Rosa bracteata Wendl.) with Aerial and Ground Applications of Picloram* (4-amino-3,5,6-trichloropicolinic acid). Tex. Agr. Exp. Sta. PR-2083. 9 pp.

175. Lehmann, V. W. 1965. Fire in the range of Attwater prairie chickens. *Proc. Tall Timber Fire Conf.* pp. 127–142.

176. ———. 1960. Problems of maintaining game on ranges subjected to brush control. *Proc. World Forest. Congr.* 5:1807–1809.

177. Leng, M. L. 1972. Residues in milk and meat and safety to livestock use of phenoxy herbicides in pastures and rangeland. *Down to Earth* 28(1):12–20.

178. Leonard, O. A., and A. H. Murphy. 1965. Relationship between herbicide movement and stump sprouting. *Weed Sci.* 13:36–39.

179. Lisk, D. J., W. H. Gutenmann, C. A. Bache, R. G. Wagner, and D. G. Wagner. 1964. Elimination of 2,4-D in the urine of steers fed 4-(2,4-DB) or 2,4-D. *J. Dairy Sci.* 47:1435–1436.

180. Lynd, J. Q., C. Rieck, D. Barnes, D. Murray, and P. W. Santelmann. 1967. Indicator plant abberations at threshold soil herbicide levels. *Agron. J.* 59:194–196.

181. McCall, H. G., and C. J. Scifres. 1975. Herbicide residues in native forages treated with various formulations of picloram. In *Rangeland Resour. Res., 1971–1974.* Texas Agr. Exp. Sta. Cons. PR-3341.

182. ———, ———, and M. G. Merkle. 1974. Influence of foam adjuvants on activity of selected herbicides. *Weed Sci.* 22:384–388.

183. McCarty, M. K. 1967. Control of western snowberry in Nebraska. *Weeds* 15:130–133.

184. ———, and C. J. Scifres. 1972. Herbicidal control of western ragweed in Nebraska pastures. *J. Range Manage.* 25:290–292.

185. ———, and ———. 1968. Herbicidal control of western ironweed. *Weed Sci.* 16:77–79.

186. ———, and ———. 1968. Pasture improvement through effective weed control. *Nebraska Farm, Ranch and Home Quarterly* (Winter). 5 pp.

187. ———, and ———. 1968. Smooth bromegrass response to herbicides as affected by time of application in relation to nitrogen fertilization. *Weed Sci.* 16:443–446.

188. ———, and ———. 1968. Western whorled milkweed and its control. *Weed Sci.* 16:4–7.

189. McCully, W. G. 1957. Chemical brush control program. *Texas Agr. Prog.* 3:14–15.

190. ———. 1950. Recovery and viability of Macartney rose (*Rosa bracteata* Wendl.) seeds passed through the bovine digestive tract. M.S. thesis, Texas A&M Univ. College Station. 45 pp.

191. McKell, C. M., A. M. Wilson, and E. L. Kay. 1962. Effective burning of rangelands infested with medusahead. *Weeds* 10:125–131.

192. McMahan, C. A. 1964. A food habits study of three classes of livestock and deer. *J. Wildlife Manage.* 28:798–808.

193. Magee, A. F. 1957. *Goats Pay for Clearing Grand Prairie Rangelands.* Texas Agr. Exp. Sta. MP-206. 8 p.

194. Martin, S. C. 1972. Semidesert ecosystems—Who will use them? How will we manage them? *J. Range Manage.* 5:317–319.

195. ———, J. L. Thames, and E. B. Fish. 1974. Changes in cactus numbers in herbage production after chaining for mesquite control. *Prog. Agr. Ariz.* 26(6):3–6.

196. Meadors, C. H. 1976. Personal communication.

197. ———, C. E. Fisher, R. H. Haas, and G. O. Hoffman. 1973. Combinations of methods and maintenance control of mesquite. In *Mesquite: Growth and Development, Management, Economics, Control, Uses,* ed. C. J. Scifres. Texas Agr. Exp. Sta. Res. Mon. 1.

198. Merkle, M. G., and F. S. Davis. 1967. Effect of moisture stress on absorption and movement of picloram and 2,4,5-T in beans. *Weeds* 15:10–12.

199. Merrill, L. B. 1976. Personal communication.

200. ———, and C. A. Taylor. 1976. Take note of the versatile goat. *Rangeman's J.* 3:74–76.

201. ———, and G. O. Hoffman. 1973. Interrelation of grazing management and mesquite control. In *Mesquite: Growth and Development, Management, Economics, Control, Uses,* ed. C. J. Scifres. Texas Agr. Exp. Sta. Res. Mon. 1.

202. Meyer, R. E., and H. L. Morton. 1967. Several factors affecting the response of pricklypear to 2,4,5-T. *Weed Sci.* 15:207–209.

203. ———, ———, M. G. Merkle, R. W. Bovey, and F. S. Davis. 1970. Brush control on forest-rangelands of East Texas. *J. Range Manage.* 23:129–132.

204. ———, ———, R. H. Haas, and E. D. Robison. 1971. *Morphology and Anatomy of Honey Mesquite.* U.S. Dep. Agr., Agr. Res. Ser. Tech. Bull. 1423. 186 pp.

205. ———, R. W. Bovey, W. T. McKelvy, and T. E. Riley. 1972. *Influence of Plant Growth Stage and Environmental Factors on the Response of Honey Mesquite to Herbicides.* Texas Agr. Exp. Sta. Bull. 1127. 19 pp.

206. ———, and T. E. Riley. 1969. Influence of picloram granules and sprays on whitebrush. *Weed Sci.* 17:293–295.

207. ———, ———, H. L. Morton, and M. G. Merkle. 1969. *Control of Whitebrush and Associated Species with Herbicides in Texas.* Texas Agr. Exp. Sta. MP-930. 18 pp.

208. Meyer, R. W. 1974. *Morphology and Anatomy of Texas Persimmon.* Texas Agr. Exp. Sta. B-1147. 54 pp.

209. ———. 1970. Picloram and 2,4,5-T influence morphology of honey mesquite. *Weed Sci.* 18: 525–531.

210. Michael, E. D. 1965. Movements of white-tailed deer on the Welder Wildlife Refuge. *J. Wildl. Manage.* 29:44–52.

211. Miller, J. H., H. M. Kempen, J. A. Wilkerson, and C. L. Foy.

1963. *Response of Cotton to 2,4-D and Related Phenoxy Herbicides.* USDA Agr. Res. Ser. Tech. Bull. 1289. 28 pp.

212. Montgomery, M. L., and L. A. Norris. 1970. A preliminary evaluation of the hazards of 2,4,5-T in the forest environment. U.S. Dep. Agr. For. Ser. Res. Note. PHW-16. 11 pp.

213. Morton, H. L. 1966. Influence of temperature and humidity on foliar absorption, translocation and metabolism of 2,4,5-T by mesquite seedlings. *Weeds* 14:136–141.

214. ———, E. D. Robison, and R. E. Meyer. 1967. Persistence of 2,4-D, 2,4,5-T and dicamba in range forage grasses. *Weeds* 15:268–271.

215. Mutch, R. W. 1970. Fire management today: Tradition and change in the Forest Service. *Proc. 1975 Nat. Conv. Soc. Am. For.,* pp. 189–202.

216. Nalewaja, J. D. 1970. The reaction of wheat to picloram. *Weed Sci.* 18:276–278.

217. National Academy of Sciences. 1968. *Weed Control.* Pub. 1597. Washington, D.C. 471 pp.

218. Norris, L. A. 1971. Chemical brush control: Assessing the hazard. *J. Forest.* 69:715–720.

219. Oefinger, R. D., and C. J. Scifres. 1977. *Gulf Cordgrass Production, Utilization and Nutritional Status Following Burning.* Texas Agr. Exp. Sta. Bull. 1176. 19 pp.

220. Owensby, C. E., K. R. Blan, B. J. Eaton, and O. G. Russ. 1973. Evaluation of eastern redcedar infestations in the northern Kansas Flint Hills. *J. Range Manage.* 26:256–259.

221. Palmer, J. S., and R. D. Radeleff. 1969. *The Toxicity of Some Organic Herbicides to Cattle, Sheep and Chickens.* U.S. Dep. Agr. Res. Ser. Prod. Rep. 106. 26 pp.

222. Parr, J. F., and A. G. Norman. 1965. Consideration in the use of surfactants in plant systems. A review. *Bot. Gaz.* 126(2):86–96.

223. Pase, C. E. 1971. Effect of a February burn of Lehmann lovegrass. *J. Range Manage.* 24:454–456.

224. Penner, D., and F. M. Ashton. 1966. Biochemical and metabolic changes in plants induced by chlorophenoxy herbicides. *Residue Rev.* 14:39–113.

225. Peters, E. J., and J. F. Stritzke. 1970. Control of persimmon with various herbicides and methods of application. *Weed Sci.* 18:572–575.

226. ———, and S. A. Lowance. 1969. Gains in timothy forage from goldenrod control with 2,4-D, 2,4-DB and picloram. *Weed Sci.* 17:473–474.

227. Peterson, G. E. 1967. The discovery and development of 2,4-D. *Agr. History* 41:243–253.

228. Peterson, G. W. 1977. Epidemiology and control of a blight of *Juniperus virginiana* caused by *Cercospora sequoiae* var. *juniperi*. *Phytopath.* 67:234–238.
229. Phillips, W. S. 1962. Fire and vegetation of arid lands. *Proc. Tall Timbers Fire Ecology Conf.* 1:81–95.
230. Polk, K. L., and D. N. Ueckert. 1973. Biology and ecology of a mesquite twig girdler, *Oncideres rhodosticta*, in West Texas. *Ann. Entomol. Soc. Amer.* 66:411–417.
231. Pond, E. W. 1955. The chemical control of buckeye, *Aesculus arguta*, on Kerr county ranch. M.S. thesis, Texas A&M Univ., College Station.
232. Powell, J., and T. W. Box. 1966. Brush management influences preference values of South Texas woody species for deer and cattle. *J. Range Manage.* 19:212–214.
233. Ramsey, C. W. 1965. Potential economic returns from deer as compared with livestock of the Edwards Plateau region of Texas. *J. Range Manage.* 18:247–250.
234. Rechenthin, C. A., H. M. Bell, R. J. Pederson, and D. B. Polk. 1964. *Grassland Restoration: Brush Control.* Unnumbered U.S. Dep. Agr. S.C.S. Publ. Temple, Texas. 39 pp.
235. Robison, E. D., and B. T. Cross. 1970. Redberry juniper control and grass response following aerial application of picloram. Texas Agr. Exp. Sta. PR-2805. In *Brush Research in Texas,* 1970.
236. ———, and ———. 1969. Juniper control with aerially applied picloram pellets. *Proc. So. Weed Conf.* 22:270.
237. Rowe, V. K., and T. A. Hymas. 1954. Summary of toxicological information of 2,4-D and 2,4,5-T type herbicides and an evaluation of the hazards to livestock concerned with their use. *Amer. J. Vet. Res.* 15:622–629.
238. Rowell, C. M., Jr. 1972. *A Guide to the Identification of Plants Poisonous to Livestock of the Texas Panhandle and South Plains.* Int. Center Arid and Semi-arid Land Studies, Cont. 107, Agr. Sci. Pub. T-9-102. Lubbock: Texas Tech Press. 23 pp.
239. Sauer, C. O. 1950. Grassland climax, fire and man. *J. Range Manage.* 3:16–21.
240. Schmutz, E. M. 1971. Absorption, translocation and toxicity of 2,4,5-T in creosotebush. *Weed Sci.* 19:510–516.
241. ———. 1967. Chemical control of three Chihuahuan Desert shrubs. *Weed Sci.* 15:62–67.
242. Schuster, J. L. 1976. Personal communication.
243. ———. 1971. Night applications of phenoxy herbicides on plains pricklypear. *Weed Sci.* 19:585–587.
244. Scifres, C. J. Unpublished data. Dep. Range Sci., Texas A&M Univ., College Station.

245. ———. 1977. Herbicides and the range ecosystem: Residues, research and the role of rangemen. *J. Range Manage.* 30:86–91.

246. ———. 1976. Herbicide nomenclature and related terminology. *J. Range Manage.* 29:173–174.

247. ———. 1975. Fall application of herbicides improves Macartney rose infested coastal prairie rangeland. *J. Range Manage.* 28:483–486.

248. ———. 1975. *Systems for Improving Macartney Rose–Infested Coastal Prairie Rangeland.* Texas Agr. Exp. Sta. Bull. 1225. 12 pp.

249. ———. 1975. *Texas Persimmon Distribution and Control with Individual-Plant Treatments.* Texas Agr. Exp. Sta. Bull. 1157. 12 pp.

250. ———. 1974. Salient aspects of huisache seed germination. *Southw. Nat.* 18:383–392.

251. ———. 1972. Herbicide interactions in control of sand shinnery oak. *J. Range Manage.* 25:386–389.

252. ———. 1972. Redberry juniper control with soil-applied herbicides. *J. Range Manage.* 25:308–310.

253. ———. 1972. Sand shinnery oak response to dicamba granules and picloram pellets. *J. Range Manage.* 25:155–156.

254. ———. 1972. Sand shinnery oak response to silvex sprays of varying characteristics. *J. Range Manage.* 25:464–466.

255. ——— (ed). 1973. *Mesquite: Distribution, Ecology, Uses, Control, Economics.* Texas Agr. Exp. Sta. Res. Mon. 1. 84 pp.

256. ———, C. R. Kienast, and D. J. Elrod. 1973. Honey mesquite seedling growth and susceptibility to 2,4,5-T as influenced by shading. *J. Range Manage.* 26:28–30.

257. ———, and D. B. Polk, Jr. 1974. Vegetation response following spraying of light infestation of honey mesquite. *J. Range Manage.* 27:462–465.

258. ———, and G. O. Hoffman. 1972. Comparative susceptibility of honey mesquite to dicamba and 2,4,5-T. *J. Range Manage.* 25:143–145.

259. ———, G. P. Durham, and J. L. Mutz. 1977. Range forage production and consumption following aerial spraying of mixed brush. *Weed Sci.* 25:217–218.

260. ———, H. G. McCall, R. Maxey, and H. Tai. 1977. Residual characteristics of 2,4,5-T and picloram in sandy rangeland soils. *J. Environ. Qual.* 6:36–42.

261. ———, and J. C. Halifax. 1972. Development of range grasses germinated in picloram. *Weed Sci.* 20:341–344.

262. ———, and ———. 1972. Root production of seedling grasses in soils containing picloram. *J. Range Manage.* 25:44–46.

263. ———, and J. H. Brock. 1972. Planting depth and soil temperature relative to emergence of honey mesquite. *J. Range Manage.* 25:217–218.

264. ———, and ———. 1971. Thermal regulation of water uptake by germinating honey mesquite seeds. *J. Range Manage.* 24:370–373.

265. ———, and ———. 1969. Moisture-temperature interrelations in germination and early seedling development of mesquite. *J. Range Manage.* 22:334–337.

266. ———, and ———, and R. R. Hahn. 1971 Influence of second-any succession on honey mesquite invasion of North Texas. *J. Range Manage.* 24:206–210.

266a. ———, and J. L. Mutz. 1979. Herbaceous vegetation changes following applications of tebuthiuron for brush control. *J. Range Manage.* 31:375–378.

267. ———, ———, and G. P. Durham. 1976. Range improvement following chaining of South Texas mixed brush. *J. Range Manage.* 29:418–421.

267a. ———, ———, and W. T. Hamilton. 1979. Control of mixed brush with tebuthiuron. *J. Range Manage.* 32:155–158.

268. ———, J. R. Baur, and R. W. Bovey. 1973. Absorption of 2,4,5-T applied in various carriers to honey mesquite. *Weed Sci.* 21:94–96.

269. ———, and M. G. Merkle. 1975. Herbicides and good management improves range pastures. *Weeds Today* 6(1):5–7.

270. ———, and M. K. McCarty. 1968. Reaction of western ironweed leaf tissue to picloram. *Weed Sci.* 16:347–349.

271. ———, and M. M. Kothmann. 1976. Site relations, regrowth characteristics and control of lotebush with herbicides. *J. Range Manage.* 19:154–156.

272. ———, ———, and G. W. Mathis. 1974. Range site and grazing system influence regrowth after spraying honey mesquite. *J. Range Manage.* 27:97–100.

273. ———, O. C. Burnside, and M. K. McCarty. 1969. Movement and persistence of picloram in pasture soils of Nebraska. *Weed Sci.* 17:486–488.

274. ———, and R. H. Haas. 1974. *Vegetation Changes in a Post Oak Savannah Following Woody Plant Control.* Texas Agr. Exp. Sta. MP-1136. 11 pp.

275. ———, and R. R. Hahn. 1971. Response of honey mesquite seedlings to top removal. *J. Range Manage.* 24:296–298.

276. ———, ———, J. Diaz-Colon, and M. G. Merkle. 1971. Picloram persistence in semiarid rangeland soils and water. *Weed Sci.* 19:381–384.

277. ———, ———, and J. H. Brock. 1971. Phenology and control of common broomweed on Texas rangelands. *J. Range Maange.* 24:370–373.

278. ———, ———, and M. G. Merkle. 1971. Dissipation of picloram

from vegetation of semiarid rangelands. *Weed Sci.* 19:329–332.

279. ———, R. W. Bovey, G. O. Hoffman, and C. E. Fisher. 1973. In *Mesquite: Distribution, Ecology, Uses, Control and Economics,* ed. C. J. Scifres. Texas Agr. Exp. Sta. Res. Mon. 1. 84 pp.

280. ———, ———, and M. G. Merkle. 1972. Variation in bioassay attributes as quantitative indices of picloram in soils. *Weed Res.* 12:58–64.

281. ———, and T. J. Allen. 1973. Dissipation of dicamba from grassland soils of Texas. *Weed Sci.* 21:393–396.

282. ———, ———, C. L. Leinweber, and K. H. Pearson. 1973. Dissipation and phytotoxicity of dicamba residues in water. *J. Environ. Qual.* 2:306–309.

283. Shaw, W. C. 1964. Weed Science—Revolution in agricultural technology. *Weeds* 12:153–162.

284. Sheffield, W. J. 1970. The nilgai antelope in Texas. Caesar Kleberg Research Program in Wildlife Ecology, Ann. Rep. Texas Agr. Exp. Sta., College Station (mimeographed). pp. 147–167.

285. Silker, T. H. 1955. *Prescribed Burning for the Control of Undesirable Hardwoods in Pine-Hardwood Stands and Slash Pine Plantations.* Texas Forest Ser. Bull. No. 46. 19 pp.

286. Smith, H. N., and C. A. Rechenthin. 1964. *Grassland Restoration: The Texas Brush Problem.* Unnumbered U.S. Dep. Agr. S.C.S. Publ. Temple Texas. 33 pp.

287. Smith L. L., and D. N. Ueckert. 1974. Influence of insects on mesquite seed production. *J. Range Manage.* 17:61–65.

288. Sosebee, R. E., B. E. Dahl, and J. P. Goen. 1973. Factors affecting mesquite control with Tordon 225 mixture. *J. Range Manage.* 26:369–371.

289. Spedding, C. R. W. 1971. *Grassland Ecology.* Oxford: Clarendon Press.

290. Sperry, O. E. 1967. *Control of Mescalbean* (Sophora secundiflora) *with Herbicides.* Texas Agr. Exp. Sta. MP-830. 8 pp.

291. ———. 1966. Importance and control of plants poisonous to livestock in the southwest. *Down to Earth* 22(1):16–17.

292. ———, D. E. Ruerson, and H. A. Pearson. 1962. *Distribution and chemical Control of Coyotillo, a Range Shrub Poisonous to Livestock.* Texas Agr. Exp. Sta. MP-594. 10 pp.

293. ———, and F. W. Pond. 1957. *Buckeye: Its Distribution and Control.* Texas Agr. Exp. Sta. MP-188. 7 pp.

294. ———, J. W. Dollahite, G. O. Hoffman, and B. J. Camp. 1965. *Texas Plants Poisonous to Livestock.* Texas Agr. Exp. Sta. Bull. 1028. 57 pp.

295. Springer, M. D. 1975. Food habits of wild hogs on the Texas Gulf Coast. M.S. thesis, Texas A&M Univ., College Station. 71 pp.

296. Stankey, G. H. 1976. *Wilderness Fire Policy: An Investigation of Vistor Knowledge and Beliefs*. U.S. Dep. Agr. Forest Ser. Res. Paper INT-180. 17 pp.

297. Stevens, R., B. C. Giunta, and A. P. Plummer. 1975. Some aspects in the biological control of juniper and pinyon. *Proc. Pinyon-Juniper Symp.*, Utah State Univ., Logan, pp. 77–81.

298. Stinson, K. J., and H. A. Wright. 1969. Temperatures of head fires in the southern mixed prairie of Texas. *J. Range Manage.* 22:169–174.

299. Sultemeier, G. W. 1976. Personal communication.

300. Swanson, C. R. 1969. The benzoic acid herbicides. In *Degradation of Herbicides*. New York: Marcel Dekker, Inc. 394 pp.

301. Taylor, T. W. 1973. Vegetational, edaphic and topograhic relationships of a 25–year exclosure on the Edwards Plateau, Texas. M.S. thesis, Texas A&M Univ., College Station. 94 pp.

302. Teer, J. G., and N. K. Forrest. 1968. Bionomic and ethical implications of commercial game harvest programs. *Trans. North Amer. Wildl. and Natur. Resources Conf.* 33:192–202.

303. Thomas, G. W. 1970. The western range and the livestock industry it supports. In *Range Research and Range Problems*. Madison, Wis.: Crop Sci. Soc. Amer.

304. Timmons, F. L. 1970. A history of weed control in the United States and Canada. *Weed Sci.* 18:294–307.

305. Trichell, D. W., H. L. Morton, and M. G. Merkle. 1968. Loss of herbicides in runoff water. *Weed Sci.* 16:447–449.

306. Trlica, M. J., Jr., and J. L. Schuster. 1969. Effects of fire on grasses of the Texas High Plains. *J. Range Manage.* 22:329–333.

307. Tschirley, F. H., and S. C. Martin. Germination and longevity of velvet mesquite seed in soil. *J. Range Manage.* 13:94–97.

308. Ueckert, D. N. 1977. Personal communication.

309. ———. 1974. Influence of defoliation by the cutworm *Melipotis indomita* on control of honey mesquite with 2,4,5-T in West Texas. *J. Range Manage.* 27:153–155.

310. ———. 1973. Effects of leaf-footed bugs on mesquite reproduction. *J. Range Manage.* 26:227–229.

311. ———, and A .D. Chamrad. 1973. Defoliation of creosotebush by walkingsticks increases forage production. *Texas Tech Univ. Noxious Brush and Weed Control Res. Highlights* 4:10.

312. ———, and H. A. Wright. 1974. Wood boring insect infestations in relation to mesquite control practices. *J. Range Manage.* 27:383–386.

313. ———, K. L. Polk, and C. R. Ward. 1971. Mesquite twig girdler: A possible means of control. *J. Range Manage.* 24:116–118.

314. Upchurch, R. I. 1966. Behavior of herbicides in soil. *Residue Rev.* 16:46–85.

315. Vallentine, J. F. 1971. *Range Development and Improvements.* Provo, Utah: Brigham Young Univ. Press. 516 pp.

316. Vanden Born, W. H. 1965. The effect of dicamba and picloram on quackgrass, bromegrass and Kentucky bluegrass. *Weeds* 13:309–312.

317. Vines, R. A. 1960. *Trees, Shrubs and Woody Vines of the Southwest.* Austin: Univ. of Texas Press. 1104 pp.

318. Waddle, J. P., and H. A. Wright. 1970. An evaluation of five methods to retreat sprayed mesquite. *J. Range Manage.* 30:214–217.

319. Walker, E. A. 1962. *Brush control and wildlife.* Ann. Meet. Nat. Audubon Soc. 58 (mimeographed). 21 pp.

320. Wapshere, A. J. 1972. Biological control of skeletonweed. In *Rural Research in CSIRO, June, 1972.* Canberra, Australia. 32 pp.

321. Weed Science Society of America. 1966. Standardization of common and botanical names of weeds. *Weed Sci.* 14 (1966):347–386.

322. White, L. D. 1969. Effects of a wildlife on several desert grassland shrub species. *J. Range Manage.* 22:284–285.

323. Whitson, R. E., S. L. Beasom, and C. J. Scifres. 1977. Economic evaluation of cattle and white-tailed deer response to aerial spraying of mixed brush. *J. Range Manage.* 30:214–217.

324. Wicks, G. A., C. R. Fenster, and O. C. Burnside. 1969. Selective control of plains pricklypear in rangeland with herbicides. *Weed Sci.* 17: 408–411.

325. Wiedemann, H. T. 1976. Personal communication.

326. ———, L. F. Bouse, R. H. Haas, and J. P. Walter. 1973. Spray equipment, herbicide carriers and drift control. In *Mesquite: Growth and Development, Management, Economics, Control, Uses,* ed. C. J. Scifres. Texas Agr. Exp. Sta. Res. Mon. 1.

327. Wiese, A. F., and R. G. Davis. 1964. Herbicide movement in soil with various amounts of water. *Weeds* 12:101–103.

328. Wilson, C. L. 1963. Persimmon wilt—friend or foe? *Ark. Farm Res.* 12(5):9.

329. Wilson, F. 1970. The nature and advantages of biological control. *Adv. Soc.* 26:374–378.

330. ———. 1964. The biological control of weeds. *Ann. Rev. Entomol.* 9:225–244.

331. Wink, R. L., and H. A. Wright. 1973. Effects of fire on ashe juniper community. *J. Range Manage.* 26:326–330.

332. Wright, H. A. 1976. Fire as a tool to manage tobosa grasslands. *Proc. Tall Timbers Fire Ecol. Conf.* 12:153–167.

333. ———. 1974. Effect of fire on southern mixed prairie grasses. *J. Range Manage.* 27:417–419.

334. ———. 1974. Range burning. *J. Range Manage.* 27:5–11.

335. ———. 1971. Why squirreltail is more tolerant to burning than needle-and-thread. *J. Range Manage.* 24:277–284.

336. ———. 1970. A method to determine heat-caused mortality in bunchgrass. *Ecology* 51:582–587.

337. ———, and K. J. Stinson. 1970. Response of mesquite to season of top removal. *J. Range Manage.* 23:127–128.

338. York, J. C., and W. A. Dick-Peddie. 1969. Vegetation changes in southern New Mexico during the past hundred years. In *Arid Lands in Perspective.* Tucson: Univ. Ariz Press. 166 pp.

339. Young, V. A., F. R. Anderwald, and W. G. McCully. 1948. *Brush Problems on Texas Ranges.* Texas Agr. Exp. Sta. Misc. Pub. 21. 19 pp.

340. Zwölfer, H., and P. Harris. 1971. Host specificity determination of insects for biological control of weeds. *Ann. Rev. Entomol.* 16: 159–178.

Index

classifications of, 144–145
combinations of, 15, 173, 174, 270, 306
contact type of, 145
development of, 141, 144
dry formulations of, 177, 191
early compounds of, 140
foliage-active type of, 145–146
nomenclature for, 142
phloem translocation of, 145
properties of, 141
and range vegetation, 13
residues of, 197, 203, 205, 212
soil-active type of, 145–146
spray mixtures of, 188–189
timing of applications of, 192
translocation of, 145
See also specific herbicide. (For effects on particular species, see species name.)
Hercules'-club, 21
hexaflurate, 82, 143, 171
High Plains, 38, 268
Hilaria, 8
Hippocastanaceae, 105
hog plum. See Texas colubrina
hogs, feral, 262, 271
honey locust: See common honey locust
honey mesquite
  biological control of, 251–253
  as browse, 265–266
  effects of fire on, 72, 238, 244
  grazing management following control of, 282
  crown of, 70
  description, distribution, and ecology of, 16, 21, 26, 29, 30, 34, 38, 39, 69–70, 127
  environment and herbicidal control of, 194–195
  foliar absorption of herbicides by, 149
  general control of, 70–72
  herbicides for control of, 70–72, 160–161, 163, 165–166, 168, 172, 174, 194–195
  invasion of grasslands by, 14

management systems for, 305
secondary succession and, 14
seedlings of, 14, 70
seeds of, 8, 14, 17, 70
hooded windmillgrass, 36, 173
horsetail conyza, 242
huisache
  as browse, 272
  description, distribution, and ecology of, 6, 21, 26, 72, 73
  general control of, 74
  herbicides for control of, 74, 163, 167–168, 172
  seeds of, 73
  soil preference of, 73
humidity
  and burning, 222–223
  and herbicide activity, 148, 160–161
hydrogen peroxide, 170
Hymenoclea monogyra. See burrobrush

Ilex vomitoria. See yaupon
increasers, 279
insects for biological control, 251
invaders, 279
invert emulsions, 151
isopropyl ester of 2,4-D, 156
Italian ryegrass, 167

Jatropha dioica. See leatherstem
javelina, 81, 262, 271
javelina brush, 21, 34, 74–76, 172
junipers, 222, 243, 256, 268
Juniperus ashei. See Ashe juniper
Juniperus pinchotii. See red-berry juniper
Juniperus virginiana. See eastern red cedar

Karwinskia humboldtiana. See coyotillo
kerosene, 74, 191
key area–key species range management, 281–282
kidneywood, 21
Klamathweed, 247, 260